CW00818891

FORD ESCORT

FORD ESCORT

Dennis Foy

For Pat, who never lets me down

Acknowledgements

THREE YEARS AGO, I swore that I would never write another book. This is it.

As with any book, there is a healthy list of people to whom I am indebted. Firstly, for their help in providing me with information, technical detail and snippets of what, to them, may have been trivia, there are such people at Ford Motor Company, Ford of Europe and Ford of Britain as (purely in alphabetical order, so that nobody can be offended) Kenneth S. Brown, Harry Calton, Kenneth Cannell, Clive Ennos, Hans Fleischer, Nick Fry, Bob Howe, Don Hume, Rod Mansfield (and several members of his team), Jim McCraw, the Photographic Unit, Barry Reynolds, Helmuth Schrader and Steve Woolmington. Thanks go to three former Ford men whose help was much appreciated—Stuart Turner, who retired early from his directorship of Ford Motor Company at the end of 1990, John Southgate, now enjoying life at a major industrial concern, and Sam Toy, who is hopefully making the most of his well-earned retirement by catching up on his salmon fishing in Scotland.

Nick Collins, my editor and mentor at Osprey, is singled out for thanks for persuading me to take on this tome—which is the biggest single project I have ever attempted—and so is my old friend Jeremy Walton, whose occasional words of encouragement and guidance were worth more than perhaps he appreciated. Somebody who helped, and who has probably long since forgotten my existence, is my college English lecturer, Mike Taylor, for it was he who taught me that whilst starting sentences with words such as 'And', 'If', 'Yet' and 'But' were technically wrong—along with the one-sentence paragraph—they did make a story more readable.

And I hope that he was right.

The biggest thanks of all, though, go to my beautiful wife Pat and son Benjamin. Both have endured my bouts of frustration and short-temperedness whilst writing this book, and Pat has also ensured that everything else in both the home and in our magazine carried on smoothly whilst I opted out to sit at my tripewriter and produce the final 80,000 words of manuscript. For her love, affection, tolerance, understanding and encouragement, I will be forever grateful.

Page 1 An early 1300L in action. The shot was to signify the nature of the beast, a fun car that would appeal to the younger end of the market. Interestingly, the filler cap on this car is on the opposite wing to that of other production models

Page 2 Stuart Turner's faith in the RS Cosworth package has been vindicated—although two years ahead of full series production. A

Boreham-built, one-off RS Cosworth Escort, in the hands of unknown driver Joseph Mia Bordelet, beat all comers in the Spanish Talavera Rally in September 1990. Although a solid research and development programme on the rally cars was only just getting under way when this book went to press, the supremo of the rally team, Peter Ashcroft, was cautiously optimistic about it becoming a world-beater

Published in 1991 by Osprey Publishing Limited, 59 Grosvenor Street, London W1X 9DA

© Dennis Foy 1991

British Library Cataloguing In Publication Data

Foy, Dennis
Ford Escort.
1. Cars, history
I. Title
629.2222
ISBN 1–85532–143–2

Typeset by Keyspools Ltd, Golborne, Lancs
Printed by BAS Printers Limited, Over Wallop, Hampshire
Editor Nicholas Collins, Designer Simon Bell

Contents

Introduction

As far back as 1907, Henry Ford began work on a new car; his concept of a people's car, a tall, rangy and loose-framed sort of machine developed by a tall, rangy and loose-framed sort of man. Ford's ideal was to produce a vehicle which would revolutionize the way that people perceived the car by taking it out of the exclusive domain of the rich and into a much wider ownership. Basically, anybody earning a good wage ought to have been able to afford one of Mr Ford's Model T automobiles. And buy them they did—by the million. In creating the Model T, Henry Ford also revolutionized the way that cars were made, by inventing the production-line.

A few months short of 60 years after the Model T was announced, the Ford Motor Company introduced a new model which was destined to fulfil the same role of offering practical, sensible and durable transport for the proletariat. There were different variants of Model T back in the early part of the century, and there were different variants of Escort available six decades later. The difference was that whilst the Model T's different models were all based on practical considerations and all developed following Henry Ford's 'nose' for such matters, those of the Escort—not just the 1967 model, but the other four generations which have followed it—have had their creation rooted in far more scientific techniques; marketing, customer clinics and organized motorsport have all had a hand in developing the Escort and its derivatives. Yet beneath the skin, each and every model which has ever been available has had a selection of common components, and a common identity.

In the middle of the 1970s, the decision was taken to enlarge the scope of the Escort—which hitherto had been essentially a European product, although it had also gone on sale in a variety of non-European countries—to become a serious global project; the Escort for the 1980s was to be a real world car. The same machine would be manufactured and sold in every one of the five continents. Yet it never quite came off.

Although this book is essentially a celebration of the Ford Escort as the single biggest-selling car which Ford has had since the Model T—that car sold 15,000,000, a figure which the Escort has yet to beat—I have also undertaken to ask the question of why the Escort became the world car that never was. I hope that you gain as much pleasure from reading the finished story as I did from researching and writing it.

Dennis Foy
Cheshire
July 1990

1 Antecedency

On the heritage trail

WITH CLOUDS of dry ice vapour pierced by waving lasers and electronic music reaching a crescendo, Ford of Europe proudly unveiled its version of what was being trumpeted as that manufacturer's first *real* world car.

Although there would be slight variations to suit specific local market requirements (what Mr and Mrs Smith in Akron, Ohio, sought from a car would be different from the desires of Mr and Mrs Smythe in Accrington, Lancashire, and different again to the tastes of Herr and Frau Schmidt in Aachen, Westphalia), the new car, codenamed Erika, essentially would be the same machine the world over. Heralded as a dramatic automotive concept for the 1980s, the front-wheel-drive Escort range was jointly developed in a variety of research and development facilities dotted around the Western world. Whilst much of the car was developed independently in those various facilities, there was a considerable degree of co-operation, with international computer link-ups being consolidated by much telephone and face-to-face contact. It has been said that the main beneficiaries of the vast budget allocated to the Erika programme were the telecommunication and airline companies of America, Britain and Germany!

Yet hadn't we heard the 'world car' concept being proclaimed by Ford before 1980?

The entire Escort range—which had first appeared in 1968—had been mooted as being machines ready for springing upon a world market. The original Escort was a car of compact dimensions which, if allowed, could have helped conserve the world's already-dwindling resources of fuel and ore. What stopped that one in its tracks

was the intransigent attitude of Mr and Mrs Middle America—their idea of a small car in the mid 1960s was something which measured less than 18 ft from bow to stern, and which tipped the scales at under two tons. To suggest to them that they ought to be going to work or to the shopping mall in a machine measuring a mere 157 in. and weighing a modest three-quarters of a ton would have been as well received as the notion that they give up cars altogether and use roller-skates instead.

In Europe, the Escort was much better received. Ford of Britain had been building compact cars right from the time of the Great Depression, cars which were suited to the developed cart tracks which criss-crossed the verdant islands with a different landscape over every hill.

Henry Ford had begun operating in Britain in 1911, setting up an assembly plant for his legendary Model T in Trafford Park, Manchester. This car was followed, in turn, by the Model A, another American design, after which was to come the Model B, again an American machine. The Model B was the first series production car to use a V8-format engine as a powerplant. By the time it arrived in 1932, though, the writing was already on the wall for American cars in Britain—they were too big, too heavy and generally quite unsuitable for British roads. They were also on the wrong side of punitive British taxation classes which had been introduced in the previous decade, and which favoured small engines. As the 1930s dawned, the cries for a small, purpose-designed car for the British market became louder, to the point where Henry Ford and his people in Dearborn could no longer ignore them.

During the earliest days of the Ford Motor Company in Britain, it was based in Manchester. This photograph, taken in 1912, shows a Model T Tourer emerging from the showrooms on Deansgate—the factory was in Trafford Park

In 1931, Ford opened its new, purpose-built car manufacturing plant on a green-field site alongside the Thames at Dagenham—before too long, the Trafford Park assembly plant would close and its output be integrated into Dagenham. Much of the attraction of Dagenham (or Little Detroit, as Henry Ford christened it) was that it had its own deep-water quay, allowing components and equipment to be brought straight from Dearborn to the plant. On most occasions, the ships left Dagenham with empty holds, but on a couple of occasions they took with them examples of the new cars which were being produced by other manufacturers expressly for the British market.

Working from these examples, and adding a sizeable amount of their own knowledge and talents, Ford's technicians designed a new car to suit prevalent (and projected) British tastes and requirements. Early in 1932, a half-dozen examples of the prototype were built in Dearborn and shipped to Europe for evaluation by customers and dealers alike; even that long ago Henry Ford displayed his company's predilection for market research exercises. The new car, which was to become known as the Model Y, became immediately popular (pardon the pun) and was approved for production with only a small number of changes.

The first examples of production Model Y Fords rolled out of the Dagenham factory later that year, and they proved every bit as successful and appealing as the market research had suggested. With its flowing lines and swept-back radiator grille and windscreen, the car was undeniably

In fact, the Model T was Ford's first world car, being built in every one of the company's areas of operation world-wide. It would be the mid 1970s before Ford would try to resurrect the concept with the Escort—and the attempt was thwarted by local requirements overlooked in the initial Grand Plan

American in its styling, yet its diminutive lines made it appropriate for use on narrow British streets and lanes. Better still was its engine, a practical, fairly basic, valve-in-block, cast-iron device which displaced only 933 cc and which was rated at just under eight horsepower, ensuring that only the minimum rate of motor taxation applied. Best of all were the prices of the new cars; in two-door form, the car cost only £120, and in four-door form, the price was a reasonable £135.

The high level of sales achieved by the Model Y (or Ford Eight, as some of the advertising of the time described it) made Dearborn realize immediately what the potential was, so a stablemate for the Model Y was designed. This was as short as the Y, but had a wider bodyshell and a bigger engine; although basically the same as the eight-horsepower unit, the new engine's block was designed to allow a greater bore (2.5 in. rather than 2.23 in.), so an additional two horsepower was added to its taxation rating.

The prices of the new car, which was designated the Model C, but which was more commonly known as the Ford Ten, were keen; the two-door model sold for £135, while the four-door variant was £10 more. Incidentally, the British company had attempted to use the common American nomenclatures for the two variants, Tudor and

Fordor, but these had failed to fire the imagination of the public, who preferred to call them by their literal names.

By the time that the Model C arrived, William Morris had introduced his latest eight-horsepower car, and this had been acclaimed as a successful and sophisticated design; it had such features as hydraulic brakes, whereas the Ford models still relied on an arrangement of cables to operate their brake shoes. The Ford response had been to undercut Morris by a substantial margin, the net result being that the £100 car arrived. Needless to say, much use of this line was made in the advertising copy of the period.

By offering a comprehensive range of cars—as time progressed, other body variants of the two basic cars were introduced, such as open tourers and wood-panelled estate cars—Ford of Britain was able to open up a commanding lead in the sales field, particularly at the lower end of the market. This suited Henry Ford perfectly, for he considered himself to be very much the champion of the common man—after all, he was the person who had described his Model T as being as 'useful as a good pair of boots'. Of the same car, he also said that he would 'build a car . . . so low in price that no man making a good salary will be unable to own one and enjoy with his family the blessing of hours of pleasure in God's open spaces . . .'

The basic philosophies, of mechanical simplicity, clean styling and most of all perceived value for money, which had started with the Model T and which were to be found in the eight- and ten-horsepower cars, never really went away. Even today, they can be applied to the more basic models of the smaller cars in the present Ford line-up.

The design parameters of those early British-market Fords were carried over to subsequent models that wore the famous blue oval badge, and right up to the middle 1950s there were still Fords on sale which had transverse-leaf springs, only the most fundamental of braking systems, the familiar sidevalve engines and tall, upright bodyshells. What saved the day was that Ford consistently undercut the products of its rivals by a considerable margin. Production of the old 'sit-up-and-beg' Popular finally ceased in the middle of 1959, no less than 155,000 examples having been sold.

The Popular was nothing more than a low-cost development of the Model Y, and since it continued to sell at a more-than-acceptable rate in the late 1940s and early 1950s, it enabled Ford to turn all of its attention to developing a radically new range of cars, cars which would have low-line styling and which would be constructed on the monocoque principle. Rather than having a separate chassis upon which the body would be mounted, the new cars would have a central tub comprising the floorpan, inner front wings, door pillars and front and rear bulkheads. Between them, these would be able to hold the engine, driveline and suspension components. Although such methods of construction had been used successfully in racing, they were relatively new for mass-produced cars in Britain at the beginning of the 1950s.

The first to appear were the Consul and Zephyr/Zodiac models, which débuted in London at the 1950 Motor Show. They were indeed radically different to any previous British Fords, for they had sleek, low styling, abundant curves (there were precious few flat panels to be found on the cars), and had a totally new suspension arrangement with MacPherson struts at the front and a leaf-sprung live rear axle.

Five years later came the car which was the direct antecedent of the Escort range, the 100E.

Following on from the Model T was the Model A. This was more of a car than the Model T, which had been derived from Henry Ford's idea for a tractor. It was made available in a wide variety of different body styles, this particular example being a two-seat roadster

The peculiar needs of the British market were first served by a specific model in the form of the Model Y. This was powered by a small sidevalve engine backed by a three-speed gearbox. Once again, several different bodyshells were available—this one is a four-seat tourer

2 The die is cast

A new age in small Fords

WITH ITS compact dimensions and up-to-the-minute styling, the 100E was an immediate success. Available in two-door Anglia and four-door Prefect formats, the model measured only 157 in. from one bumper to the other, and a modest 60 in. wide. Thus, it was of smaller overall dimensions than the model which it was destined to replace—I say destined because for the first three years of the 100E's lifespan, the old sit-up Popular model would continue to be sold as the cheapest Ford. Only when the new model had been able to recoup a substantial chunk of its development budget would Ford's British management be able to offer a low-specification, low-cost version of the car through its dealerships.

Under the car's forward-hinged bonnet was the trusty old 1172 cc sidevalve engine that had first appeared in the mid 1930s—although by the time that it reached the 100E, it had developed such sophisticated assets as a full lubrication system, a water pump, which was driven by the fan belt (earlier models used a syphonic cooling system!), and a relatively high-compression cylinder head (7.0:1 as distinct from the earlier 6.1:1) with increased inlet-valve sizes. These amendments allowed the diminutive block to produce a reasonable 36 bhp at 4500 rpm, and a usable 54 lb/ft of torque. Interestingly, although the block was externally the same as that of the earlier car's engine, in fact, it was not interchangeable, but was a development dedicated to the 100E range.

Backing up the engine was a three-speed transmission, again of similar vintage to the engine. This had synchromesh on its upper two ratios, but not on first or reverse gear. At the back of the car was a live axle with tall (4.4:1) final drive gears, and

Ford's first small monocoque car was the 100E, shown here in Anglia form. The author has owned several of these machines and remembers them as being very tough, in a 'belt and braces' way, with crossmembers akin to those on the Forth Bridge

the overall package was such that the machine could eventually achieve a little over 70 mph with quite acceptable mid-range performance and acceleration which was at least as good as that of its competition.

If the driveline was nothing new, then the rest of the car's hardware was state-of-the-art. The rear axle was mounted on longitudinal springs, controlled by a pair of telescopic hydraulic dampers, and its location was very good; there was no swaying of the body, and ride quality remained good even at fairly high speeds over rough surfaces. At the front of the car was a pair of the latest Macpherson struts, devices which had coil springs sitting on the upper part of a robust telescopic damper. Compact and efficient, these were a world apart from the transverse beam axle and cart spring which had previously featured on small Fords. They allowed the two sides of the car's nose to act independently of each other; hitting a pothole with one wheel would not make the front wheel on the other side of the car skitter off line.

The tops of the struts were mounted in bushings to turrets formed as part of the inner wing sheetmetal, while at the bottom, they had spherical ball joints attached to the outside ends of track control arms. The inside ends of the track control arms were mounted via rubber bushes into the inverted U-section, pressed-steel crossmember, providing accurate lateral location. Positive fore-and-aft location was taken care of by an anti-roll bar which was bolted into the track control arms, again with rubber bushings, close to their outer ends. The anti-roll bar was mounted to the front cross-plate of the car and also gave an additional

A linchpin in Ford's Escort programme was the plant at Halewood, close to Liverpool Airport. Built on a green-field site, the plant has been home to the Escort since its inception

amount of springing. A steering box with idler arm had a ratio that combined a light action for the driver with a reasonably efficient turning circle. Apart from the steering, the same basic suspension arrangement would be found on equivalent cars for the next 20 years.

As with earlier small Fords, braking was taken care of by drums at each corner, but unlike its predecessors, the 100E's brakes were actuated by hydraulic pressure rather than by an arrangement of cables. They worked, too. However, an inspired burst of hard driving (and the 100E could be made to travel quite quickly, thanks to its good power-to-weight ratio and, by the standards of the day, excellent handling) could generate whiffs of smoke from the overheating friction shoes; they did not actually fade very much at all.

I have owned several of these little cars over the years, and in every case I have worked on them myself; one was restored to standard specification, another converted to a pickup truck, and the third was built into an Essex-engined drag race car. What was apparent from any close scrutiny was

Ford's belt-and-braces approach to their first small monocoque car. The front bulkhead was a relatively huge box-section of pressed steel—even with the middle cut away to accommodate the V6 of my racing version, the concept of scuttle shake was alien to the 100E, so much strength was there engineered into its basic design.

Substantial box sections were permanently attached to the floorpan of the car, the fore-and-aft members designed to aid the suspension location being augmented by lateral members (outriggers, as they were described) which prevented any tendency for the floorpan to twist. The rear bulkhead was made of a particularly thick grade of pressed-steel sheet, again welded positively into place, and there were reinforcing plates to be found around the rear damper mounts, the door hinge and lock areas, and the sill corner flitches. Looking at one of these cars closely today, it seems that Ford was paranoid about anything flexing and subsequently breaking on what, at the time, was a radical departure for them in small car building.

It was within the 100E range that the model name Escort was to be found on a Ford for the first time. This was the estate version of the Anglia—the equivalent model to the Prefect was the Squire, a name that has never been used since by Ford.

It was the next generation of small car from Ford which took the manufacturer closer to their world car concept. This was introduced in 1959 as the 105E Anglia, or 'angle box' as it was immediately nicknamed.

The 105E had been on the drawing boards since 1956, and it was to become the first fully-fledged product of the then-novel Ford Product Planning Department. As part of its overall strategy, the department had decided that by the middle of the 1960s there would be a new range of cars one size up from the 100E, a range which would slot in neatly between the Anglia/Prefect/Popular-sized machines and the top-sized Consul/Zephyr/Zodiacs. This meant that whilst the generation which would evolve from the 100E would still have to be a full four-seater, it did not need to be a four-door car; that aspect of the marketplace would be taken care of, in due course, by the middleweight which was to become the Classic in 1961.

The then Chairman of Ford, Sir Patrick Hennessy, was one of the hands-on executives who were common in the motor industry of the 1950s, and during one of the early planning meetings for the car which would become the 105E Anglia, he made it known that he felt very strongly about the welfare of rear-seat passengers in two-door cars.

So that Ford could begin production virtually from the day that the Halewood plant was complete, staff were hired in advance and trained in an aircraft hanger rented from the airport authority. Naturally, the city council was enthusiastic about the idea of Ford operating on Merseyside and bent over backwards to help

This was based on feedback from dealers and from the buying public. Mindful of his influential position—and no doubt of the fact that if the new car did not make adequate provision for those in the back, he would catch some flak—he suggested to the leader of the Product Planning Department that they ought to ensure ease of access to the rear seats and sufficient room for passengers once ensconced. However, they still had to keep to similar overall dimensions to the range of cars which the 105E was to supersede.

Therefore, the new Anglia had a pair of doors which were appreciably wider than those of earlier two-door cars; this created a precedent which is still being applied today, the doors of a two-door Escort being some 25 per cent longer than the front doors of a four-door example. It was the provision of adequate headroom for the back-seat passengers which led to the controversial reverse-angled rear window of the car. This design allowed the roof height to remain constant from front to rear, and interestingly also allowed the adoption of a slightly lower overall roofline which improved the aerodynamics of the car; although such factors as drag coefficients were not in everyday use at that time, manufacturers were becoming increasingly aware of the effect which wind resistance could have on the overall performance of a car.

The Anglia was endowed with a wheelbase longer by 3.5 in. than that of the 100E, at 90.5 in. This vital dimension would be stretched further when the Escort arrived eight years after the Anglia, but it was considered satisfactory for the market in which the Anglia would be competing.

The body of the new car was to be a monocoque again, and the suspension system first seen on the 100E would be employed. This time, though, Ford was not quite so apprehensive about building that type of car, and when it arrived it was obvious that a number of substantial weight savings had been made without sacrificing integrity or strength. The adoption of pressed-in swages, creases and integral box-sections enabled the car to be made without recourse to the relatively massive structures found on the 100E.

Once again, the steering was by a box, but this time it was a Burman recirculating-ball design, which reduced wheel effort and did away with some of the stiction which had dogged its predecessor. The rest of the front suspension layout remained as that of the earlier car, but at the rear, the cart springs were longer, and the axle was located ahead of their centreline to minimize axle tramp—a condition which was further controlled by the siting of rubber bump-stops between the front spring eye and axle on each side of the car.

Under the bonnet of the Anglia was a new engine. In place of the reliable and torquey little sidevalve device was a reasonably sophisticated pushrod unit with overhead valves and a displacement of just under a litre. This engine's block was designed from the outset to allow a variety of different capacities, so it had widely-spaced bore centres; the idea was to increase the engine size by the simple process of changing the crankshaft. The initial engine was extremely oversquare in its dimensions, the bore measuring 80.96 mm to the crankshaft's very modest stroke of 48.4 mm. The concept of an oversquare engine (which was designed to rev at high speeds by reducing

connecting-rod inertia) was rare in those days; most of the other manufacturers with whom Ford was competing were using undersquare dimensions, the stroke being greater than the bore. Undersquare engines are extremely good at developing torque, but in consequence feel lazy; in contrast, the free-revving Ford overhead-valve engine felt positively sporty.

In comparison with the other small engines of the day, the new engine had an extremely lightweight crankshaft; in fact, this central component was hollow. Initially, the crankshaft ran in three main bearings, an arrangement which was perfectly adequate given the inherent strength of the component and the fact that its dimensions were chosen to minimize whip and, thus, extremes of stress. As the engine family grew over the years (for this was the first example of the now-legendary Kent series of powerplants which would still be in use several decades later), its crankshaft was redesigned, along with the bottom end of the block, to allow another pair of bearings to be used as support.

Something else that was new to Ford was the fact that the engine had separate bearing caps with two-piece bearing shells. This meant that in the long term the crankshaft could be given a new lease of life quickly and easily; for the old sidevalve, specialized machining facilities were necessary. The new arrangement made it easy for the local garage or even the able home mechanic to effect a change of bearings.

Sir Patrick Hennessey, Chairman of Ford when the 105E Anglia project was in its gestation period. It was his insistence on a fair deal for the rear-seat passenger that led directly to the strange angle of the rear window which, in turn, led to the car's nickname of 'angle box'

FIRST CAR MADE ON MERSEYSIDE

N°1

The very first car to roll off the line at Halewood was this green Anglia, seen being presented to the then Mayor of Liverpool (it was hoped that he would drive it off the line, but the timing wasn't quite right!). This particular car is still in the charge of the city council

The Kent block was designed to be robust, yet light in weight and modest in its overall dimensions. The camshaft was positioned just above and to one side of the crankshaft, being driven by a toothed chain running between the pair of shafts. The oil pump and the distributor were driven from a gear on the camshaft, and the pump assembly also included a bolted-through oil filter. By arranging the oil system's primary components in unit, Ford was able to use various pickup pipes and sumps over the years to suit different applications of the engine; to keep the car's centre of gravity as low as possible (and, thus, improve its handling) the engine needs to sit low over the front crossmember, and this would call for a variety of sumps to suit specific underbonnet layouts.

Below Introduced in 1962, the Anglia was the immediate predecessor of the Escort; in fact, within Ford, the Escort was known as New Anglia until 1967 when it was re-christened. Initially available with only a 1200 cc overhead-valve engine, the Anglia was subsequently endowed with a 1500 cc development of the powerplant which, via several evolutions, would still be in use three decades later in the MkV Escort!

The Escort Mexico was a popular machine with clubman racers, thanks to its eminently tuneable 1600 cc Kent crossflow engine. This car is seen on the 1973 Avon Motor Tour of Britain—an event which Autoglass tried to resurrect a decade and a half later

The early examples of the Kent engine were equipped with a cylinder head design which had inlet and exhaust manifolds on the same side, but in time a new head would appear which was a crossflow design that offered superior gas-flow characteristics. But that would come later; all Anglias had pre-crossflow heads.

In terms of power output, the new engine was able to produce a creditable 39 bhp at 5000 rpm—a 3 bhp improvement over the old sidevalve engine, despite giving away 15 per cent in capacity. The torque characteristics of the new engine were surprisingly similar to those of the sidevalve, with 53 lb/ft at 2700 rpm. In real terms, this meant that the new engine was producing some 24 per cent more power than its predecessor.

Backing up the new engine was another novelty; the 105E was the first Ford saloon to come out of the factory with a four-speed gearbox as standard issue. Part of the reasoning behind this was that Ford was keen to shake off its reputation for clothing antiquated drivelines with modern bodyshells, and the management was convinced by its executive engineer, Fred Hart, that much of the impact of the new engine would be dissipated by the use of the old three-speed transmission. Hart siezed the opportunity and specified a set of ratios which endowed the new car with quite nippy acceleration from both standstill and whilst already on the move, and which also allowed a maximum speed of almost 80 mph. The earlier examples of the car came with a final drive ratio of 4.125:1, but later another ratio of 4.4:1 was offered

in estate models when they appeared in 1961.

Because of the sophisticated running gear (well, this was 1959) and its racy looks, the Anglia was an immediate success. Despite its modest overall dimensions, the car was able to accommodate four full-sized adults in comfort—for years to come, Ford would base its design parameters for that class of car on the internal measurements of the Anglia saloon. More than a million examples of the car were built and sold during its eight-year lifespan.

In 1962 came another derivative of the car with the introduction of the Anglia Super. This was powered by a 1200 cc engine, a powerplant which had appeared a month prior to the Anglia Super's October début when the Cortina arrived on the scene. As was to be expected, the increase in size was achieved by installing a longer-throw crankshaft which had a stroke of 58.17 mm—although this was greater than that of the original engine, the 1200 was still substantially oversquare and, thus, was able to rev freely, thanks to its low inertia and piston speeds. The power increase was in proportion to the extra 20 per cent of capacity, being just over 48 bhp at 4800 rpm, and the torque was up to 65 lb/ft at 2700 rpm.

By the time that the Anglia Super hit the streets, work had already started on another model of small Ford, which would eventually replace the Anglia towards the end of the decade. That car was to become the Escort, and it was to revolutionize Ford's marketing strategy.

The RS1700T undergoing serious testing in Portugal in 1982. The car's shape had already started to alter, the NACA ducts of the show car having given way to far more functional Fibresports bonnet scoops

3 Brief encounters

Evolution or revolution?

FORD'S PHILOSOPHY had always been to develop a car from the previous model, ironing out the areas of weakness or criticism and developing superior components as and when necessary. The Product Planning Department had assumed responsibility for the Anglia programme during its infancy, but the car, like others before it, had been a development of its predecessor. For the forthcoming Escort range, things would be different; the Product Planning Department would lay down fresh ground-rules for the new model, drawing up a package of requirements and the means of fulfilling them before any of the hands-on people would become involved.

Because the car would be taking over from the Anglia, it was clear that the overall packaging of the Escort would not be dissimilar to that of the earlier model, but there would be a few vital changes. The first of these concerned the ability of the bodyshell and suspension package to minimize noise, vibration and harshness from the road surface (NVH); Ford was the first major manufacturer in Britain to take the matter seriously, and to treat it as a scientific subject in its own right.

The bodyshell would again have to be of monocoque construction; Ford had discovered that this method of building cars offered a substantial number of advantages over the old separate body and chassis type of production, and was firmly committed to using the design throughout its European product ranges. The car would have to be a full four-seater with adequate luggage space for that number of occupants. It would also have to be adaptable enough to ensure that it could be satisfactorily built in four-door as well as two-door formats (Ford had realized that the lack of rear doors in the Anglia had harmed, or at least inhibited, sales) and as an estate car.

The new Escort would have to be very flexible in its choice of driveline, too. At the same 1959 Motor Show that had seen the Anglia unveiled to the public, the Mini had also been introduced. By the early 1960s, it was becoming crystal clear that there was a potential market for sporty versions of small cars, which was beginning to be exploited by the Anglia's co-débutant in the form of the Mini Cooper. If Ford was to capitalize on this new market segment, it would have to offer at least one, and possibly several, versions of the Escort which provided something of interest to the driver with sporting pretensions. It also occurred to the marketing people at Ford that having uprated versions of their cars active—and successful—in motorsport could generate more interest in the showroom models.

Finally, the car would have to be produced to a finely-controlled price; it is a fact of life in the motor industry that the smaller the car, the lower the profit margin, and it has been proven time and again that even the price of an ashtray, or a few pence on the cost of a set of tyres, can make all the difference to the profitability of a basic model. As the specification of the car climbs, profitability rises accordingly, but the tenet of being prudent with the pennies at the beginning was a Ford philosophy. And anyway, at that time, the vast majority of Ford car sales were provided by the basic models in each of their product lines.

The eventual brief ran to a dozen typed pages, and the heads of all the departments involved had the overall goals impressed upon them at a series of product planning meetings. Only when everybody

The world car concept is apparent in these clay model studies which were released a year after the car had gone into production. The Anglia designation, which was still being used at that time, is apparent from the plates on two examples. Looking at the options, it is safe to say that the correct choice was made for the final car

was fully aware of the need to meet their specific objectives within the brief were the teams allowed to start work on the car itself.

The styling of the car, which at that point was known as the New Anglia/1968 programme, was supposed to have been handled jointly by the staff at Ford of Britain's studios in Aveley and the Ford of Germany stylists at Merkenich. However, shortly after the Anglia/1968 programme was officially instigated in 1963, the Germans were handed a half-finished Taunus concept from Dearborn and told to finish it so that it was ready to sell on the Western European market by the later part of the decade.

As a result, virtually all of the responsibility for what would eventually become the Escort passed to Ford of Britain. Working closely with their colleagues at Advance Vehicle Studies in Birmingham, and with the engineering team at Dagenham, the stylists at Aveley began to draw up ideas. However, at that time, the final format of the car had still to be decided, for the late 1950s and early 1960s had thrown up all manner of driveline configurations, ranging from the transverse, front-wheel-drive arrangement, championed by Issigonis and his Mini, to the rear-drive, rear-engine of the Hillman Imp.

As still happens today, the moment that it was possible to do so, Ford's engineers would get hold of an example of a rival's car, carefully dissect it and analyse its make-up and potential. The same thing happened with every other manufacturer, and doubtless the British Motor Corporation, Standard Triumph, Vauxhall, et al, had taken apart examples of the Anglia back in 1959. Having studied every feature of every competitor's products, and tried out a few of the ideas for itself using its own production or home-built components, the Ford engineering team kept coming back to the same conclusion; the only format which would really work for the New Anglia would be that of the old one. Thus, it would have an in-line, four-cylinder engine driving through the rear wheels, the whole shebang being kept off the ground by a suspension system that was basically the same as that already employed in the existing Anglia model.

Once there was a basic set of dimensions from which to work, the styling ideas came thick and fast. Some were outright flights of fancy, whilst others were downright fundamental. Eventually, the best of the sketches were picked by the Product Planning Department, and the laborious process of making three-dimensional clay models was begun; drawings and sketches can deceive the eye, so it was essential to have a full-size representation of each of the short-listed ideas to walk around, to view from every conceivable angle, and to generally nit-pick over before a final decision could be made. Today, the process has been simplified greatly by computer programmes that generate three-dimensional impressions of a car from scaled plan and elevation data inputs.

In addition to demonstrating the aesthetic advantages of a styling idea, a full-size mock-up also gave the production engineers the opportunity to evaluate the feasibility of actually producing a favoured design. In this respect, smaller manufacturers, able to mould bodyshells in fibreglass or other plastic materials, were, and are, far better off than those producing cars from sets of pressed-steel panels.

Eventually, a body style was settled upon, one which fulfilled all of the requirements by being readily adaptable to two- and four-door, and estate-car formats (the vehicle also subsequently became available as a van), and which was easily broken down into the required number of small panels to allow mass-production at a reasonable cost. Meanwhile, work had been going on in the engineering department to sort out the details of the car's underpinnings.

The MacPherson strut front suspension from the Anglia would be carried over to the new car, but with a vital difference; instead of having the fore-and-aft location taken care of by the anti-roll bar, the New Anglia would have a compression strut which would run rearwards from each track control arm. The British engineering team felt that this would reduce kickback through the steering wheel whenever the car hit a bump in the road and,

thus, would make it less susceptible to road harshness. Unfortunately, although the earliest examples of Escort were equipped in this way, cars produced from late 1969 onwards reverted to the older method of location, which utilized the anti-roll bar and which was forced upon the British designers by their counterparts at Merkenich.

Totally new was rack-and-pinion steering in place of the previous box-and-idler-arm arrangement. This took up less space than the latter and was altogether more precise in its action. Furthermore, with volume purchases, the unit cost could be held to slightly below that of the earlier system, while the time taken to install the rack on the production line could be reduced because of its simplified mounting arrangement; rather than having to bolt in first the steering box itself and then its idler assembly, the entire rack assembly was located by a pair of saddle clamps attached to the front suspension crossmember. Ford has long held to a policy of dual-sourcing their vital components, and the steering rack of the Escort was no

Today's cars spend much of their early development life in the new test facility at Dunton, or in the similar 'punishment cell' at Merkenich. In 1967 this instrument was strapped to the back of the car, and its print-out read at the end of each session

exception; it came from either Burman or Cam Gears, the two makes being interchangeable.

At the rear of the car was the familiar solid rear axle, which could accommodate a wide variety of different final drive gear sets. The axle was attached to the bodywork by a pair of in-line cart springs measuring 2 in. across and almost 4 ft in length. These were available in a variety of different poundage rates for specific applications, and there were either three or four leaves to each spring depending upon its pressure rating. The springs were controlled by dual-acting hydraulic dampers, mounted with their upper eyes forward of the line of the lower set as an aid to positive location; Ford's chassis engineers had favoured the use of a pair of forward-running tie bars to help control axle tramp, the syndrome where the torque from the engine forces the pinion gear to climb up the crownwheel, causing the axle to twist so that the tyres break contact with the tarmac. The strict rules on noise, vibration and harshness set by the Product Planning Department made such a system unacceptable, so the forward rake of the dampers and the way in which the axle was mounted forward of the spring centre-line was the accepted compromise. To minimize noise transmission from the road, and to absorb harshness, the dampers and springs were mounted to their respective floorpan brackets via rubber bushes.

Interestingly, a number of vital changes were made to the floorpan during the Escort's lifespan which seemed to be at odds with the rules on noise, vibration and harshness—but more of those later.

On basic models of Escort, the same 8 × 1.5 in. drum brakes, carried over from the Anglia, were used to provide stopping power. With the small engines which powered those cars—and with the type of driving which generally goes with low-powered cars—these were perfectly adequate. However, on the first of the 'hot' Escorts, the 1300GT which formed part of the original line-up at the car's London Motor Show début in 1967, disc brakes were to be found at the front, a servo being provided to relieve the pedal pressure. Discs were also to be found on the 1300 cc estate version of the Escort.

Under the bonnet of the new car could be had any one of several variants of the same Kent engine. Although engineering prototypes of the car were to be seen running around Western Europe in general, and Essex in particular, with the Anglia-specification engine as motive power, by the time the car reached production, the engine had been updated and featured the crossflow

cylinder head. There had also been a change of the available sizes; with a common bore size of 80.98 mm (only fractionally greater than that of the original engine from which it had evolved), but with a choice of either 53.29 mm or 62.99 mm stroke crankshafts, the engine's displacement was either 1098 cc or 1298 cc. The five-bearing crankshaft was used in this engine and, combined with the oversquare dimensions, ensured a pleasing free-revving nature.

For the first time in a small production car, Ford offered buyers a choice of engine specifications, providing the option of a low or high compression ratio, which meant that the cars could operate on either low-grade fuel or on a high-octane diet, depending upon local conditions. The standard compression ratio of the engine was 9.0:1, but in the low-compression variants it was 8.0:1. Additionally, the GT version of the 1300 cc engine was available with a standard compression ratio of 9.2:1.

The power outputs of these engines were quite reasonable, considering the period and their modest dimensions; the low-compression 1100 gave 47 bhp at 5500 rpm, whilst the high-compression version of the same car was rated at 2.5 bhp more. Torque figures were 54.5 lb/ft and 58.5 lb/ft respectively. The three 1300 cc engines were rated proportionally higher: 53.5 bhp at 5000 rpm for the low-compression version, 58.0 bhp for the high-compression model, and no less than 71 bhp (albeit at 6000 rpm) from the GT engine. Torque figures were 68 lb/ft for the low compression engine, 71.5 for the high-compression version, and 70 for the powerplant in GT trim.

As had been anticipated when the Kent engine block had first been designed, the oil sump for the Escort was at the opposite end to that of the Anglia, as the engine sat slightly further back in the chassis than it had done in the earlier car. This was in the interests of better front-rear weight distribution. Because of Ford's policy of multi-sourcing, there were two possibilities for the oil-feed system; depending on the car, there was a choice of either rotary or sliding vane pump. In either case, the design pressure within the system was between 35 and 40 psi, a figure which caused one or two raised eyebrows among the informed of the day because it was appreciably lower than that for other engines from rival makers. That so many Kent engines went on to achieve 100,000 miles of faithful service during the ensuing years, without recourse to major surgery, was vindication of Ford's engine designers.

Studio shot of a pre-production model for evaluation; not a single badge in sight. This may have been one of the cars that were used during the many market research clinics prior to the model launch

The basic engine range achieved its power output with very modest valve sizes and valve timing, but to extract the 20-odd per cent more power needed to endow the GT version of the Escort with acceptable performance, both of these were changed. The standard 1300 cc valve face diameters were 1.4 in. for the inlet, and 1.25 in. for the exhaust, but in the GT engine, the former was increased to 1.5 in., while the latter remained the same. The cam timing was changed from the standard engine's 17/51/51/17 degrees to a far more radical 27/65/65/27 degrees.

The fuel system was also changed for the GT version. On the standard engines, slightly different variants of the same Autolite C7AH single-choke carburettor were specified—these could have either manual or automatic cold-start devices, depending upon application. Neither of these, however, was man enough to feed the much-improved top end of the GT version, so Ford turned to the Italian carburettor manufacturer Weber SpA for help, which duly arrived in the form of a 32DFE twin-choke unit. On the other side of the engine block, the modest (and noise-suppressing) cast-iron manifold of the standard range was replaced by a complex, four-tube fabricated manifold, feeding into the same basic silencing system as that of the 1300 cc saloon.

Regardless of engine specification, behind it was a compact, four-speed transmission with synchromesh on all four forward gears. This was effectively the work of one man, in that it was Ford staff engineer Ken Einchcombe who was responsible for the smooth-as-silk gearshift for which the car will always be remembered. That the rest of the transmission worked well was purely incidental to most people; what counted was the way in which the appropriate gear could always be selected quickly and cleanly.

Rather surprisingly for a new and purpose-designed transmission, the unit was not actually as strong as it felt from within the car; its design capacity was in the region of 80 lb/ft of torque, and at much beyond that, it would start to break up, albeit slowly. The other weakness of the transmission was one which was only normally found by enthusiastic drivers who were keen on making the occasional powershift up or down the ratios; at some point, the somewhat disturbed driver would find that the gear lever had divorced itself from the rest of the box and would end up being waved about in mid-air rather than being where it ought to be, sticking up through the car's central tunnel.

The reason for this was the way in which the lever mechanism was mounted to the gearbox tailhousing. Because that part of the transmission casing was cast in aluminium alloy rather than the iron of the bellhousing and main body, and because cast aluminium is weaker than the steel which would normally have been used for making the lower part of the gearlever, a nylon threaded bush was used. This would tear out of its home as soon as too much force was applied to it. Ford eventually developed a permanent method of fixing, but the early examples of the transmission were dogged by the problem.

From the tail of the gearbox which, incidentally, was fed its power by a cable-controlled clutch rather than the previously-favoured hydraulically-operated unit, led a single-piece propshaft on the 1100 cc models, or a two-piece propshaft with supported centre bearing on the 1300 cc cars. At the other end of this was the rear axle, and it was this third member which caused more than the occasional argument between the various teams responsible for engineering the overall package. The problem was not the axle itself, which was a robust piece of hardware, but rather the ratios which were to be used in its final drive arrangement.

On one side of the camp were those for whom NVH was sacrosanct and who felt, quite justifiably, that the best possible reduction in NVH would be gained from having as tall a set of gears as possible; that way, the engine would be running at a leisurely pace when the car was cruising—and as the engine was one of the main noise generators in the car, that had to be the way to go. In the other

camp were those arguing that to go to a tall set of final drive gears would exact too high a cost in drivability; the lower the overall gearing, the sharper the acceleration, and vice versa.

In the end, compromises were struck and the car came to the marketplace with a variety of standard and optional gear sets, varying between a tall 3.77:1 and a short 4.44:1—at least, that was the theory. In practice, few dealers bothered to let potential customers know that options were there for the taking, so most of the cars that were sold came with their standard build ratios. The 1300 saloons, in manual transmission form, came from the factory with 3.77:1 gearing (the option was 4.125:1), and the 1100 cc cars, because of their relative lack of power, came as standard with 3.90 gearing—the NVH camp arguing successfully that the buyers of 1100 examples of the car would care more for economy than for acceleration capabilities. Probably they were right.

Having won that particular battle (as well as the earlier one concerning the layout of the rear suspension), the NVH addicts lost the war through no fault of their own; although they could effectively control the way that the three qualities of noise, vibration and harshness were transmitted into the car, the costs involved in carrying their creed through into the cabin precluded matters. So far as the car manufacturers of the day were concerned, the interior trim of the car was dictated by the overall price of the machine (such things haven't really changed even today, but more of that later), and if you wanted a deep-pile carpet which covered a thick layer of soundproofing felt, then you bought a big car. Conversely, if you bought a small car, you got rubber mats.

Similarly, if you wanted an array of clocks ahead of you which told you everything that was going on out of your immediate line of sight, then you bought an expensive sportscar. If you bought a cheap car, you were told the basics of how fast you were going, how much fuel you had and, if you were really lucky, whether or not the engine was close to overheating.

Given that basic philosophy, it should come as no surprise to anybody to learn that the purchaser of the lowliest model of Escort gained only the lowliest level of trim. The more you paid for the car, the more you received, but even the original top-of-the-line model in the standard range, the 1300GT, was hardly plush.

Externally, it was a different story; the more you paid for the model, the more embellishments there were to tell the world precisely so.

4 Launching the fleet

The Escort arrives

THE FORD ESCORT RANGE was officially announced at the Brussels Motor Show in January 1968, and an advertising campaign rolled out across Britain at the same moment using the copy line 'The New Ford Escort. The Small Car That Isn't'. Despite the fact that the then-Prime Minister, Harold Wilson, and his Foreign Secretary, George Brown, were in Rome discussing the possibility of Britain becoming a member of the European Common Market, it was Ford's new baby that was grabbing most of the headlines in that day's newspapers.

The car's styling was certainly modern and immediately attractive, and for those curious to see the real thing rather than photographs in the newspapers, Ford had ensured that there were more than 11,000 examples of the range disseminated through the dealer network. There were an additional 8000 cars on display throughout Europe at the same time—production of the car had commenced in November of the previous year at Ford's Halewood plant, on Merseyside, to ensure adequate supplies by the launch date.

As is typical of the industry, the more attractive models, those with a higher perceived value such as the Super and the GT, made up the bulk of those cars sitting on showroom floors; it is easier to draw the punter into the dealership with an attractive model from the range, and then trade down to the amount of money that the customer has to spend, than to attempt the exercise from the opposite direction.

At the time of the launch, the full line-up comprised five cars—although only four of these were in plentiful supply. These were, in ascending order of cost, the 1100 De Luxe at £635, the 1100 Super at £666, the 1300GT at £647, and the 1300 Super at £690. The fifth car was the Twin Cam, a rare and desirable beast that deserves its own chapter, which follows. For now, it is worth investigating the four mainstream cars.

As its price indicates, the 1100 De Luxe was the most basic model obtainable. In common with all the others, this was available initially only with two doors. In contrast to its name, there was precious little luxury to be found in the cabin of the car, but in fairness to Ford, it was no worse than any other car on the market at the price. On the floor was a rubber mat—moulded to shape and colour co-ordinated, but still a rubber mat—while the driver and passengers sat on moulded vinyl seats with fixed backrest angles and squabs which were crucifyingly flat and lacking in support. The same vinyl was to be found trimming the door panels, complete with moulded-in stitch marks—the description 'hand-tooled vinyl' was coined by one wag at the time.

The fascia comprised a curved metal panel, the upper surface of which was covered in a non-reflective plastic. In the centre of this was a pair of swivelling air vents, through which heated or ambient air, or a combination of both, could be directed at either the screen or the occupants of the front seats. Immediately ahead of the driver was a moulded binnacle which housed a pair of circular instruments of about 4 in. in diameter. One of these was a speedometer able to register up to 110 mph (optimistic!), whilst the other told the driver the coolant temperature and how much fuel remained in the nine-gallon tank. The rest of the fascia comprised a strip of imitation wood, perhaps 1½ in. deep, running from the passenger door to the instrument pod and into which were set the sliding heater controls. Indicators were controlled by a stalk mounted on the steering column on the blind side of the deep-dished, spindly, three-spoke steering wheel, but all other primary functions were taken care of by a selection of rocker switches scattered along the fascia. The only exception to this was the screen washer, which on the early cars was controlled by a floor-mounted switch adjacent to the clutch pedal. I have lost count of the number of times that I have involuntarily washed the windscreen whilst making a rapid gearchange when driving any of the half-dozen early Escorts which I have owned over the years!

In keeping with the juke-box styling favoured at the time, much use was made of chromium-plated strips, both inside and outside the car—on the fascia were thin edges of the stuff, and the window and door handles were similarly brightly-finished. Externally, the full-width bumper bars were

chromed, as were the surrounds of the rear lights. The radiator grille—which also incorporated surrounds for the 7 in. diameter headlamps—was produced from a bright metal alloy, to give the effect of chrome at appreciably reduced cost. Finally, the door handles were chrome-plated, as were the (optional) door mirrors.

There were a number of extras available for the car, the list starting with a push-button radio, although in those days it was still described as a wireless. This worked tolerably well and cost £20 by the time that purchase tax had been added to its basic ex-factory price. Because the car had been conceived as a low-cost form of transport for the masses, there was no provision for such an instrument; it would be several years before Ford cottoned on to the notion of customers liking to mount the radio in the fascia itself. Therefore, when it was specified, it came in a moulded carrier which allowed it to be slung beneath the fascia, outboard of the driver.

Other popular extras were front disc brakes (complete with servo assistance), which endowed the car with the same means of stopping as the GT model for a premium of £15 7s. 6d. (£15.37), and metallic paint at just over £6.

Then there were the wider wheels. As part of the cost-paring exercises which had been an ongoing feature of the car's entire development pro-

To a fanfare from the Household Cavalry, the Escort is announced to the press at a gala ball in London in 1967. Only the basic range was shown at this point; for some years, it has been a Ford policy to progressively unveil models, partly to suit the manufacturing process, but mainly to extend the amount of potential publicity

gramme, there had been considerable controversy within the department concerning the wheel size. Originally, the notion of carrying the 13 in. diameter rims of the Anglia over to the new car had been favoured, but those concerned with reducing noise, vibration and harshness were pushing in favour of 12 in. diameter wheels. They argued that these would offer more precise control of ride, handling and surface noise, and also would allow the use of slightly smaller wheelarches and a small reduction in overall body length. Additionally, there would be an overall weight saving in the region of 13 lb in the unsprung weight of the car.

Countering those arguments were the facts that Ford would have to invest £40–60,000 of the total development budget in tooling up for new wheels and would have to put pressure on the tyre manufacturers to ensure the supply of 12 in. tyres—which, at the time, were an uncommon size—at an acceptable price. Eventually, the first argument won the day and the standard cars would roll out of the Halewood plant on 12 × 3.5 in. wheels, shod with 5.50/12 crossply tyres. A concession to the greater power of the GT version was made by fitting it with 4.5 in. wide wheels with 155/12 radial-ply rubber.

For an extra £12, Ford provided the standard saloons with the wider, radial-clad wheels of the GT model. Another option in that area provided whitewall crossplies for base models, but these were already considered *passé* by so many potential owners that few took up Ford's offer. That option soon disappeared from the list.

Purchasers of the Super version of the Escort, in addition to the choice of either 1.1 or 1.3 litre powertrains, also received one or two other worthwhile additions to their cars over the De Luxe models. Externally, the cars were immediately identifiable by their rectangular headlamps, which measured 9 in. across and which, on paper at least, were more efficient than the smaller round lamps of the lesser car. In practice, however, their performance was not sparkling, and before long Escort Supers were to be seen whizzing about with pairs of rectangular Lucas spotlamps mounted in front of the grille.

On the inside, the main advantage of spending the extra for the Super trim package was to be found on the floor; in place of the rubber matting was a loop-pile carpet. The seats of the car were also uprated to offer a small amount of lateral support by having moulded-in 'bolsters' at the sides of each squab.

Naturally, all of the extras which were available for the base model were also on offer to those purchasing the Super variants.

The buyers of the 1300GT models got the best deal. Although the interior trim was the same as that of the Super versions, the driver was provided with a good deal of additional instrumentation; in place of the standard two-gauge binnacle was one of similar dimensions housing a speedometer (again reading to 110 mph for those who liked to brag about such matters in the pub), next to which was a tachometer of equal size, redlined at 7000 rpm. To the right of the two main clocks were four smaller ones which monitored engine coolant temperature, battery condition, oil pressure and the usual fuel tank contents. A special steering wheel centre boss with a pair of crossed flags and a GT badge completed the sporty image. Externally, the special badging and the wider wheels formed the first impressions of the car, and the image was completed by a pair of overriders on each bumper bar.

The curvaceous lines of the new car were in total contrast to the stark angularity of the Anglia, and in consequence Ford had decided at an early stage of the development programme that a new name was in order. The issue of what to call a new model is thorny to any manufacturer. Firstly, the title must not offend in languages other than its mother tongue; the embarrassment at Rolls-Royce still reverberates when the matter of the Silver Mist is brought up—the company discovered too late, and to its chagrin, that whilst the name evoked images of Highland mystery in Britain, in Germany it translated into something else entirely, for 'mist' is a teutonic slang word for the results of a basic bodily function. Being an international manufacturer keen to develop a pan-European market for the new car, Ford was keen not to put itself into any similar situation.

Because of the international flavour of the new car, which was being promoted as a true European effort and just a step away from being a true world car, the obvious nationalistic connotations of the name Anglia were undesirable. Few of the earlier model names used by Ford, such as Prefect, Popular, Classic or Pilot would do, and the name Capri had already been reserved for the forthcoming sporty coupé which was due to arrive at about the same time as the Escort. Ford had started to explore the possibility of using place names for cars, with Cortina (a skiing resort in the Italian Dolomite mountains) already being in use, and Granada being reserved for the ultimate replacement for the Zephyr/Zodiac range. The potential

Interior shot of a basic model of the first Escort. The large, spindly steering wheel and instrumentation, which have been retrospectively dubbed 'jukebox style', are offset by a plain rubber floorcovering and simple vinyl-covered seats

in that area was limited, however; most place names were either too cumbersome or too nationalistic—could you imagine the reaction to the Ford Cannes, or perhaps the Ford Florence?

Two possibilities did emerge from the list of already-used names, though. One was the Squire which, although it had possibilities, was a little too 'quaintly English' for most European tastes. But Escort, that had potential. The name was innocuous in any language, and it had only been used in the low-quantity estate car market for a short time. It was eventually adopted for use on the new model range.

As is common practice in the industry, the press were allowed to see the car a short time before the

rest of the world, being flown out to a pan-European launch in Morocco in the middle of January 1968. Initial reaction to the new car was very favourable, judging by the reports which followed as soon as the embargo allowed; a voluntary code of conduct exists within the more responsible areas of the motoring press even today, with journalists respecting the wishes of the manufacturers not to disclose significant details of a forthcoming model until it suits the makers.

The light and responsive steering of the Escort range gained immediate favour, as did the lively performance of even the most basic models. The test cars were all equipped with disc brakes (they were an option, remember, and Ford has always tended to load its press demonstration vehicles with all of the available options), and these also attracted praise for their light pedal feel and effective stopping power. Having already tested various examples of the car in varied conditions (desert tracks in Australia, arctic work in Finland, and so forth) Ford was unafraid of the cars

The up-market instrumentation gave the driver a set of four additional instruments, and a third design of door liner panel. Even though this was the top-of-the-line fascia, there was still no provision for a radio, which would be underslung from the dash panel if required

breaking, despite the gruelling press tests which they would be put through in North Africa; in two days, the assembled journalists would cover more than 700 miles of hard desert driving.

In addition to the press appraisals in Morocco, planeloads of dealers were also flown out to the North African kingdom to try the car. Although a select number of influential importers and dealers had already sampled prototypes—and been able to advise Ford of specific strengths and weaknesses within the range for their market needs and requirements—this was the first opportunity that most dealer principals and salesmen had been offered to examine the newcomer which Ford hoped would open up a substantial market lead

during the next decade. They, too, went home suitably impressed.

In addition to the mainstream production cars, the visitors to Morocco had also been shown what was to become an extremely useful tool in Ford's Escort marketing strategy—the Twin Cam.

The Escort GT, which had wider-section tyres, black window trim, and overriders. That brightwork around the wheelarches looked very nice, but it soon proved to be a water trap, leading to a healthy trade in new wheelarch repair sections in bodyshops throughout Europe

5 Twin cam, twin cam, little star

Starting point for the RS Escorts

EXCITING was the most widely-used adjective during conversations concerning the Twin Cam Escort when it made its début. The story had really started earlier in the decade, when Ford and Lotus had joined forces to create the Cortina Lotus, a marriage of the Ford all-purpose saloon and the sophisticated, Harry Mundy-designed, dual-overhead-camshaft engine which Lotus Cars, under the leadership of the mercurial Colin Chapman, had created for their road and race cars. At the time, Walter Hayes was running Ford's Public Affairs Department and was keen to generate as much publicity as possible for the newly-announced Cortina. Chapman and Hayes were old friends, so the alliance was fairly easy to forge under such circumstances. The car which resulted was everything that both parties had aimed for and generated masses of press coverage for Ford. The car also spawned the entire Rally Sport range (the 'e' of Rallye came later) when sales supremo Sam

The car which started the RS revolution was the Cortina Lotus, a marriage of Ford's middleweight contender and the latest in high-technology, twin-overhead-camshaft engines from Lotus Cars, the specialist concern which had been founded by Colin Chapman.

Toy press-ganged a select number of dealerships into handling not only this highly-strung hybrid, but also the special range of parts which competitors intending to use the Cortina Lotus in racing and rallying would require.

Powerful and fast by the standards of the day, the Cortina Lotus was a highly effective tool in the hands of the right driver. When the legendary Jim Clark spent time in one during the 1964 British Touring Car Championship, it came as no surprise to anybody that he and his car became overall champions.

From those beginnings, Ford had rapidly evolved a special team based at Boreham, a decommissioned wartime bomber base just north of Chelmsford in Essex. It had campaigned the Cortina Lotus with great effect, but by the mid 1960s it was becoming apparent that the formula was beginning to weaken a little, affected by increasingly successful products from the competition. There was another generation of Cortina on the way, a squared-off development based on the original's floorpan, but this would not be able to do any better than the earlier car, even if the engine was taken further. Being aware that the Escort was on the way, the team turned its attention to the new car to determine whether the magic already generated by the Cortina Lotus could be repeated by building a Lotus-powered Escort.

By the time that the concept was thought up, in January 1967, by Bill Meade and his then boss Henry Taylor, the Escort was almost ready for production and the tooling was already being installed at the Halewood production plant, which would be the only home for the Escort in its infancy. However, virgin bodyshells were scarce and in great demand. Although the car was signed off for production in its final prototype form, the engineering team was not entirely happy with it and wanted to develop things further. Consequently it tended to nab any spare bodyshells that were left standing for longer than a few minutes. That the project was conceived by Boreham and not by Product Planning did not help matters, and internal politics created obstructions to the team at the Competitions Department. However, it persevered in its quest to get hold of a full bodyshell and eventually managed to 'borrow' (possibly through the back door) a full-size mock-up of a final-state bodyshell and floorpan from the newly-opened Dunton Research and Development Centre.

By working through the weekend, the team was able to establish that the hybrid could be built and that the engine and transmission of the Cortina

Henry Taylor and Bill Meade, of Ford's Competitions Department, hatched a plan to evolve the Cortina Lotus concept into the two-door Escort. The result was the Escort Twin Cam. Early development work was carried out on a borrowed bodyshell mock-up, all the work to establish the feasibility of the concept being undertaken in a single weekend!

Lotus could be shoehorned into place within the narrower confines of the Escort's engine bay. However, it was found that the bigger and beefier gearbox paired with the Lotus twin-cam engine would not fit in the Escort's central tunnel, which was a close fit around the original, smaller gearbox. Had there been the time to develop a suitable pressing, it would have been done, but as time was tight—and development money tighter still—the team conceded that the extra space would have to be provided by using what, at the time, was referred to as a 'labourer's screwdriver'. You and I would know it as a 4 lb lump hammer.

Because the Lotus engine, with its twin side-draught Weber carburettors, was substantially wider than the Kent crossflow for which the Escort engine bay had been designed, the team at Competitions soon realized that there would be more to the project than was apparent at first glance. Once it had a real bodyshell on which to work, it was able to start building up a prototype of the vehicle, and to ascertain exactly what was involved. The major problem was that the rearmost carburettor choke fouled against the brake master cylinder, and even moving that component across the bulkhead failed to make enough clearance. The problem was finally solved by moving the entire engine block sideways by a couple of inches at the front, thus

drawing the offending carburettor clear of the bulkhead!

Various other bits which normally lived under the bonnet of the Escort needed to be either shuffled about or moved completely, and the most conspicuous of these was the battery; by the time that the Lotus lump was *in situ*, there was no longer any room for the battery. Therefore, the Competitions Department employed an old racing trick and relocated this vital component in the boot. This not only solved the initial problem, but also improved weight distribution and traction.

Having squeezed the engine and gearbox of the Cortina Lotus into the bodyshell, the team then turned its attention to the rest of the underpinnings. The axle from the Cortina Lotus could be

The eight-valve, twin-overhead-camshaft engine sits at a slight angle—the nose of the engine is offset slightly to the car's nearside so that the rearmost carburettor clears the inner wing. It also proved necessary to relocate the battery in the car's boot

persuaded into the space at the back of the Escort's bodyshell (the 50 in. rear track of the donor car left a space within each wheelarch, but the axle was a snug fit within the confines of the smaller car's bodyshell. In the interests of keeping a balanced package, the final drive ratio of the Escort Twin Cam (or Lotus Escort, as it was commonly referred to at Boreham) was left the same as it had been in the Cortina at 3.90:1. However, once the car had finally met with the approval of the Product Planning people, this was changed to a 3.77:1 set of gears which better suited the lighter weight of the Escort.

Although the Boreham team would have dearly loved to have installed the axle on coil springs, the format of the Escort's floorpan precluded this, so the car utilized the same arrangement of leaf springs and angled dampers which were to be found beneath the standard versions of the Escort. The team would also have liked to locate the axle more positively by using a panhard rod and a pair of radius rods. In the end, however, it had to settle for the latter items only, as it was not possible to

install a panhard rod 'twixt axle and floorpan.

At the front end of the car, the team was able to dispense with the production car's compression struts and to revert to the anti-roll bar as a means of controlling the fore-and-aft movement of the suspension legs. They were also able to make use of the big disc and caliper sets which were specified for the Cortina Lotus—although their adoption would involve the use of the 13 in. diameter wide steel wheels of that car, as the smaller road wheels of the standard Escort line-up would foul the calipers. Because the Escort came as standard with a fast-acting steering rack, requiring but three and a half turns of the spindly steering wheel from lock to lock, and because the car had a design turning circle of 31 ft, Competitions utilized the standard issue equipment.

Ford's Competitions Department, in common with its counterparts in other car manufacturing companies world-wide, has always considered that the way a car goes is more important than its levels of comfort. However, it had a burning desire to see the project become a production reality, and to do so needed to gain the approval of first the entire Product Planning Department and then of the main board of directors of Ford Motor Company. To achieve these ends, it needed to present a finished package, so the final prototype was built with the full range of interior appointments already specified for the 1300GT Escort. This meant that the car had the GT's superior seats along with the six-clock instrumentation. As a concession to the NVH advocates in Product Planning, the Twin Cam was treated to a carpet; this, they hoped, would make it seem less like an all-out competition car and more of a very fast road machine.

Because the Competitions Department worked as a close-knit team, it was able to conclude the first, and biggest, phase of the programme in a very short period of time. Whilst the initial concept was discussed in January 1967, it was March before the team managed to get its hands on the borrowed dummy shell, and another three months before a real bodyshell, the one upon which it could actually start work, came into its possession. Even with these hurdles, it was able to show its finished and trimmed prototype, and gain approval, by October of that year. The car was complete right down to the appropriate badges; they acquired a set of Twin Cam badges which were destined for the MkII Cortina Lotus and affixed them to the bootlid and wings of the Escort, along with the Escort's own bootlid badge!

Despite the fact that the Lotus name was appended to the cam cover of the engine, it did not appear anywhere on the exterior of the car, which was known simply as the Escort Twin Cam. Perhaps this was because the Cortina Lotus was usually referred to as the *Lotus Cortina*, and not as a Ford

As part of the conversion, Competitions had strategically reinforced the bodyshell with additional welding around the suspension pickup points. However, for the production run, the special heavy-duty bodyshell, which had been planned for adverse overseas use, would be employed; this would be far more suitable for the running gear of the new car. It became known to fans of the hot Escorts as the Type 49 bodyshell, and subsequently it would be adopted for all of the uprated Escorts that were to follow.

Once the decision had been taken to manufacture the new model, there arose the issues of where and how; although Boreham had the facilities to produce and maintain very small numbers of complete cars for race and rally use, there was no way that it would be able to sustain series production. The answer to the problem lay at Halewood, which had been open for only four years—the first car produced there, an Anglia in that awful shade of lime green so popular at the time, had been accepted off the line by the Lord Mayor of Liverpool on 8 March 1963.

Because the Escort Twin Cam would be built from a bodyshell which rolled off the regular production line at Halewood, and because there existed the space to allocate a dedicated workshop—a mini production line—adjacent to the main manufacturing lines, that option was taken up. However, the wheels of industry grind slowly, and it was impossible to instigate the scheme immediately, so for the first few months, the cars were assembled from knock-down kits of parts at Boreham. This interrupted the activities of the Competitions Department to the point where it proved impossible to prepare any Escorts for the 1968 rallying season. This was ironic, as the whole idea of the machine was to enable Ford to homologate it and compete in such events as the Monte Carlo, the Tulip and the other big international events. However, the chance would come.

In all, 25 cars were prepared by Boreham before Halewood's new facility was ready to roll on 17 January 1968.

The final production specification of the Twin Cam was surprisingly close to that of the prototype, which had been so proudly (yet apprehensively) displayed to the management by Henry Taylor and his team. The 1558 cc engine (it had oversquare dimensions of an 82.55 mm bore and a 72.8 mm stroke, which showed how much spare meat there was in the cylinder walls of the Kent block) retained its twin 40DCOE carburettors and a tubular exhaust manifold, the latter being all but concealed by the massive air cleaner assembly. Although equipped with a mild set of camshafts, the engine was able to pump out just under 110 bhp—an impressive output by the standards of the day, when even a six-cylinder, two-litre Triumph Vitesse would be giving out only 85 bhp.

The clutch, unlike that of the rest of the Escort

The entire RS network—which, in embryonic form, produced the MkI Escort Twin Cam—was the brainchild of Sam Toy, then General Sales Manager, Cars, for Ford of Britain. He went on to become supremo of Ford of Britain, and after his retirement from the Ford board, he headed the SMMT

A late example of the Twin Cam, with plain rims rather than the Rostyles which normally kept it off the ground

range, was hydraulic in operation, which meant that a special pedal block was required for the car. The close-ratio gearbox had a first gear ratio of 2.97:1, a 2.01:1 second, a 1.40:1 third gear, and a direct 1:1 top gear. The final drive was set at 3.77:1, although subsequently it would be possible to buy alternative shorter gear sets, right down to 4.4:1, through the growing Rallye Sport dealer network.

Suspension was exactly as detailed previously, with specially-chosen spring rates and uprated, oil-filled dampers. The braking system, with its substantial 9.625 in. solid front discs, 9 × 2 in. rear drums and full servo assistance, was also exactly as it was on the prototype.

Ford's top brass obviously concurred with the Competitions Department (or were persuaded by it) that the GT interior trim was the right package for the 'Twink', as that, too, was carried over into production. Perhaps it was easier and more cost-effective not to over-complicate matters by introducing yet another trim variation on to the Halewood production line. Finally, the badging used by Competitions, the legend 'Twin Cam' with a chequered flag symbol which had been borrowed from the MkII Cortina Lotus, was approved for the production model.

The car had been conceived as a competition machine, and it was the first of many Fords to be accurately described as a 'wolf in sheep's clothing'. Mechanic and driver Mick Jones, along with others, had already done a considerable amount of track testing of the new machine at Boreham (the rest of the range had been tested at Lommel, but the Belgian proving ground never got to see the early examples of twin-cam Escort) to the point where the first prototype was destroyed when a defective weld collapsed. Therefore, it was obvious that by the time the car was first seen outside Ford's own premises—when it was displayed and made available for testing in Morocco in January

1968—its chassis was exactly as the Competitions Department had wanted it to be for general consumption.

Everybody loved it.

For a substantial number of those who were flown out to Morocco, the newcomer was the closest that they had ever come to driving a real competition car—and even those journalists and dealers who had prior experience of racing and rally cars were impressed by its raw energy.

Autocar described the performance as 'startling' in its road test, the American magazine *Car & Driver* was impressed by its flexibility and its overall balance, and the Australian publication *Sports Car World* described the machine as able to see off 'all the big noise, stripey stuff'. The press, quite simply, heaped praise upon the new machine, which was the first car to be developed for production by Ford's own Competitions Department. By no means was it to be the last.

The only area of criticism of the car came in the thorny area of its cost; although designed for competition use and the nearest thing to an all-out race car that anybody could walk into a high street dealership and buy, there were still those who considered that the asking price, at £1171 including all taxes, was too high. In bald terms, this made it almost twice the price of a base-model 1100 cc Escort, and it was also £300 dearer than its nearest rival, the Triumph Vitesse. But then it kicked all of the competition into the weeds as it hared past.

Several different trim finishes were tried during the car's gestation period. This specimen with its blacked-out window trim and bonnet, and its striping overkill fortunately never made it into production. The 'Mary Quant' influence still prevalent in 1968 was obvious, especially on the section beneath the grille

6 Changes one

The range changes with the times

ON THE BACK of every Ford new-car brochure is a statement which effectively reserves the right of the company to change the specification of a car or the price whenever it suits. Ford says that this is because it operates a policy of continuous product development, but cynics consider that it simply gives Ford Motor Company the opportunity to get it right next time.

There were certainly quite a few changes made to the Escort range during the couple of years following the car's launch in 1968.

Initially, the changes were confined to offering additional models in the range, starting with the estate car, which arrived at the end of March 1968. This was based on a special floorpan which drew on both the saloon car and the forthcoming van. The vehicle was some 4 in. longer than the saloon, all of the extra length appearing behind the rear axle to provide the optimum amount of load space.

The styling of the estate followed closely that of the saloon, the roofline being continued (and subtly straightened) to a point several inches ahead of the end of the floorpan. A one-piece tailgate extended down to the level of the floor and opened with the aid of a torsion-bar arrangement concealed within the roof. The rear window area of the estate was of similar proportions to that of the saloon, the light and airy feel of the interior being aided considerably by the use of single-pane side windows which extended from the B-posts (the panels where the trailing edges of the doors meet the rest of the bodywork—the other ends of the doors meet the body at the so-called A-posts) right through to the slim rear quarter pillars.

The rear seat of the estate car could be folded flat, the squab tilting forwards to abut the back of the front seats, while the back folded to fill the space vacated by the squab. This facility made the car a true dual-purpose machine and ideal for those who were running small businesses, as it gave a useful amount of carrying capacity for work purposes during the day, yet offered the practicality and comfort of a conventional saloon for evening and weekend use.

Although it did not have quite the same carrying capacity as the van which would follow a few weeks later, the estate's load space could be augmented by using a roof rack; the car had been designed to allow another 100 lb or so of evenly-distributed weight on the roof. It soon became a firm favourite among such tradesmen as painters and decorators, window cleaners and plumbers.

There were two driveline options available for the estate: the 1100 cc with 4.44:1 final drive ratio, and the 1300 cc with 4.125:1 overall gearing. Heavy-duty rear springs were fitted to the estate car, complemented by the 4.5 in. wide steel wheels of the GT saloon—although these were fitted with 6.00 in. crossply tyres rather than radials. The advocates of NVH preferred things that way— they felt that the improved performance of the radials increased noise and harshness to a level

These overhead shots of the Escort two-door saloon and the estate car, which was introduced at the end of March 1968, show the slightly longer floorpan which was developed for the latter model. This provides an extra couple of inches in the load area. All subsequent Escort estates have had similarly longer aft sections when compared to the saloons upon which they have been based

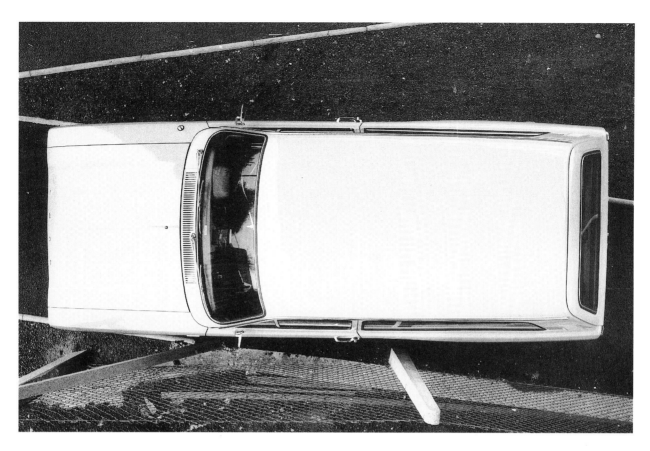

An automatic transmission was introduced in June 1968. A three-speed unit controlled by a floor-mounted shifter (rather than the hitherto popular column-mounted control), this opened up a new market sector for the Escort

which was acceptable on the sporty version of the saloon, but not on the estate, which was targeted at drivers with more mundane needs.

Because it would be carrying more weight and, when empty, it tipped the scales at about 200 lb more than the saloon (a result of the increased areas of sheetmetal and glass), the estate came with a 7.5 in. clutch as standard.

To maximize the load-carrying potential of the estate, it had an underfloor fuel tank—in the saloons, petrol was stored in a nine-gallon tank which lived inside the rear offside corner of the boot, opposite the upright spare wheel. The spare in the estate was still stored upright, just behind the rear nearside wheelarch, but it was housed within a special moulded plastic cover to protect it

from any sharp objects which might be among the loads carried. With the rear seat folded flat, there was a 5 ft run of flat floor; at its narrowest point, between the rear wheelarch tubs, it was just under 40 in. wide. The load capacity, in weight terms, was set at 6 cwt for the 1100 and 8 cwt for the 1.3 litre car. Initially, the estate was available only in De Luxe trim, which meant that vinyl and rubber abounded—it would be another year before a Super variant would be offered.

After the estate car came the van, which appeared in April. This was a natural progression, for Ford had already carved an enviable slice of the market sector for itself with the Anglia van; when compared to the other light vans on the market in the 1960s, the Anglia had immediate advantages because its load area was longer, wider, higher and altogether more capacious than those of its rivals, such as the Austin A35 and small Bedford. The same format as that employed by the Anglia was carried over to the new van, but taken further still. By extending the floor and making full use of the longer wheelbase of the Escort, Ford was able to give the Escort van a 9 cu. ft advantage over its predecessor.

The vans were available in two weight capacities, either 6 or 8 cwt. Although identical externally, save for the badging, the variation was achieved by offering the two engine options of the saloons; the smaller-capacity van used the 1100 cc engine with 4.44:1 final drive gears, and the larger one came with the 1300 cc with 4.125:1 overall gearing. Ostensibly, the interior of the van was the same as that of the basic Escort De Luxe saloon, but closer inspection proved otherwise. Whilst the fascia followed the same basic format of the saloon, its instrument pod had only a speedometer and fuel gauge, and even the heater system was an optional extra; if a van came with a means of warming the cab, the purchaser would have had to pay a premium of £10–12 for the privilege. Because the vans attracted no tax burden from the exchequer, their prices were lower than those of the cars at £450 for the 6 cwt model and £525 for the 8 cwt version.

Externally, the van had almost as much brightwork as the saloons from which it had been derived, with a brightly-finished grille and lamp surrounds, and chromed bumpers—although in additional to the full-width blade of the front bumper, the van had twin quarter bumpers at the rear, which protected only the outside corners of the bodywork. The van also had the round headlamps of the base model saloons. As with the estate car, the van was an immediate success, and a staggering number of small businesses not only bought them to replace their old Anglia vans, but also made the shift from their Austins and Bedfords to Ford's newcomer.

After the van, the next major change came in June 1968, when all of the cars became available with the option of automatic transmission—only the 1100 cc van could not be ordered with this.

The transmission was not a Ford product, but was made by the American-owned Borg Warner Corporation. Costing a premium of £87, a price for the facility which has been held in proportion even today, the Type 35 automatic was quite satisfactory when used with the 1300 cc Escorts, but altogether underwhelming when used with the 1100 cc engine—that particular model was to remain in the catalogue for only 15 months before being quietly dropped.

As with most self-selecting gearboxes of the time, there were only three forward ratios available within the casing; first gear was set at 2.393:1,

second was 1.450:1, and top was a direct drive. A neat floor-mounted shifter was employed, and as with any other automatic, it was possible to override the self-selection facility and to use the gearbox as a clutchless manual. All automatic Escorts came with the same 4.125:1 final drive ratio, which meant that maximum speeds were slightly lower than those of manual Escorts; whereas a 1300 manual would achieve perhaps 87 mph, an automatic would find difficulty in getting to within 5 mph of that figure.

Although the car had been in the showrooms since the late winter of 1967–8, the first time that the Escort range appeared at a British exhibition was in October 1968, at the Motor Show. In a bid to display something new, Ford's marketing department instigated a number of minor changes to the line-up ready for Earls Court. These included such things as colour-keying more bits of the fascia (all of the dull plastic which surrounded the ashtray, and the shelves which ran from each side of it) as well as extending the theme to the steering wheel and column shroud. More use was made of the plastic woodgrain finish which had been used spasmodically on the fascia strip, too. The door

By the middle of 1968, a variety of Rally Sport accessories was beginning to filter through to the Escort options list. These included two different types of sports seat: the fixed-back type, nearest the camera, and the semi-reclining version on the far side with adjustable headrest

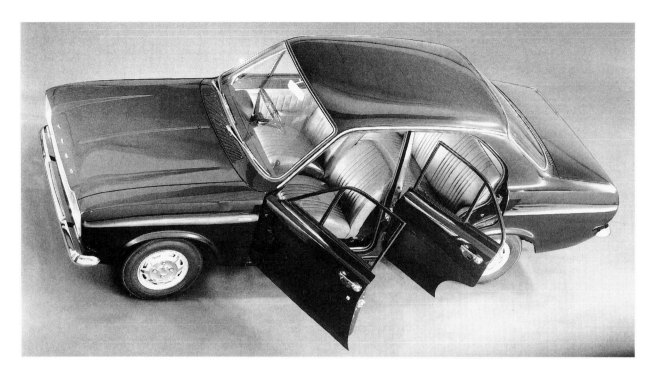

Above **The GT model was added to the list of available packages using the new four-door bodyshell. From the MkIII Escort onwards, the mantle of the four-door GT model has been transferred to the Orion 1.6i, as sports models of Escort have been only in the two-door format**

Top **Instigated by the German Ford operation, a four-door Escort was added to the line-up in the Autumn of 1969, the car débuting at the London Motor Show. The additional set of doors created a major problem, as the tooling was horrendously expensive. The front doors also had to be redesigned, as the originals were too wide to allow the rear doors to be installed.**

handles and window winders were treated to a minor redesign to ensure that they would break off under impact—the effects of Ralph Nader's crusades in America for more safety-consciousness by manufacturers were beginning to filter across the Atlantic—but it would be several years before owners realized that as well as being a safety factor, these alterations would also add considerably to the trade in replacement parts when drivers were forced to pay for any heavy-handedness by buying new handles.

A new range of colours was added to the fairly limited launch selection and, at the same time, the radiator grilles were treated to a sporty matt-black finish, which had already been applied to the GT and TC models. Finally, the chrome drip-rail trim was deleted from the car, but bright chrome-effect surrounds appeared on the side windows.

Interestingly, if only as an indication of how inflation was running in that period of the 1960s, by the Motor Show in 1968, the prices of the range had risen quite sharply; when *Autocar* tested an example of the 1300GT in November 1968, the price had risen from its original £647 to £833. However, the car was loaded with all of the available options, so the 'real' price was nearer £760—even so, it represented an increase of about 18 per cent in ten months. Prices settled down thereafter and rose at a more acceptable ten per cent per annum over the next couple of years. To put those prices into perspective, at the time of writing (mid 1990), the nearest direct equivalent in the MkIV Escort range was the 1600 Sport, and that cost a shade under £10,000 by the time that it was road-ready!

Escort activity appeared to have quietened down after the flurry of events in readiness for the 1968 Motor Show, but behind the scenes arguments were going on between the British design and engineering teams and their counterparts in West Germany. The main bone of contention was the front suspension arrangement, and in the event, the Germans won; at the time, the sun rose out of Merkenich as far as the American directorate of Ford was concerned, while Britain was all but a waste of time. A decade later, that situation had been turned upon its head, but in 1968–9, the Germans got what the Germans wanted. The compression-strut arrangement, so heavily favoured by Britain, was dropped in favour of the old-style layout which used the anti-roll bar.

Of greater magnitude was the Germans' pressing need for a four-door version of the Escort. From a styling viewpoint, this was not problematic, as the original design had been conceived to be adaptable to a variety of configurations. Engineering the new model, however, would be difficult, because much of the Escort's ease of construction had been facilitated by its large, one-piece side panels. Installing a second door on each side of the car would be darned awkward, and it would also call for the front doors to be rejigged, making them narrower by perhaps 20 per cent. Ford of Germany convinced Dearborn that the addition of a four-door Escort would be essential to developing the sales potential of the model range, especially in mainland Europe. The car went into production immediately after the mid-summer shutdown (a traditional time for installing

This German-market XL from 1970 shows clearly Ford's aftermarket (afterthought?) radio installation—a single speaker was normally mounted on the back shelf. The picture also shows the use of wood-effect appliqués on the fascia and the door cappings

new equipment in Ford plants) in 1969, being built at Halewood. The original plan was for the range to be built from day one at both Halewood and at Saarlouis, but in the event, the new German plant (it had been built in 1965 on virgin land on the banks of the River Saar near the French border) was not ready. Escort production eventually began at the latter facility in the middle of January 1970, some two years later than intended!

The four-door version of the car went on sale in the autumn of 1969, after being shown at the London Motor Show. At the same show, Ford unveiled a package of amendments to the range which had also been integrated on to the restarted production lines in September. These included revised spring rates for the rear of the car; they were uprated slightly—although they were still of three leaves on the lighter vans and the estate, they were changed to a four-leaf design for the saloons in both standard and heavy-duty applications. Damper rates were revised at the same time, and the bump-stops were redesigned to take some of the shock out of the system when running over rough surfaces in a fully-laden condition.

Two-speed wipers were added to the specification of the GT model—the production version of the Twin Cam already had such a feature—and all models benefited from increased fuse protection. However, the main electrical generator in the range was still the good old dynamo. Although the more efficient alternator was fitted to an increasing number of vehicles during the next three years, it would be 1973 before that type of generator became standard issue on all Escorts.

Externally, the revised Escorts were easy to spot from the front because the tops of their grilles no longer had central cut-outs for the bonnet latch—Ford had evolved a remote catch arrangement operated from within the car by a lever tucked down low against the inner arch liner panel. Pulling the lever to operate the cable was never an easy matter, and some drivers complained about the level of physical strength required to perform the operation, but their pleas fell on deaf ears because the same basic system would stay right through to the end of the next decade. From the rear, the car which had been produced after September 1968 was identifiable by its flush-fitting fuel filler cap.

These modifications had been carried out as a result of a massive market research and dealer information programme that had been instigated shortly after the car went on sale. Other niggles which were attended to in response to the same survey were weaknesses in the exhaust system and the petrol tank brackets. A splash guard in moulded plastic was also fitted to the car's distributor to minimize the problems caused by it getting wet when the car was used in heavy rain.

Back in the mid 1960s, Ford's dealerships were being inundated with requests for versions of the Cortina estate car with a more substantial power output, and in response were able to offer special-build examples which utilized the GT saloon's running gear. These were built under the umbrella of Special Vehicle Orders, a small department which specialized in fulfilling such requests.

A similar demand was experienced for the Escort during the first year or so that it was on sale, but this time the response was slightly different; instead of being a special-build car, a GT estate was added to the mainstream line-up and was available through the national dealer network from April 1970. The car cost just over £1000 and gave an acceptable hike in performance compared to the standard 1300 estate. In mechanical terms, the entire 1300GT driveline was simply slotted into the 1300 Super estate, while inside the car were to be found the fascia and six-clock instrumentation of the GT saloon.

In the autumn of 1970—again coinciding with the resumption of work after the annual shutdown—a new engine specification was to be found beneath the bonnets of all of the Escorts. The relatively mild camshafts of the standard engines had been replaced with new items which increased duration from 248 to 256 degrees, while overlap was also increased from 34 to 43 degrees. The camshaft of the GT was also altered, duration staying at 272 degrees, but overlap being reduced from 54 to 50 degrees. However, the overall timing was totally different; from dimensions of 27/65/65/27, the revised engine had a shaft with 29/63/71/21. The reason for these changes was that the design of the combustion chambers within the pistons (the crossflow Kent engine had a flat head face) had been altered to improve the pattern of burning and then evacuating the mixture. The valve diameters of the 1300 cc engines had also been changed, and the engine had been metricated. From an original inlet valve size of 36 mm, both 1300 cc units—GT and standard—now had 38 mm valves. Exhaust valves remained at 31.5 mm. Finally, the 1300 standard engine gained a slight increase in its compression ratio, sharing the 9.2:1 of the GT version.

The net result of these changes was that the 1100 cc engine gained 3 bhp to give 48 bhp, the 1300 went up to 57 bhp from 52, and the GT went up from its original 71 bhp to 73 bhp—although by the time that these increases were announced, the GT's power output had been reassessed at 64 bhp, for reasons which have never been satisfactorily explained. The given reason was that the company had revised its method of measuring power outputs. To go with these revised power levels, all Escorts were standardized at 3.90:1 for their final drive ratio. Wheels were still 12 in. in diameter. The engine changes were made obvious by a fresh set of body badges. The De Luxe variant was laid to rest, and henceforth the basic model of Escort would be known simply as Escort, being available in all three body derivatives. Then came the Escort L, which was substantially the old Super with added value items. These included full interior carpeting (right through to a boot floor mat for either of the saloon models), a dipping rear-view mirror, overriders and reversing lights. The L could be had with either the 1100 cc or 1300 cc engine packages. Beyond the L came the XL (extra luxury, according to Ford's special acronym codes), which had everything of the L plus a cigarette lighter, a vanity mirror inset into the passenger-side sun visor, a slightly thicker-pile carpet and, for two-door models, hinged rear side glass that could be opened an inch or two for additional ventilation.

Both of the basic models retained the standard round headlamps, but from there up the range,

In 1971 Ford achieved substantial publicity by teaming up with Britain's leading formation aerobatic team, the Red Arrows. The crack RAF unit was loaned a fleet of 1300L Escorts by Bristol Street Motors of Bromley, Kent

rectangular lamps still featured; even though their efficiency was pronounced inferior by all manner of people, Ford's marketing experts still felt that they gave a more up-market image. The perceived value of the XL models, which were available in either two- or four-door form, but only with the 1.3 litre engine, was added to still further by various chrome strips. These ran along each sill and across the edge of the back panel. The GT

version remained much as previously (although it benefited from the extra bits and pieces fitted to the other cars) and stood out from the others in the line-up by having a matt black tail panel to match the blacked-out front grille centre. As with the XL, the GT was available with two or four doors.

Whilst all of this mainstream activity was going on, another range of Escorts was being developed around the same basic bodyshell, the RS cars. As with the Twin Cam, their story merits its own chapter, but there is one car which doesn't fit easily into either the mainstream or the Rallye Sport ranges, the Escort Sport.

Because of the way in which they had been developed and made, the RS cars were expensive, but they had a distinct—and enviable—cachet. To capitalize on this, the decision was taken to produce a model which would fall into the mainstream range, but which would allude to being an RS in all but name. The packaging needed to be simple, tried and tested, and built up from off-the-shelf parts. In building the car, Ford shot itself in its corporate foot and did little to enhance the image of the Escort range.

At first glance, the car was a Type 49, in that it looked as though it was based on the same heavy-duty bodyshell already used for the Twin Cam. However, scratching the surface revealed that the Sport was built on the standard-grade bodyshell with a pair of the bigger-arched front wings found on the Type 49. Under the bonnet was the 1300GT engine with its close-ratio transmission, but at the back of the car was an axle centre-unit with 4.125:1 gearing, rather than the newly-rationalized 3.90 set.

Launched in 1973, the Escort 1300E was a deliberate move up-market by Ford. Based upon the mechanical package of the Sport, the car featured a set of rectangular driving lamps, sculpted road wheels, much chrome, a vinyl roof (although not every example came with such a lid) and dedicated badging.

The flared front arches were not the only allusion to the serious performance Escorts, for the Sport also had a set of 13 × 5 in. sculpted steel wheels with 165/SR/13 radials and the round headlamps favoured by the AVO people. The image was completed by a special set of decals which shouted 'Sport' in big letters on each front wing.

On paper, the Sport was a highly-successful package, especially considering that it undercut the 1300GT two-door by about £35. On the road, however, the package was an unmitigated disaster.

Running a Sport hard through a series of bends immediately highlighted just what a poor recipe had been concocted, for the suspension, designed to work in conjunction with 155/12 tyres, was patently outclassed by the 165/13 SR rubber, and a burst of spirited driving would soon have one of the inside wheels wagging in mid-air. Furthermore, the taller tyres raised the gearing to an unacceptable level, which meant that the normally fine acceleration of the GT was dulled almost to the point where boredom set in. The only praise that the car drew was for its braking system which, like that of most other Escorts, was excellent at bringing the car to a halt from virtually any speed without fuss or drama.

The interior of the car was as much of a *mélange*

The inside of the 1300E was downright opulent by Escort standards, with deep-pile carpeting, a centre console, fabric trim, and abundant planks of American Light Cherry trim appended to just about every flat area. Alas, there was still nowhere to fit a radio

as the mechanical specification. To keep costs down, the basic two-clock instrument pod was used. However, to satisfy the need to know what the engine was up to, Ford bolted a little pod-mounted tachometer to the top of the dashboard just to the right of the main binnacle. This, and the spoked steering wheel, made it look as though someone from Ford had spent Saturday morning shopping at Halfords for go-faster goodies—all that was missing was the 12 ft long whippy glass-fibre aerial favoured by boy racers of the day.

The next major arrival from Ford with the Escort badge on its rump was a far more interesting machine. This was the 1300E, and it was a blatant attempt by Ford to move the name up-market and to develop a following for the pocket-sized executive car. Once again the car was based on the 1300GT, and once again the cocktail of

5 × 13 in. wheels with radial 165SR tyres was used—but as the 1300E was to be a sort of 'mini-limousine', the deficiencies of the Sport were well-masked. What also helped matters was that the car was a good deal heavier than its cheaper counter-part. In fact, viewed as a small luxury car and not as a sporty saloon, the 1300E was very successful.

Externally, the car was identifiable by its badging; in addition to title badges on each front wing, there were intricate crests on the rear roof pillars—either the same as those of the Cortina 1600E or special ones for the 1300E, depending upon availability. The specially-sculpted wheels (which would find their way on to other Escorts) gave the car an extra edge in the car park, as did the abundant use of brightwork around the side windows, across the bootlid lip and along each rain gutter. The car was topped off, literally, by a black vinyl roof. Initially, the bodywork could be had in only three shades: Venetian Gold metallic, Copper Bronze metallic, or Aubergine metallic purple. Eventually, there would be 14 body colours, metallics and non-metallics.

The car was available in a choice of two- or four-door bodyshells, the former outselling the latter by

The Escort Sport was not one of Ford's more desirable models; its gearing was so remote from that required by the sporting driver that the car was lousy to drive. A Type 49 bodyshell was alluded to, but in fact only the wings were common to that stiffened shell, while the suspension system was ill-conceived. It did not appeal to the driver in search of excitement

a ratio of almost two to one. Regardless of the number of doors, opening them revealed thick wooden trim cappings at waist height on the insides. Wood veneer also featured on the fascia, not only across the bit which in lesser Escorts would be in imitation zebrano walnut, but also on the instrument binnacle (which was the six-clock type) and even on the switch and ashtray panel. A modest centre console was featured (although, in reality, this was little more than a moulded plastic tray atop the tunnel), and the car had a leather-rimmed steering wheel after the style of the Capri.

In addition to the copious use of Light American Cherry veneer panels, Ford also used Beta cloth for the seat facings, although door liner panels and the outer surfaces of the seats were trimmed in the more familiar vinyl. Beneath the carpet, which was about as thick as Ford was able to provide for use in Escorts, was an adequate amount of soundproofing felt, for sweet and quiet as it was when new, the engine could produce intrusive noise levels when worn. The padding also helped mask the bumps and thumps from the tyres and suspension.

Had it not been for the fact that the car cost £1199 when new—and, thus, was appreciably more expensive than other mainstream Escorts—it may have gone on to sell more than it did. As it is, the remaining cars are fast becoming collectable, and there is a burgeoning owners' club.

The same package would be repeated more than 15 years later in the Orion, but whereas the Orion was a limited-edition car, the 1300E was a series-production model which went on to achieve no less than 11,133 sales in the British market. There were also another 50 built for export, two of them being in left-hand-drive format.

Part way through the 1300E's production run, which had commenced in February 1973 for a March launch, Ford revised the entire floorpan of the mainstream Escort range in readiness for the next generation (codenamed Brenda), which was already taking shape.

Nobody had been altogether happy with the rear suspension arrangement of the early Escort range, primarily because whilst the forward-raked dampers undoubtedly aided axle location and the control of axle tramp, their efficiency was impaired by their attitude. The Competitions Department had overcome this long before by relocating the dampers vertically in specially-fabricated turrets, which were welded to the inner wheelarches. The job was usually completed by fitting two pairs of links, one above the axle line and the other below, from the halfshaft tubes forward to the central floor cross-bracing tubes. This system worked extraordinarily well, but had the effect of increasing noise transmission into the cabin. Because the work was being carried out on race and rally machinery, this hardly mattered (aural comfort was fairly low on Competitions' list of priorities), but the noise, vibration and harshness people just could not countenance the adoption of such a system on road-going, production cars. They could, however, capitalize on some of the ideas.

The outcome, which was realized in October 1973, just in time for the British Motor Show, was a rear suspension arrangement which had vertical dampers living in a production derivative of the Competitions Department-originated damper turret design. However, instead of having the complex and precise four-bar linkage, additional location control was provided by a rear anti-roll bar, which was attached via brackets to the axle casing, and then joined the main bodyshell in special brackets which had been designed into the floorpan adjacent to the front spring eyes.

This arrangement gave the best of both worlds. The anti-roll bar, which provided a degree of springing, absorbed a good deal of the road shocks rather than pushing them through into the bodywork. Furthermore, those shock loads which did make it along the bar were absorbed quite effectively by the substantial rubber bushes which insulated it from its mounting points. The damper arrangement allowed those components to function correctly, without any tendency to stick or bind. As a result of this improved efficiency, the spring design was modified, gaining an extra $\frac{1}{3}$ in. of width to improve location, but losing one of the four leaves to reduce any binding effect. The main benefits of the system were felt not at the beginning of an outing, but later, after a long run when the old damper arrangement would have been feeling distinctly jaded because of the amounts of friction—and thus heat—which would have been generated by their uncomfortable angle. Damper fade on the post-October 1973 cars was much-reduced.

There were also changes at the front of the car, although nothing as radical as at the rear; amendments were limited to slightly redesigned bump-stop rubbers, which were more progressive in their action, and to the use of a larger-diameter anti-roll bar. This latter move was in readiness for the increasing adoption of radial tyres, the sidewalls of which offered greater compliance than those of crossplies. By 1973, the radial was already becoming the rule rather than the exception, and by the time that the next generation of Escort

arrived, the crossply tyre would have been consigned into Ford history.

There were few other changes to come during the next two years of Escort production; all of the engineering and design teams' efforts were being directed towards Brenda, the next generation of the car which was due to appear in the winter of 1975–6. There were, however, a couple of major causes for celebration within Ford at the time, the first being on 20 September 1973 when the millionth example of mainstream Escort rolled off Halewood's production line. Then, on 10 June of the following year, the company announced that there had been no less than 2,000,000 Escorts produced, the majority being built at Halewood, with Saarlouis contributing the rest. Those figures also included estates and vans, but what the heck, they were all Escorts. There was one other major landmark for Ford to celebrate, and that came on 25 November 1974 when it was announced that Halewood had set a new Ford of Britain production record by building 1,288,957 examples of Escort since the lines had started rolling in late 1967. This bettered the previous best-ever figure established by the Anglia 17 years previously.

Meanwhile, other records were being set, albeit very quietly, in deepest rural Essex, where the Ford Advanced Vehicle Operations team was busily building a range of cars under the Rallye Sport banner.

The idea of an Escort van, based on a panelled-in estate, could have been worthwhile; it was found in production in the late 1980s as the Escort IV Combi. This exercise from 1974 predated that one by more than a decade. Part of the appeal to purchasers at the time was that vans did not attract purchase tax, whereas estate cars did

7 The Rallye Sport revolution

Adding a little spice!

'WHO do you think you are? Roger Clark?'

Aah, if only I had a pound for every time I was asked that question by traffic policemen when I was running my RS1600. And why shouldn't I have been asked that? After all, I was driving a car with the Rallye Sport emblem and the Rallye Sport bits inside and underneath—just like Roger's. And I was probably going too fast anyway—a common hazard with an RS car.

The Twin Cam Escort had been the first hot example of the machine, and although never designated as an RS model, it had been supplied and serviced through the Rallye Sport network, which had been established in the early part of the 1960s. In January 1970, the first RS-badged Escort appeared—the now-legendary RS1600.

The Twin Cam had been a success in competition, but its tuning potential had been more or less exhausted. However, the fast-rising tuning company of Cosworth Engineering felt that it might have an answer; just like Lotus, it had taken a standard production Escort engine block and designed a special cylinder head for it. The vital difference was that it felt that, ultimately, its powerplant would develop more power than the Lotus product.

Cosworth Engineering was no stranger to Ford—the company had been retained at the beginning of the decade to carry out tuning work on the pre-crossflow engine, the result being the Cortina GT. For the Escort project, Cosworth had started with the latest version of the Kent cylinder block, the 116E, from the Cortina MkII GT. This would allow Ford the best of both worlds, for by taking the minimum/maximum manufacturing tolerances and turning them to advantage, the engine could have a displacement of either 1599 cc or 1601 cc. This ensured its acceptability across several different classes of motorsport. It was all a matter of interpretation.

The cylinder block was basically the same as that in any other application, and its original block-mounted camshaft was retained to drive the distributor and oil pump assemblies, just as it had been in the Lotus version, which had been in service for some years. A nodular crankshaft was a standard feature of the block, and this vital component had been tuftrided for longevity. Heavy-duty bearing shells were fitted in the carriers for the same reason. The dimensions of the block were the familiar 80.98 mm bore and 77.7 mm stroke—although, as mentioned earlier, the outside tolerances were sometimes quoted to 'enlarge' the block's capacity.

On the top of the engine was the new Cosworth-designed cylinder head, a complex, multi-decked affair cast in aluminium. The basic head casting carried the valves and their specially-hardened seat/inserts, the valves sitting at 20 degrees from the vertical on each side of the spark plug—there were two inlet and two exhaust valves per chamber. A slim gasket sat on top of the head, and above that was the camshaft carrier, again an aluminium casting. This carried the pair of camshafts, one to operate all eight exhaust valves, and the other the inlets. After another gasket was inserted, a third casting topped off the whole assembly rather neatly. The intake manifold was cast integrally with the head and could accept either a pair of Weber 40DCOE/48 carburettors or a pair of Dellorto 40 DHLA/E units; both makes were used, depending upon Ford's predilection.

Valve sizes of the standard engine were good and gave a large swept area; intake valves measured almost 31 mm, while the exhausts were 27.4 mm across. These sat in valve seats angled at 45 degrees and formed most of the semi-hemispherical chamber's surface. The solid-skirted pistons were flat topped with carefully-designed cutaways to ensure no valve contact. The engine differed from the Twin Cam and, indeed, from any other member of the crossflow engine group in its method of driving the camshafts, for in place of the usual tooth-and-chain arrangement was a neat, single, broad nylon toothed belt. This actually drove three shafts (the two camshafts and the auxiliary shaft which ran the oil system and distributor) in the same direction as the crankshaft. It was this method of operation that led to

One of the most charismatic of all Escorts was the RS1600. This example was lovingly restored by Bob Quirk, head of the Manchester Ford dealership H&J Quick at Old Trafford. Quick has been associated with Ford since the very early days, being the first-ever British dealership appointed by Henry Ford

the engine being named the Ford-Cosworth BDA (Belt-Driven series A).

The engine was certainly powerful in its standard form, giving a creditable 115 bhp at 6500 rpm and a useful 112 lb/ft of torque at 4000 rpm; a small, but worthwhile, gain over the previous dual-cam, 16-valve Escort. What was even more important was its tuning potential, for by enlarging the valve sizes, increasing the camshaft's lift, timing and duration, and raising the compression ratio from the standard block's 10.0:1 (together with all of the other tuning tricks), it was possible to obtain appreciably more muscle from the modestly-sized unit. Later, when the Hart-designed aluminium cylinder block was added and capacities of two litres and more could be achieved, the power output would be double that of the original car!

Behind the engine—which, incidentally, followed the precedent set by the Twin Cam in being installed at an angle—was the same basic arrangement of an 8 in. single-plate clutch (with hydraulic actuation) followed by a close-ratio gearbox with syncromesh on all four forward gears. The ratios were 2.972:1 for first gear, 2.010:1 for second,

The Mexico was developed as a direct spin-off from Ford's success in the London–Mexico World Cup Rally. This example, affectionately referred to as 'The Mistress' by David Hensley of Bristol (secretary of the Ford AVO Owners Club), is equipped with Minilite wheels and quadruple Cibié driving lamps. These were available from all RS dealerships, and were almost *de rigueur* for the serious enthusiast

1.397:1 for third, and 1:1 for a direct top gear. The final drive ratio was also shared with the Twin Cam at 3.77:1.

Braking was taken care of by substantial 9.625 in. front discs matched to $9 \times 1\frac{3}{4}$ in. rear drums with servo assistance, also carried over from the Twink.

In fact, much of the RS1600 was carried over from the previous 'hot' Escort; both the Competitions Department and the sales to the public had proved that the packaging was successful.

However, what had emerged during the $2\frac{1}{2}$-year, 1100-strong sales lifespan of the Twin Cam was that customers wanted a little more on the inside of the car. Ford provided it in the form of a new steering wheel with a deep dish. Aah, the benevolent nature of the world's biggest motor manufacturer. It seemed to know no bounds!

The first batch of new cars was assembled at Halewood, alongside the main track, as had been the case with the Twin Cam. The new Advanced

Vehicle Operations unit, located in the old central stores building at Aveley, opened officially on 14 January 1970, but it would not actually start producing cars for some months to come. The BDA engines were shipped to Merseyside not from Ford's foundries or from Cosworth's plant, but from Harpers, a sub-contract builder in Hertfordshire—this pattern of using small subcontractors for engine building was to continue for some time, as neither Ford nor Cosworth was geared to producing finished powerplants in the required numbers; too few were needed for Ford, and too many for Cosworth to cope with.

As is often the case, there was a degree of delay in the supply of some of the little bits and pieces which were designated for the car, and some of the earliest examples which appeared—they rather trickled out of the factory during the early part of 1970—came with Twin Cam badging because the special RS1600 castings were not quite ready! On the inside of the car, there was a slight change from the previous specification of the instruments (the familiar six-clock cluster) in the form of a 140 mph speedometer and a tachometer red-lined at 8000 rpm. In standard form, this didn't make much difference, as there was an 'engine saver' electrical cutout which brought proceedings to a halt at 6000 rpm. In terms of performance, the car was a little quicker than its predecessor—about 8.5 seconds to 60 mph and 34 seconds to 100 mph—but times could vary wildly for two reasons. One

We brought it back from Mexico.

We spent two years building an Escort for the London to Mexico Rally and, after it had cleaned up down there, it suddenly occurred to us: wouldn't it be a shame not to offer this kind of car to everybody? Yes, we decided it would. Gentlemen, the Escort Mexico—except for a more economical power plant and a few other nice little improvements, the same car that beat

the world. 1600GT engine uprated to 86 bhp (din) at 5,500 rpm, close ratio gearbox, stiffened and lowered suspension, specially strengthened body, servo assisted brakes, 5½J wheels with radials, uprated half shafts, radius arms, stone-deflector plates—the whole shooting match. All of which will wind up to a hundred. And hit sixty in less than eleven seconds.

How much does a rally winner cost? You'd expect it to cost a bomb. (That's what it cost us.) But we're only asking £1,150. So, if you've always regretted missing out on the world's toughest rally, cheer up. At least now you can own the car that won it!

The Escort Mexico.
The road version of the rally winner.

RECOMMENDED RETAIL PRICE IS £1,150.6.5. PRICE INCLUDES PURCHASE TAX AND DELIVERY TO FORD DEALERS IN THE UK (EXCLUDING N. IRELAND). ACCORDING TO STATUTORY REGULATIONS FRONT INERTIA REEL SEAT BELTS ARE FITTED. THESE ARE SUPPLIED AT EXTRA COST.

Straight out of the crate, a car just like those that had blitzed the rest of the field in the Mexico rally . . . or so Ford would have liked us to believe from this 1971 advertisement. This was the first of a short series of marketing specials which Ford produced during the 1970s

was the variation in actual cutout speed (which could be anything from 5500 to 6500 rpm), while the other was that the car soon went off-song. My own RS1600 needed to be retuned every 1000 miles if the best was to be made of its packaging. I also did away with the rev-limiter . . .

The package worked, though, and it was not long before examples of the first real RS Escort were to be found on racetracks and in rallies. Although it was not homologated (approved) for competition use until October 1970, the RS1600 made its competition début in March 1970 when Roger Clark drove his 180 bhp machine (making use of the rules, Ford had stretched the rated 1601 cc block to 1.8 litres by overboring it to 85.6 mm) in the Circuit of Ireland. With its widened arches covering a set of Minilite wheels, the car was immediately identifiable as an RS Escort, and it won the event convincingly.

According to Clark, the white machine (most of the early cars could be had in any colour you liked,

so long as it was white!) never missed a beat. Ford capitalized on the win—they did not, however, mention that the Clark car had a five-speed ZF transmission and a non-standard, altogether tougher, German rear axle.

Perhaps of greater significance than that début win for the RS1600 was the factory assault on the London–Mexico Rally later that year. Timed to coincide with the World Cup, the event was sponsored by the Daily Mirror newspaper and was a gruelling event covering 16,000 miles.

Ford fielded a seven-car team, with such names as Hannu Mikkola, Gunner Palm and Tony Fall providing the professional expertise, and such footballing stars as Jimmy Greaves giving the team a broader canvas on which to paint a publicity picture. Stuart Turner (until recently head of Motorsport, Ford of Europe) masterminded the operation in his usual forceful manner—he was determined that Ford of Britain would win. Ford had been robbed of an outright victory in the London–Sydney Marathon two years previously when the Cortina Lotus of Roger Clark and Ove Andersson had been beset by reliability problems, so a more reliable package was the first requirement in what amounted to a full-scale battle campaign.

The chosen vehicle was an Escort, the familiar Type 49 bodyshell which had been tried first on the Twink and then on the RS1600, while the suspension package was equally heavy-duty. However, there were reservations about the long-term reliability of both of the dual-cam engines on such an arduous event, so the final selection of powerplant was made in favour of the good old pushrod Kent crossflow. The thick-walled blocks, which could be overbored in the manner of Clark's Irish-event RS1600, were used and overbored to give 1850 cc. The power output was kept to a deliberately modest 140 bhp—that way, everything was under-stressed, but the cars were still endowed with adequate performance.

The Escorts romped home in first, third, fifth, sixth and eighth positions overall—not a bad result by anybody's standards, especially considering that some 80 per cent of the 96 cars which had left London on 19 April had fallen by the wayside. The winning team of Mikkola and Palm took abundant honours, while Ford received the Manufacturer's Award. Stuart Turner was able to justify the awesome amounts of money which had gone into the event, and the marketing people began to see that they might be able to make some long-term capital from the victorious outing.

RS customers gained fuller, altogether more comprehensive instrumentation than purchasers of lesser Escorts. RS cars could be had with a choice of steering wheel: either a flat, three-spoke item or this deep-dished, drilled-spoke model. The centre console was another special RS part, as were the bucket seats with cloth facings. So who cared if they didn't recline?

The result was the Escort Mexico. In showroom form, it bore more than a passing resemblance to the event-winning cars—at least, it did if you squinted and cocked your head to one side. Under the bonnet was a standard 1600GT crossflow engine taken straight from the Cortina GT, which had the standard bore of 80.98 mm and a stroke of 77.62 mm. A reasonably modest camshaft grind of 27/65/65/27 degrees was used along with the 1300GT Escort's cylinder head, a twin-choke Weber downdraught carburettor and a good exhaust design to give a power output of 86 bhp. Behind this was the same gearbox as that found in the RS1600, although a smaller clutch (7.5 in.) was

Below **The Rallye Sport packages for the MkI Escort included this set of heavy-duty driving lamps on suitably heavy-duty mounting brackets. The pins holding down the bonnet on this car were** *de rigueur*, **as the bonnet would tend to fly open when the car was 'yumped' if the original locking mechanism was relied upon**

used, and at the back of the car, the 3.77:1 final drive gears of the RS1600 were employed. In standard trim, the car came on wide steel wheels, measuring $5\frac{1}{2} \times 13$ in. and shod with 165/13 Goodyear G800 tyres—although a popular option was to spend another £145 and have a set of Minilites just like those of the rally cars.

Externally, the car was striking. The round headlamps which, by that time, had been specified for all RS Escorts were on the nose of the car, as were the sporty quarter bumpers. The Type 49's slightly flared arches gave more away about the nature of the beast, and in case anybody was still unsure about the pedigree of the car, there was a set of broad stripes running the length of each side of the car in a contrasting shade to the main body colour. The name 'Mexico' was emblazoned just ahead of the door handle on each side, and there were matching stripes across the bootlid and over the outer edges of each side of the roof. Fortunately, these were what Ford called a 'Delete Option', which meant that if you specifically asked

Right A favourite trick in racing and rallying is
to remove the battery from under the bonnet and
to site it in the boot to enhance traction. Ford
used this as a selling point for the Escort RS, but
they were being a shade economical with the
truth—the real reason it was there was because it
would not fit in the engine bay! The spare tyre
consumes a good deal of the luggage space

for the car to be delivered without them, it would
come with far more subtle pinlining on each flank.

Ford had introduced the RS Escort programme
under the banner, 'The Potent Mix', and this was
carried over to the Mexico, for which there was an
abundant range of factory-fitted optional extras.
These included Minilite wheels, batteries of Cibié
Oscar driving lamps (£33 for four, including
brackets), a sump guard (£36), and special seats.
The last items could either recline (£31) or have
fixed backs (£18), and they were far more supportive than the standard items. The trim on these was

Below The RS1600 was set apart from all other
Escorts by the phenomenally sophisticated
Cosworth BDA twin-overhead-camshaft engine.
In full race trim, this could produce awesome
amounts of power for a 1.6 litre unit

cloth rather than the usual slippery, black vinyl, which was still commonplace at the time.

Motor magazine used one of these machines—loaded with all of the options—as a chase car during the RAC Rally in 1970. By this time, the car had only been on sale for about three weeks, and all production came from the AVO plant at South Ockendon/Aveley. The magazine was generally very complimentary about the car, and although the event spanned only five days, it led to the journalistic team from *Motor* covering some 2000 miles, which is usually long enough to find any weaknesses. Initially, it was found difficult to match Ford's claimed performance figures of under 11 seconds for the sprint to 60 mph and a maximum speed of more than 100 mph, but eventually they did manage to coax 11.5 seconds and 101 mph. Praise was high for the roadholding and handling, while the steering was described as 'razor sharp', although it was felt that the ride was very firm. The overall impression that *Motor* gave was that the car provided all of the advantages of owning an RS1600, save for the expensive twin-cam engine. At the time of its launch, the Mexico cost £1150, whereas by the end of 1970, the RS1600, in standard trim, cost nearer £1550. The Mexico was an immediate success (it exuded the right image) and went on to sell by the thousand.

What is already apparent is that Ford was adhering strictly to its policy of evolving new models, of using as many common parts as pos-

Special four-spoke alloy wheels were developed by Ford for the models. Some cars came with them as standard, whilst others were offered with them as optional extras. Although originally they had a natural metal finish overall, some owners preferred to blacken the centres of the wheels, leaving only the spoke faces and rims in bright alloy finish

sible. 'The Potent Mix' was used to describe the RS car-then-accessories package, but the same phrase could have been applied to the entire Escort programme. This is why the next RS car to come along also featured the same package of parts (except, of course, for the engine) as the existing models—and those models had already inherited a good deal of their specification from the Twin Cam Escort. Incidentally, production of that particular car did not cease completely when the RS1600 appeared, but continued to the end of 1970. But I am becoming sidetracked. Back to the plot, and to the next RS,

Some years before, Ford of Germany had been searching for a new overhead-camshaft engine and had been given one of the then-new American Pinto single-overhead-camshaft engines upon which to base their research. The result had been the European Pinto engine, a cast-iron lump of undistinguished abilities which, eventually, became available in sizes from 1600 cc to 2000 cc.

By far the most popular model of RS Escort was the RS2000. This example belongs to Paul Corkhill, of the RS Owners Club, and has been superbly restored. The car was an ideal package, offering plenty of unstressed power (over 100 bhp) from a 2.0 litre sohc engine, mated to a strengthened bodyshell and uprated driveline

Right **That rudimentary lip beneath the bumper was what Ford called a spoiler in 1974; compared to today's complex mouldings, it looks positively puny. However, it did help keep the nose of the car down at speed. Those abbreviated bumpers were essential fitments on any sporting Ford of the time**

This underbonnet view of the RS2000 shows how easily the German-developed engine (which, in turn, was an American hand-me-down from the Pinto programme) slotted into the allocated space—and left room for a battery alongside the radiator!

It was the Germans who were responsible for the creation of the RS2000.

Impressed by the competition history of the Twin Cam and of the RS1600, and by the promising start to the Mexico's sales life, the Germans felt that there was room for a third RS car, one which would give the showroom performance of the RS1600, but without its mechanical complexity. They wanted a more luxurious interior than that of the existing RS models, but they wanted the lot for a price which would fall neatly between that of the Mexico and the cost of the RS1600. The brief was thrown at AVO to see if a suitable package could be engineered.

In typical fashion, the team at South Ockendon delivered the goods. The physical aspect of slotting the altogether taller Pinto engine into the

compact bodyshell of the Escort was nothing that the engineers at AVO could not deal with, but there were complications. For a start, the Germans wanted to use the newest model of gearbox to back up the 2.0 litre sohc engine, and they wanted a cable clutch operation.

To achieve the installation, the first move was to design and make a new oil sump for the engine that would clear the Escort's crossmember. The sump was cast in aluminium and contained anti-surge baffles as standard. At the same time, a new cast-aluminium bellhousing was designed and made; this gave a reduction in weight (the Pinto is a heavy lump of iron) and also reduced the amount of space required around the bulkhead. The gearbox could be made to fit if the odd intruding bit of floorpan could be persuaded out of the way with a lump hammer. An electric cooling fan, ahead of the radiator, released more underbonnet space—and gave a 2 bhp gain as well.

Whereas the RS1600 and the Mexico shared common standard spring rates and dampers, the set called for by the heavier two-litre engine needed to be uprated by some 30 per cent at the

Spotlessly clean and totally original in its appearance—the Mexico engine was able to take a substantial degree of uprating without showing too much; this particular one has been increased in size to 1.7 litres

front. To reduce the understeer which would be generated by the nose-heavy car, the rear suspension was softened slightly. The car was also lowered overall—it sat an inch nearer the ground than either the Mexico or RS1600.

One of the advantages of the new engine, when compared to the other two in the RS line-up, was its improved torque at lower speeds; this allowed a taller final drive ratio to be used in the rear axle, and that, in turn, gave relatively unstressed autobahn cruising. The ratio was set at 3.54:1, and by the time that this was teamed with the big radial tyres—on newly-designed, four-spoke, aluminium-alloy wheels—the car could achieve a maximum speed of almost 110 mph whilst still being able to sprint to 60 mph in nine seconds or less.

The interior of the RS2000 offered a number of

major improvements over its stablemates, starting with the carpet. This was thicker and more luxurious than that in the other Escorts, and it concealed appropriate amounts of soundproofing, particularly around the bulkhead area. The seats had been completely redesigned for the front occupants, being wider than in previous RS models and also cloth-faced. A flat, three-spoke steering wheel was provided, as was the familiar six-clock instrumentation. There were also a number of extras listed which were quite alien to the motorsport leanings of AVO, such as wood-effect fascia trim fillets and a centre console for a radio and time clock. Judging by the number of these cars which survive, quite a number of owners were attracted by the additional luxury which these parts afforded.

The RS2000 actually débuted at the beginning of July 1973, and it was keenly priced at £1500 when the Mexico cost £1275 and the RS1600 £1721. United Kingdom deliveries commenced in October of that year, and reaction to the new car was generally good, although some road testers tended to compare the car a little too closely to the

RS1600 for comfort; the RS2000's engine, although able to produce similar overall power levels to the 'out of the box' twin-cam RS car, tended to deliver its power in a totally different manner, generating more torque and generally feeling less 'lively' than the more exotic engine from Cosworth.

There were mixed feelings about the appearance of the car, too, for it was anything but subtle—that description could never be appended to any car which had 8 in. high contrasting decals running the full length of each side. The Mexico's striping set was positively understated in comparison.

What did gain universal praise was the car's road behaviour. It was a package worthy of the RS tag, displaying a pleasingly neutral stance through most bends; only when a corner was attempted on a trailing throttle would the nose start to run wide in the dry, or when too much power was applied would the tail swing outwards in wet weather. Rough surfaces, however, did bring out the worst of the original rear suspension design of angled dampers, as the rear of the car would be thrown off line if a pothole was encountered mid-bend. This would cause the driver to become involved in a battle of skills to prevent the disturbed rear end from upsetting the nose of the car. An unskilled driver could easily come to grief in such a situation.

The amended specification of the car included smaller rear brake drums. The official reason for this was that the original 9 in. items prevented snowchains from being attached to the alloy wheels, but it was felt by a number of road testers (including Ford's own people) that equally responsible for the 8 in. items was a desire to apply more of the braking effort to the nose of the car, where it would be easier to control.

Although the research and development work on the car had been carried out at AVO's plant in South Ockendon, where the Mexico and RS1600 were being manufactured, it was decided that production would take place in a similar facility within the Saarlouis plant. This was partly because the Germans thought that they could make a better job of building the cars, and partly because AVO was already stretched in fulfilling orders for the existing two models. Then international politics came into play, and the result was that the RS2000 was built at South Ockendon after all. In total, Ford built some 3500 examples of the car, 2000 of them going to Germany in left-hand-drive form. Quite how Ford managed to persuade the governing body of motorsport that they had built the 5000 examples required to gain its

homologation certificate is a mystery still unsolved today. There is a rumour that completed cars were pushed out of the factory past the 'man with the clipboard and counting machine', and then, when he wasn't looking, they were pushed around the building and in through the back door, but this could well be an apocryphal tale ...

Within a very short time of the RS2000's launch, the entire Escort range, including the AVO cars (which were all taken off the line at Halewood fully-built but for their engines, transmissions and a few other bits and pieces), was treated to the new rear suspension arrangement which revised the angle of the rear dampers. Thus, the mainstream cars gained the type of suspension which the Competitions Department had favoured all along. This improved the ride quality of the RS cars every bit as successfully as it did the regular, mundane showroom stuff and countered one of the main criticisms attached to the product range.

With the tall final drive gears and the overall wide-spread ratios within the Cortina transmission, the RS2000 was a surprisingly frugal car, many owners being able to combine brisk progress with mpg figures in the upper 20s or even low 30s. This had not been a major criterion of the car's design brief from Germany, but had been a side-effect of the desire to keep engine speed—and thus noise levels—to an acceptable level when cruising. However, the fuel economy of the car turned into a major selling point within days of it reaching British showrooms. At the time, the Arabs and Israelis had engaged in the Yom Kippur War, the Israelis attacking Egypt, Syria attacking the Golan Heights, and all hell letting loose in the Middle East. The first major ramification of this was that the OPEC countries—which then were almost exclusively Arab—announced a drastic cut in oil exports until Israel withdrew from its battlefronts in occupied territories. This multiplied the cost of crude oil, leading to a radical hike in pump prices.

With Britain on the brink of petrol rationing—coupons were issued, but never actually employed—and with a blanket 50 mph speed limit imminent (it was introduced on 5 December), people suddenly started to take notice of the mpg figures of cars. It is fair to say that until then, the distance covered per gallon had been generally ignored, as petrol had been relatively cheap and plentiful. Thirsty cars were suddenly anti-social, and most sporty cars tended to be less than frugal with their fuel.

Yet here was Ford offering a serious sporting saloon car, complete with wide wheels and bold

The début of the RS1600. The subtle keylining, detailed wheels and discreet badging whispered rather than screamed that this was a serious performance Ford. The author's own example was specially finished in black with gold keylining, after the then-trendy JPS Lotus colour

body striping, which was actually cheaper to run than many of its mainstream sisters!

If the RS2000 did well out of the fuel crisis, its stablemates were eclipsed by its success; commanding only a small price premium, yet offering so much more performance, the RS2000 began to steal sales from its 'Mexican' sister. At the other end of the scale, only the serious, competition-orientated driver would still consider the more expensive RS1600; unless the car was to be radically uprated for racing or rallying, it made more sense to buy the cheaper RS2000, which offered similar levels of performance with increased comfort and considerably less complexity.

The Yom Kippur War also affected more than just the Mexico, for car sales plummeted at the end of 1973 and stayed low until 1978; in 1974, sales were more than 25 per cent lower than they had been in 1972. And it was the bigger, more profitable cars which had borne the brunt of the sales slump.

When Ford opened its AVO facility in 1970, it had been seen as a long-term proposition, a small-run, specialized plant which would enable specialized cars to be produced alongside quite different models, a plant with the flexibility to build individual cars to order. If a customer wanted an RS2000 with full forest arch kit, the widest wheels in the catalogue, a quick steering rack, a sump guard and, indeed, anything else in the comprehensive range of RS add-ons, then AVO would build it. Unfortunately, as with any business venture, it takes time for a facility such as South Ockendon to achieve profitability, and although Ford of Britain's management were initially prepared to give the plant more time to start making

By 1974, when this car was shot on the Arctic Rally in the hands of Hannu Mikkola, (it failed to finish), the RS1600 (overbored to 2.0 litres) was already a legend. The team's other cars finished third and fourth in this event, in the care of Timo Makinen and Markku Alen respectively

money, the sudden downturn in profits, caused by the slump in big-car sales, had caused a radical reappraisal of all of the company's activities. Indeed, similar operations were going on in the boardrooms of other manufacturers throughout the Western world, as well as in the other areas of Ford Motor Corporation.

With reluctance, it was decided that instead of carrying on with the MkII Escort, which would have been a natural progression for AVO when production of the MkI ceased at the end of 1974,

the plant would be mothballed. Originally, it was hoped that there would be some kind of miracle in the Middle East and that oil prices would drop back to 1972 levels, with a corresponding return to the glory days of 1.7 million new car registrations that had been such a profitable activity. But miracles were pretty thin on the ground those days, as they are now, unless you count those performed by bible-punchers on American cable TV, and none came. Instead of South Ockendon (Or Aveley—the two names are interchangeable) being reopened, the plant was quietly dismantled three years later, and all RS production of MkII Escorts went to lines alongside the mainstream ones in Germany. Sad.

Some 15 years on, when Ford was sending batches of partly-trimmed Orions to the coach-building concern of Tickford in Coventry, for conversion into 1600Es, more than one old hand at Ford quietly voiced the sentiment that AVO would have been the perfect place for such an operation to be performed.

Or was Ford never really that interested in having ongoing series of special programmes coming out of its own facility at Aveley?

The MkI RS in full race specification. This particular example, now owned by Ken Shipley and seen at an RS Owners Club day, was, in fact, a Lotus-engined machine prepared by Alan Mann Racing. The wide arches were popular with racers and rally teams alike

8 Squaring up

A new style for the late 1970s

THE MkII ESCORT, at least in its basic form, was not one of those pieces of body styling that would ever set the world on fire. Codenamed Brenda, it was conceived in December 1972. In fairness, the replacement for the MkI Escort which, by that time, had established itself as a firm favourite across Europe (the millionth European example had rolled off Halewood's production line a little over a year before) would only be a temporary facelift, as distinct from a totally new model, for the world car concept was already in the air and, no matter what, it would not be a conventional three-box, rear-drive, front-engined car.

The same floorpan would be used for the MkII car, although something would have to be done to reduce the noise, vibration and harshness (good old NVH again) from the chassis. In fact, this aspect of the car was attended to surprisingly quickly. By the middle of 1973, it had been modified to relocate the rear suspension and installed on the existing MkI range as a mid-life improvement. The body styling, although of the same basic dimensions, would perforce be significantly different from the MkI in appearance, even though the inner wings would have to share certain vital dimensions if the running gear was to be carried over from the older car. The new car would also have to better the existing model in terms of accommodation and equipment—or at least give the illusion of doing so.

Because the drivelines of the various models would be carried over from the MkI Escort, the entire project was completed in a very short time indeed; stylists began to produce ideas almost immediately they had received their copies of the production brief, and by early 1973 matters had progressed to the point where full-sized clay models had been made—there had been similar progress in such areas as trim design, electrical systems, seat design and even the badging. This entire operation had been a major logistical exercise, the various teams responsible for the project—which were British and German—being given specific deadlines for each task. The car was finally signed off for production in June 1974, and examples were rolling off the actual (as distinct from pilot) production line at the German factory by early December 1974—exactly two years to the day from the date of the first concept briefing being published.

What the press saw at the car's launch, in January 1975 (two months before the model started to appear in the showrooms, and about the same time that the last RS2000 came off the production line at South Ockendon), was a flat-fronted, slab-sided machine which was a world away from the curvaceous car which it was replacing. There was something of a compromise about the whole car's appearance, in that whilst the engineering people were keen to improve the aerodynamic efficiency of the new shell, the marketing people—who would have to answer to the dealerships—wanted a car which was up-to-date in its looks and, most of all, one which was totally different to its predecessor. In the end, the engineering people lost out, for the 'house-brick' aerodynamics of the MkII were more than 5 per cent worse than the older car. In fact, it was rumoured that even the old 100E Popular had a better drag coefficient, but that would have been simply sour grapes.

What had improved tremendously, compared to

the old car, was the glass area; sensitive to comments about the MkI Escort having a slightly claustrophobic interior, the company increased the window areas of the car by almost 24 per cent. Unfortunately, this had a negative effect on the car's overall weight—automotive glazing is appreciably heavier than sheetmetal, which just goes to show that you can't win 'em all.

Much was made of the amount of extra soundproofing which had gone into Brenda; in addition to the expected sound insulation on the bulkhead (to minimize the thrashing sounds which were transmitted by the valvetrain of the ageing Kent engine), there were also pads attached to the floorpan, to the inside of the doors, to the rear bulkhead, over the rear wheelarches, over the transmission tunnel, and even to the roof panel. Many of these were expressly designed to cancel out panel 'thrum' and resonance—areas in which the earlier car had been criticized—and were surprisingly effective. Unfortunately, those in the footwells tended to absorb moisture (windscreen leaks were common on the MkII) and would eventually lead to the floorpan disintegrating in a cloud of powdery rust. However, at the time of the car's Algarve press launch, in the early part of 1975, such revelations were still to come.

Unlike the MkI, which had débuted as a minimal range, the launch selection available to the customers for the MkII car was broad and comprehensive. Three engine sizes were offered, all variants of the familiar Kent unit which had been carried over virtually unchanged from the previous car. All shared the same 80.98 mm bore in their 117M cast-iron blocks, the differences in capacity being achieved by varying the stroke; the 1100 had a 53.29 mm stroke, the 1300 a 62.99 mm stroke, and the 1600 a 77.62 mm stroke. As previously, there were low- and high-compression versions of the two small engines; there were also twin-choke carburated versions as well as the standard single-choke units.

Compression ratios had been rationalized to 8.0:1 for the low-compression (low-octane fuel) engines, and 9.0:1 for all high-compression versions. Power outputs ranged from a modest 44 bhp (52 lb/ft torque) for the 1.1 litre LC to 84 bhp (92.5 lb/ft) for the 1.6 twin-choke. The most popular model, the 1300 cc HC, gave a good 57 bhp in single-carburettor form.

The suspension systems of the range were carried over from the later models of MkI Escort, although spring rates were uprated slightly to cope with the increased body weight. On average, every MkII Escort derivative weighed some 200 lb more than its corresponding model in the previous line-up.

Ford introduced a new range of model designations with the car. Gone were the old XL and E tags, and in their place came GL and Ghia. Ford

A styling concept of Brenda, the MkII Escort (or an illustration of the finished compromise perhaps?). Sharing the same floorpan and with very similar overall dimensions to the first Escort, the car had a projected lifespan of five years from its introduction

Right **Some cars set the world on fire, and others throw a bucket of cold water over it; Brenda did the latter. The Popular, seen here in a launch-time studio shot, was about as basic as it was possible to be, with a minimum of brightwork offsetting an underwhelming range of colours**

had taken over the Italian styling house some time previously, having acquired an 84 per cent interest in the *carrozerie* (along with Vignale and one or two other little businesses) from Alejandro De Tomaso. The latter had been using his family funds to develop a range of business interests which were leading to the supercars that would carry his name, but by early 1970 his need to hold on to the Ghia interest had diminished, so he sold it to Ford via his friendship with the company's then-golden boy, Lee Iacocca.

Although Ford was making limited use of the styling and design talents of the Turin studios, it was felt that appreciably greater use could be made of the brand name. Therefore, the decision was taken to exploit its charisma by using it to describe the top-of-the-line models in each of their current ranges; the practice continues to this day, with the familiar crest signifying additional luxury. In the case of the MkII Escort, this meant velour seats, a deep pile carpet and much additional brightwork, both inside and outside the car. The interior was completed by a set of neat wooden fillets on the dash trim, and the exterior was distinguished by the use of square headlamps, when almost all of the

One of the early grille concepts being tried in a corner of the pilot plant at Aveley, where the pressing and assembly tools are tested prior to a full-scale factory installation. This grille was a dummy (as its wavy edges indicate) and was not chosen for the production models

The automotive equivalent of a monastic cell. The Popular's interior was an exercise in minimalism, with much moulded rubber and durable vinyl

rest of the range wore round ones. A vinyl roof, tinted glass and chromed wheel bezels completed the picture.

In all, there were 19 cars in the original line-up, starting with the 1100 basic model, which came with rubber mats and basic everything. Even the front brakes were drums. Next up was the 1100L, which offered the benefit of a carpeted floor and one or two other little bits and pieces. Then there was the GL, which had better levels of trim than the other two cars. Heading the fleet was the Ghia, making a total of four cars. Double this, since each car was available in four-door as well as two-door format, while the permutations of engine size brought the total to 17 cars; the remaining two were the Sport models, available with either 1.3 litre or 1.6 litre engines, but with only two doors.

Closer inspection of the cars showed that more changes had been made to the specification than

met the eye. For a start, the entire car was fully metricated to ensure inter-plant compatibility between Halewood and Saarlouis; essential for Ford's embryonic plans to change over to a 'just in time' method of stock control, whereby essential parts for as little as 36 hours production are held at the factory, the remainder for a longer time scale being held by supplying Ford or external contracted plants. By being able to multi-source parts on a pan-European basis, Ford was able to overcome localized supply difficulties without having to shut down any production lines—at least, that was the idea.

Then there was the suspension system. Although this appeared to be just as it had been on the last of the MkI cars, in fact, there was precious little interchangeability. For example, the anti-roll bars were bigger on the newcomer by 2 mm, which meant that their bushes were proportionately larger. Little details such as the steering rack rod ends, the tie-bar balljoints and so on were changed for the new car. The damper rates were uprated to suit the different springs, and at the rear an anti-roll bar increased springing as well as improving location which, again, called for a revision in damping. In all, the MkII was appreciably firmer than its predecessor, and roll was substantially reduced,

The handling was further fine-tuned by altering the geometry of the front wheels to increase toe-in (or reduce toe-out when running), which improved straight-line stability; but the biggest single improvement over the previous model was the adoption of radial-ply tyres as standard across the range. Although by today's standards, the tyres specified (primarily on the grounds of cost) were extremely average in their performance, in 1975 such products as the Michelin ZX, the Goodyear G800 and the others that were fitted to the cars were a quantum leap forward from the crossplies which used to be standard issue. Interestingly, of the half-dozen different types of tyre which were fitted, only two—the offerings of Uniroyal and of Michelin—were really favoured by Engineering. The rest were the idea of the accountants.

If the body styling (which had been carried out under the direction of the affable German Uwe Bahnsen who, at the time, was Vice-President of Design at Ford of Europe) was teutonic in its appearance, so was the car's revised fascia. This had been developed from the award-winning dashboard of the Cortina and featured a single clear cover over a simple arrangement of black gauges with white markings. There were two alternatives in the line-up: the low series, which

The Sport was available in either 1.3 or 1.6 litre versions—this is the latter. Two-door variants only were offered, and the driveline was carried over from the earlier Escorts, being the old GT and Mexico engines respectively, backed up by four-speed transmissions. The Sport had a cloth-trimmed interior and a reasonable level of equipment

had a speedo on one side and a combined water temperature/fuel gauge on the other, and the high series, which had the latter items located centrally, while the space vacated by them was taken by a tachometer of matching size to the speedometer. This assembly sat in a heavily-cowled pod ahead of the steering wheel, and it was claimed to be totally glare-free. Much of the time it was, too, although a low rear three-quarter sun could be reflected into the driver's face from the single pane of the panel.

The rest of the fascia was an exercise in simplicity. Most of the scattered switches of the earlier car had been combined into neat, column-mounted flick-switches, while those rocker switches which remained were positioned in two pairs, one on each side of the central spin-out ashtray. The (optional) radio was underslung beneath the pod which housed these, while the heater controls were located above the pod in the middle of the expanse of flat metalwork. Cortina-style pods at each end of the fascia controlled and directed cool-air ventilation, and the screen was demisted by concealed ducting in the dash top. A capacious shelf was positioned ahead of the front seat passenger. Depending on the car, a two-spoke spindly steering wheel, a thicker-rimmed two-spoke wheel, or a three-spoke affair topped off the steering column; the three-spoke version was for the Sport models, the thick-rim one came with the Ghia models, while the remainder of the range received the spindly item.

The front seats were good, especially if the car happened to be a GL or a Ghia, which benefited from having semi-reclining backrests. In the back the accommodation was a little cramped, but not to the point of being intolerable—in this respect, the car was certainly no worse than the MkI. Boot space was said to be ten per cent better than the earlier Escort, but to capitalize upon this, a driver would have had to pack it with a selection of soft bags of varying sizes. In all but the Ghia models, the boot was equipped with rubber floor matting—the top-of-the-line car gained a cut-pile carpet for the luggage area.

The MkII was a pleasant, if uninspiring car to drive (even in 1600 Sport form) for although quiet and civilized when running at moderate speeds, the engine could be made to sound clattery when pushed, and this would still make its way into the cabin of all but the Ghia models. The driving position was fine—in fact, the car should be praised for the very small length of time it takes to feel at home behind the wheel—and the seats did a good job not just of locating the occupants, but also

Ford's acquisition of Ghia of Turin gave the company access to some of Italy's brightest styling people—and a charismatic name. The first Escort to carry the Ghia badge was introduced along with the rest of the new range in January 1975, and was broadly derived from the 1300E version of the MkI

of absorbing anything which made its way up through the tyres, wheels and dampers.

Because of the weight penalty of the new car, model for model, the performance indexes were down; maximum speeds were relatively unchanged, but the amount of time it took to get away from a standstill was extended. For example, whilst the old 1300 Sport could manage to get to 60 mph in 13.8 seconds with its 4.1:1 final drive, the similarly-geared MkII 1300 Sport took more than 1½ seconds longer to reach the same speed. Interestingly, though, the even weightier 1300 Ghia was made to cover that sprint in under 14 seconds by *Autocar* in March 1975, despite its identical mechanical specification. Another of life's little mysteries.

Such inconsistencies would continue to dog Ford's products for years to come, with road testers from different publications obtaining quite different results from what were ostensibly the same car. It has even happened when the same car has gone from one magazine to another.

But back to Brenda.

The prices of the new range, when it went on sale in the spring of 1975, raised quite a few eyebrows, because Ford appeared to have totally disregarded its usual keen price-matching policy against the competition; almost without exception, the new cars were a good ten per cent more expensive than those of their rivals, model for model. For instance, although the company was able to claim new-model status for the Escort 1300L, its price of £1591 compared less than

favourably with that of the (admittedly dreadful) Marina 1.3L from British Leyland which, at that time, retailed at £1425. At the top end of the scale, the 1.6 litre Ghia cost no less than £2609—more than many of the one-size-up offerings from the other major European manufacturers.

Ford's reasoning behind this was twofold. Firstly, the company knew from inside information and past experience that everybody else would be putting up their prices anytime, and from that point on, parity would be restored. The other reason was that it was keen to hold the launch prices for quite a few months—even as long as a year, when the industry norm was to raise prices every six months—so a cushion against inflation was built into the launch price structure.

Still, the dealers did have brand-new cars which were a world ahead of their predecessors, while their good road manners undoubtedly helped the cause. They battled on and began to register the first of what would turn into a worthwhile sales total of almost 650,000.

At Ford of Britain's headquarters in Essex, plans were already being drawn up to create a loss-leader for the range, an ultra-cheap Escort which, hopefully, would appeal to those initially dismayed by the £1440 starting price of the new range. Although from looking around the 1100 Escort two-door, it was difficult to see where economies could be made, Ford's eagle-eyed cost accountants obviously thought differently. The result of their labours was the most uninspiring of all small Fords ever, the Escort Popular.

If anything, the reintroduction of the name which had served the company so well from the 1930s to the beginning of the 1960s did an injustice to those fine, serious, simple machines which had established Ford's reputation as a maker of the true people's car. Whilst the original Ford Pop' was a genuine attempt at offering value for money, the 1975 Escort Popular, which was presented to the public in July, was a cynical attempt at price paring.

Priced at £1299, the car had all of the usual brightwork replaced by matt black fittings, and the three-dimensional bootlid badging replaced by cheap-looking stickers, which rarely seemed to have been applied straight. The plain rubber mats were an obvious choice for floorcovering, but removing the soundproofing pads from the foot-wells seemed almost churlish. The final straw was when the 13 in. pressed steel wheels of the rest of the Escort range were eschewed in favour of skinny 12 in. items with—wait for it—crossply tyres.

Unlike the 1300E, the wood in the Escort Ghia was not real—and there was a lot less of it. The blonde with the fur and the Ghia handbag was not a standard feature

Grave robbing? I'll say! The occupants of the car did not even get a parcel shelf under the dash, or a dipping rear-view mirror, and if the sun came out, the passenger had to squint, for there was no drop-down visor on that side of the car!

Part of Ford's philosophy towards the car was that it was to be as cheap to run as it was to buy, and to that end the low-compression 1100 cc and 1300 cc engines were to be standard equipment. The first batch, however, came with the standard 1100 cc HC engine as a temporary measure—these were calibrated to run on as lean a fuel/air mixture as possible and had a revised throttle linkage which prevented the throttle flap from being opened fully!

Ford claimed an overall economy figure in the mid 40s for the 1.1 Popular, but few testers ever managed to match that figure. Never mind, the cheapness of the car appealed to quite a number of potential owners, and it was a particular favourite with companies that were looking for inexpensive, basic transport for junior members of staff who had just made it on to the company car ladder's bottom rung.

To confuse matters further, Ford also launched the Popular Plus at £100 more. This could be had with either two or four doors (the basic Popular came in only the two-door shell) and, again, with either the 1.1 or 1.3LC engine. Paradoxically for the Popular concept, this car had a basic carpet, the soundproofing pads replaced in the footwells, the passenger-side parcel shelf, cloth seat trim (that of the Popular was good old Ford vinyl), a dipping rear-view mirror, and so forth. Externally, the car had 13 in. radial-shod wheels and reversing lamps. It posed the question: why not simply cut the price of the base-model 1300 in the first place?

Whatever the reason, Ford never explained it adequately, but simply dropped the basic model.

Perhaps there was a greater perceived value to the Popular Plus because it had a longer name.

Although a bargain-basement Escort, the usual array of Ford extras (except black or metallic paintwork) could be specified at the time of ordering. This is why, today, there are examples of the car running around with servo-assisted disc brakes, and even the occasional automatic transmission.

At the same time that the Popular was announced to a crowd of reverentially-hushed pressmen, Ford also realigned the rest of the range to ensure that the VFM concept could be applied across the range. For instance, the 1100L and 1300L models gained disc brakes, reclining seats and additional exterior trim. The company had reached a watershed, if only they had realized it, for by the beginning of the 1990s, they would be using the trick of 'added value for no extra cash' as a major marketing tool; today, the cars are known as the LX range and account for some 60 per cent of total sales. Then, it was disc brakes and reclining seats, today it is sunroofs and central locking—it will be interesting to examine developments a dozen years

The fascia of the Escort II range was derived from that of the Cortina, a design which had won several awards. The basic models had this two-clock cluster of instruments; more up-market models were equipped with a tachometer, the fuel and temperature gauges being fitted in place of the Ford crest. There was still nowhere proper to fit a radio in the car

hence to see what Ford throws into the ring 'for free' to increase the perceived value of its mid-range models. A carphone? A portable fax? A computer terminal? I wouldn't be surprised.

To ensure that they were not identified with the loss-leaders, the Escort L models also gained the squared-off headlamps hitherto fitted to only the GL and Ghia models, but if their owners wanted the additional driving lamps of those cars, then a supplement had to be paid. The L models got rid of their plain-Jane wheels, gaining instead the sculpted rims of the Sport and Ghia models—although the chromed bezels of the latter car were an optional extra.

The estate version of the MkI Escort had been a resounding success, and Ford was keen to maintain the momentum with the new model. However, due to the cost-consciousness of the entire Brenda programme, the stylists were denied the opportunity of designing an all-new combination car. Instead, the 'new' car was the old one with the Brenda nose-section grafted into place. Interestingly, because of the likely reduction in the capacious load area of the estate, it had been denied the revised rear suspension of the rest of the range. Thus, it entered the second phase of its life with the same angled-damper design with which it had started. Unlike the saloons, the estate was available with only 1100 cc or 1300 cc engines—although the three-speed automatic option was extended to the latter variant—and was available in only basic trim.

Much the same story applied to the Escort van. This, too, had been such a success that its facelifted successor was rushed through as quickly as possible, ensuring a continuity of supply to the dealerships. Again, this was available with only 1.1 or 1.3 running gear and the low-series trim package.

Tedious machine though it was, the Popular had been a shrewd move on Ford's part, because it was instrumental in taking the Escort range to Number One in the 'sales chart', which is produced monthly by the Society of Motor Manufacturers and Traders. This breakthrough came in July 1976, and the car has been a consistent high-seller ever since in Britain, only infrequently being relegated from the top slot. Even then, it is usually deposed by another member of the Ford line-up, such as the Sierra.

In fairness to Ford of Europe, the Escort had already proven itself to be mainland Europe's best-seller in the previous May, and production of the cars at Saarlouis was improving month by month.

Although externally very similar to the earlier MkII cars, the post-1977 Escort Sport, seen here, benefited from a number of detail changes instigated by the German design team. These centred on the suspension system and were aimed at reducing stiction

Furthermore, Ford of Europe was achieving its end without recourse to loss leaders, special editions or any of the other ploys being used by Ford of Britain, But then the Europeans have always been less emotive about their cars.

For all of its success, there was no room for Ford to rest on its corporate laurels with the Escort range, and it wasn't long before a response was made to criticisms of the car's ride quality. Although these had started as gentle whispers, the sounds were getting louder and had the potential to damage sales. Ford's engineering people had been working on improving the car on a continuous basis since its introduction, but it was to be October 1977 before the public got to see the fruits of the department's labour at the Motor Show in London.

There had been two main problems to address with the car, both of which came under the general heading of 'stiction'. This is a word which is a hybrid of 'stickiness' and 'friction', and it referred to the way in which neither front nor rear suspension arrangements would operate smoothly and 'seamlessly'. A partial cure for front suspension stiction had already been effected in 1975, when the damper fluids had been changed to a thinner liquid, but to overcome the problem completely, it was necessary to relocate the top of the strut so that there was a little less side loading on its piston.

At the rear of the car, stiction was attributed to the fundamental design of the spring leaves; although the three leaves which made up each spring were an improvement on the four which had originally featured on the first Escorts, there were still two friction points too many for comfort. The only chance of completely eradicating the problem would come from replacing the multi-leaf springs with single-leaf items, and this had been done by the time of the car's Motor Show appearance. Overall damper ratings were also amended to soften the ride of the car a little, and the rear anti-roll bar was reduced in diameter for the same reason. Until that point, the single-leaf rear springs had been viewed as competition-only hardware, but suddenly even grandma's Escort 1.1 could have them as standard.

A few minor changes were made to the car

during the next couple of years, such as the provision of a rear wash-wipe facility for the estate cars (which, by then, could also be bought with GL trim), but in the main, the range was left much as it was for the autumn of its life, as attention had been diverted to the new lady in Ford's life, Erika. But more of her later.

Across the world, in Australia, two-litre versions of the Escort were also available. These were built in knock-down form (part-assembled bodyshells were sent from Halewood and Saarlouis to Campbelltown, Victoria) and were available in both GL and Ghia trim packs.

The chosen powerplant for the car was the 1993 cc Pinto engine, which had already seen service in the RS2000 Mk I Escort, and this was available in both high- and low-compression forms; with the standard 9.2:1 piston set, it gave 94 bhp, but with the 8.2:1 low-compression pistons in the block, power dropped to 85 bhp. The reason for the two options was the Australian government's emphasis on ecology, which had resulted in the need for engines capable of running on low-lead, low-octane fuels with better-than-European exhaust emissions.

To match the torquey engines, the final drive gearing was set at 3.54:1, and the Cortina transmission was installed to give a healthy spread of power on the ground. This was in response to criticisms that the range of Escorts on sale in Australia were underpowered—the 1.1 and 1.3 Kent engined variants had been dropped, which meant that from 1978, only 1.6 Kent and 2.0 Pinto-powered Escorts were available on that continent.

As with the RS2000, installing the Pinto engine involved making up a new sump for the two-litre unit, while the radiator had to be relocated slightly further forward. The MacPherson struts were

The GL model is distinguishable from its lesser stablemates by the use of square headlamps. The amount of brightwork also increased as the car moved further up the scale

The marketing specials were an innovation in the late 1970s, and the Linnet was the first of the line. This was a *mélange* of bits from the GL and the Sport, wrapped up in a standard four-door bodyshell, and finished off with its own decal set. The driveline was still that of the 1.3 Popular Plus, and the car sold for £3385

uprated from their standard settings to deal with the additional nose weight—buyers could also specify a Rally Pack ('Rally' without Ford's extra 'e') of sportier suspension settings. The pack also provided the owner with a new steering wheel, which was a flat, three-spoke item with a leather rim, and gave the car a front spoiler. The latter came with a reversed 'Escort' decal immediately beneath its number-plate mount—the driver of a car ahead of the spoiler-equipped Escort could read the model name in the rear-view mirror.

In trim packages, the GL and Ghia were very similar to those of the European examples—although there were locally-sourced fabrics and carpeting, they followed closely the style of those already on sale in Britain and Germany. One additional extra which was available for the Ghia was air conditioning. This was considered essential for the high-humidity which pervades not just Australia, but also those areas of the Far East to which Ford Australia exports its products.

1979 saw another Ford innovation which would still be with us as the company entered the beginning of the last decade of the century, the special-edition Escort. The first of these came in 1979, with a package sold under the rather curious name of Escort Linnet. As with all other special-editions that were to follow, this was a 'parts bin special', which drew heavily on the vast amount of different equipment which was available across the range.

Starting with the 1.3 litre Popular Plus model, in four-door guise, the company replaced the standard seats with those from the GL (which, by this time, had its own dedicated cloth trim in a woven diamond pattern) and, for good measure, threw in a push-button radio (combined radio-cassettes were still a rarity then) and the three-spoke sporty steering wheel from the Sport model. With the addition of a door mirror on the passenger side and some special decals, the car was put into the dealership network at £3385—not much more than the model upon which it was based.

At the end of May 1979, the Goldcrest arrived, as a sort of swan-song to the range, production of which was about to cease. This was available, as its name suggests, in only metallic gold paintwork. Its sculpted steel wheels were sprayed in the same shade. The car was based upon either the 1.3L or 1.6L model and, like the Linnet, could be had with only four doors. On the inside, the GL seats were finished in a light gold trim and came complete with headrests—in 1979 the latter items were still options on the mainstream models. A Ghia centre

Neither a MkI nor a MkII, this was the Sunshine Special, photographed at Ford's Boreham motorsport facility in 1978. The car is something of a mystery, but was definitely based on Escort running gear. There is speculation that the badge on its wing is that of the famed coachbuilding house Pininfarina

consol with integral clock and push-button radio was fitted to the car, and the Sport steering wheel was a feature once more. As with the Linnet, the Goldcrest came with special graphics, special literature and a price that was not much different to the standard GL's £4256.

Britain wasn't the only place where special-edition Escorts appeared, though—on the other side of the globe, in Malaysia, there was another. In fact, this had predated the Goldcrest slightly, going on sale at the end of April 1979. It was known as the Anniversary Escort.

This was based on the 1300GT two-door—the Oriental 1.3 Sport—and only 150 were offered for sale to help the Australians celebrate Ford's 75th birthday as a car producer. Available only in Executive grey with a black vinyl roof, the car also featured front and rear spoilers, foglamps to match the square halogen headlamps, and special side badging at the base of each rear pillar. As with the British specials, the additional items were sold at only a nominally higher price.

There was one other special-edition, the Harrier, but, in many ways, that was more of an RS car than a mainstream Escort. And speaking of RS cars, perhaps it is time to investigate how these made the transition to Brenda's clothing . . .

9 Permutations

Brenda shows her sporting nature

THE ORIGINAL RS Escorts had been a tough act to follow, especially when the 'bespoke build' service offered by Ford Advanced Vehicle Operations was taken into account. And if Ford was prepared to let the AVO facility lie down and die peacefully in its sleep without any qualms, the opposite applied to the RS Escorts themselves. They were too lucrative in terms of showroom enticement to be allowed to simply slip away. No matter what, the Rallye Sport Escorts would continue in their own tradition.

The RS2000, seen here in rare flat-face form—the bodyshell was shared with that of the RS1800— and with the forest arch kit in place. In this form, it was a firm favourite amongst club-level rally drivers, and even a decade after the car went out of production was still setting the pace in local and regional events

The first of the new-generation cars appeared in October 1975 in the form of the RS2000. At the same time, Ford officially announced the existence of its new rally weapon, the RS1800.

The RS2000 followed the same formula as previously, the two-litre Pinto engine (producing 110 bhp) being backed up by the Cortina-derived gearbox and a 3.54:1 final drive ratio. Once again, braking was handled by a combination of 9.7 in. front discs and 9 × 1.75 in. rear drums with full servo assistance, and the suspension was an up-rated version of the MacPherson strut front, leaf-sprung rear arrangement found on all other Escorts.

Ford would have had an adequate cocktail on its hands if it had stuck to the bodyshell used by all the other two-door MkII Escorts, but clearly there was a desire to make the car look different from the rest of the herd. This was achieved by designing a

new nose section which increased the overall length of the car by 7 in. (to 163.1 in.) and gave the impression of being more aerodynamic. As no drag coefficient for the revised car was ever published officially, the actual windcheating value of the nose-cone is unknown, but what was obvious was its ability to transform the 'pair of shoeboxes on wheels' into a very sporty looking device. The lighting performance of the car was also improved by the new visage, because in place of the usual pair of round headlamps were four Cibié items. At least they were better on full beam; on dip, only the outer pair was active, whereas on full beam all four lamps were illuminated.

In addition to the nose-cone, there was an under-bumper front spoiler, finished in the main body colour, while on the trailing edge of the bootlid was a corresponding aerodynamic device finished in natural black neoprene. There was no brightwork anywhere on the car, save for the trim within the Ford oval badges; window surrounds, bumpers and door handles were finished in satin black—obviously what was viewed as a cost-saving move on the Popular models was considered sporty for the RS2000!

Reaction to the car was mixed, most of the controversy being centred on that nose-cone. For example, *Custom Car* described it as 'certainly not

Former RS Owners Club officer Peter Nixon, of Shropshire, is the justifiably proud owner of one of Britain's finest RS2000s. Finished in yellow with the optional black vinyl roof, the car has an uprated engine—at the time the RS2000 MkII was on sale, it was possible to buy engine uprate systems from your neighbourhood Ford dealership

a thing of rare and delicate beauty', whilst Mike Scarlett wrote in *Autocar* that it was 'funny'. Whatever anybody made of the nose-cone, the rest of the car was well-received.

The RS2000 upheld all of the virtues of the previous RS cars, combining urbanity when pottering through traffic with the ability to cut loose and go when conditions allowed. Even recently, when I renewed my acquaintance with the car after a gap of more than a decade, it felt good to drive. Its power-to-weight ratio was much the same as that of the MkI RS2000, despite the fact that the new model was bigger and bulkier; weight gains by the new bodyshell had been countered by a redesigned exhaust system which released a few additional horsepower. The car's straight-line ability was lively, the benchmark sprint to 60 mph being achieved in $8\frac{1}{2}$ seconds. In a little over a half-minute from starting, the car could be topping 100 mph, when there was enough road available, and if the driver could manage it, there was enough power to push the machine to a maximum speed in excess of 110 mph.

What was more important, however, was not that the car could do it, but how it did it; the revised exhaust system had taken peak torque to an impressive 119 lb/ft at a useful 4000 rpm—and that meant that progress need not be frantic and strained to be quick. The handling was also up to par for an RS car. More taut and responsive than the rest of the Escort range, the RS2000 (which didn't sit quite as close to the ground as its immediate predecessor) could soak up bumps quite effectively without being over-sloppy and without rolling or pitching around. The car came with the same steering rack as the rest of the Escort range, requiring three-and-a-half turns of the

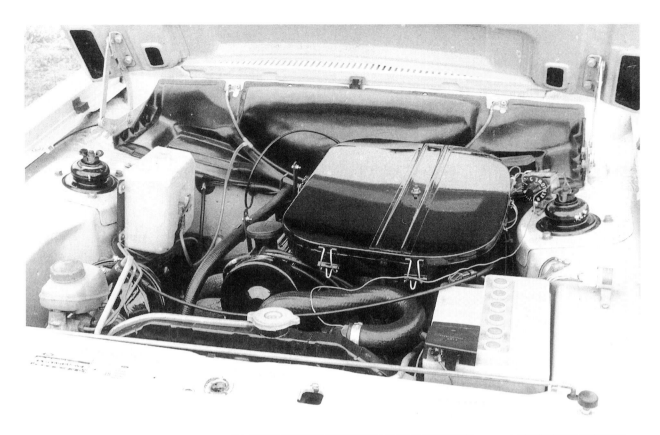

Above The works-pattern arch kit allowed the car to run appreciably wider wheels and tyres than the standard items—essential for gaining traction on loose surfaces. Although their cars often suffered a reduction in handling precision, a number of private owners, who never went rallying, were attracted by the style and adopted it for their road cars

Above left The substantial air cleaner conceals a pair of Weber downdraught carburettors—an integral part of the Group One engine package which raised power output from the usual 110 bhp to over 140 bhp

Left The interior of the RS2000 was an improvement on that of the standard Escorts by virtue of its thick-rimmed RS steering wheel, the centre console, additional stowage, and sports seats. The Beta cloth chosen for the model proved less than durable and caused problems for later owners of the cars due to its rarity

thick-rimmed wheel to get from one lock to the other, but there was also the option of a high-ratio rack which reduced the number of turns to two-and-a-half. However, the latter option increased steering effort considerably, whereas the standard rack needed a light wheel effort—the fast rack proved very good for building up a driver's biceps.

The car's brakes were less praiseworthy. Although fine for normal, light traffic use and requiring a light pedal effort, they were prone to fading when used hard and frequently; ventilated discs would not become standard on the sporting models until the next generation of Escort arrived. There was also a tendency for the rear drums to lock up prematurely under hard retardation.

Unlike the current practice with such cars as the XR3i, the smart four-spoke 13 × 6 in. alloy rims—which came shod with Pirelli Cinturato CN36 tyres as standard—were not optional extras, but came as part of the package. And the price of that package? £2857, plus extra for seat belts, number plates and delivery.

Inside the car, Ford tried hard to make the RS2000 a cut above the rest of the Escort range. Firstly, there were special front seats manufactured to Ford's specification by the esteemed German aftermarket supplier, Recaro. These had distinctive integral headrests which allowed the occupants to see through them—years later, the small ads of the specialist press, such as *Performance Ford*, are liberally sprinkled with requests from potential buyers looking for Recaro 'Fishnets'. Needless to say, the items for which they are searching are far removed from the articles of ladies' clothing to which their name alludes!

In addition to the Recaro seats, which were covered in a distinctive and durable Beta cloth to Ford's own specification, other aspects of the RS2000's interior set it apart from the mainstream models. The first of these was the instrument panel which, while retaining the overall design of the range's glare-free glazing, had three central round gauges to monitor oil pressure, water temperature and fuel level. These were sandwiched between the large tachometer and speedometer. The expanse of blank fascia which normally faced the

The Mexico, when recycled into MkII form, was a resounding failure in terms of sales; its 1600 cc sohc engine was appreciably less powerful than that of the RS2000, and its looks were equally subdued, but the price differential was not enough to justify the down-grading exercise. This immaculate example belongs to Mark Slater of the RSOC

The small neoprene rear spoiler was as much for looks as for aerodynamic effect. The next generation of Escorts, however, would have a truly efficient design, engineered by Ford following exhaustive wind-tunnel tests

front-seat passenger was cut into to provide a neat cubby-hole with integral Smiths time clock at the right-hand end, the usual shelf below the dashboard was replaced by a lidded glove compartment, and there was yet more stowage space in a cubby-hole beneath the standard push-button radio in its special centre console. The flat, three-spoke, thick-rimmed steering wheel with moulded centre-pad (bearing the new embossed RS logo) completed the picture nicely.

Down under in Australia, they had their own RS2000 model, and unlike the European cars, this could also be had in four-door form. The cars were sent to Australia from Europe in knock-down (part-assembled) form and were completed at Ford Australia's Campbelltown, Victoria, facility. Because of this, there was a significant amount of local content in the cars.

For a start, whereas the European cars came with Recaros, the Australian models were equipped with Scheel seats with conventional fixed headrests rather than see-through, net-trimmed items. The suspension was different, as was the engine specification, and there were special exterior detailing changes.

The main difference to the suspension was to be found under the rear of the car, for in place of the pair of forward-running radius arms, which featured on the European versions of the RS2000, there was an anti-roll bar of the type used beneath earlier MkI Escorts. Spring and damper rates were also uprated to cope with the more arduous conditions which prevailed in Australia; whereas the highways were smooth and straight, the outback roads could leave much to be desired.

Because of Australia's forward-thinking policy on exhaust emissions (which was modelled on that of America), the power output of the engine was reduced by some 15 per cent to 94 bhp, with a drop in torque to 109 lb/ft. This was achieved mainly by modifying the car's ignition timing and valve timing to cope with low-octane fuel.

Despite previous claims to the contrary, the RS2000 in Australia had the same wedge nose as the European car; reports that it could be had only in the flat-nose style confused it with the GL and Ghia two-litre models, which were detailed in the previous chapter. Unlike the European cars, Australian examples did not come with aluminium-alloy wheels as standard, but came on steel rims. When the optional alloys were ordered, these turned out to be special items manufactured by Globe Industries—the model name was Volante— in a size of 13 × 6 in.; the familiar four-spoke British wheels were never officially offered for sale on the Australian RS2000. The same applied to the tyres; in place of the Italian Pirellis, Australian buyers received similarly-sized Uniroyals. The Volante wheels, incidentally, were specially-finished with an ultra-hard lacquer and had black plastic centre caps—chrome-plated caps were also available direct from Globe Industries.

There were other, subtle, differences in the Australian car's appearance. It came with locally-sourced door mirrors, and there were no RS logos in the centres of the wheel caps. Bold graphic decals appeared on the car's flanks and tail, and there was no vinyl roof trim option. Inside, there was no RS logo on the wheel's centre boss, and there was no clock on the dashboard; instead, there was a blank-off plate on the centre console should the owner desire to fit one after taking delivery of the car. In fact, there was not even the dash-mounted cubby-hole, while the centre console was of a different design to that of the European cars. The glass content was all locally-sourced, and there were such fine-detail changes as the makes of the headlamps (Hella outer, Lucas inner, rather than Cibié lamp sets) and the absence of screw head covers on the rear bumper bars.

Under the bonnet of the RS, close scrutiny would elicit that the cast-aluminium bellhousing and similarly-made sump were absent; in their places were a cast-iron assembly and a sheetmetal pressing respectively. The air cleaner assembly was round, there was no RS logo cast into the exhaust manifold (these cars used the same manifolding as the mainstream models), and some of the plumbing arrangements were slightly different.

Despite the lower power output of the engine, the car was well-received, most of the praise going to the sharp and responsive handling. More than one owner bemoaned the fact that, unlike European buyers, the Australians could not go down to their local RS dealership and buy a Stage One engine tune-up package. In fact, they could not go down to their RS dealership at all, because no such infrastructure existed within the Ford Australia dealer network.

The South African Ford factory also produced its own variant of the RS2000. As with the Australian car, it was made from a knock-down kit of parts which had been shipped in from Halewood, via Dagenham; bodyshells were put together at Halewood then sent to Dagenham where the rest of the package was put together and then loaded on a ship for South Africa.

Unlike the Antipodean car, which was much-modified for its own market, the South African

More than 10,000 examples of the RS2000 were produced during the car's lifetime. This example (the property of *Drive & Survive*'s Phil Newton) gave the author the opportunity of re-aquainting himself with driving a standard example. It was enjoyable!

By inserting a 1.8 litre development of the Cosworth BDA engine into the MkII bodyshell, Ford happened upon a package which was to win a phenomenal number of international rallies. The RS1800, disappointing and expensive in standard roadgoing form, proved a perfect starting point for an excellent rally car

version was very similar to the British and German models; the main external difference was that the front quarterlights opened, whereas the European models had fixed glass. A large fuel tank was fitted—a Capri unit which sat between the rear wheelarches—and an anti-roll bar was used to locate the rear axle rather than the European twin radius arms. Uprated rear dampers featured on the car, and the final drive ratio was a taller 3.77:1 rather than the usual 3.54 item.

The car was in production for only a year or so, and according to Ford's figures, less than 2000 examples were built.

Back in Britain, the next new arrival was the RS1800. Although it had been announced at the same time as the RS2000, it was some months—in

fact, the early part of 1976—before the new rally weapon was made available. And when it did arrive, reaction was mixed. With the benefit of hindsight it is clear that most of the adverse press coverage was attributable to the machine having been misunderstood; whereas it ought to have been viewed as a basic package upon which to build, the car was looked upon as a complete and finished entity which, on paper at least, offered no real advantages over its RS2000 stablemate. Perhaps the marketing pitch wasn't as precise as it might have been.

The car was a straight development of the old RS1600—in fact, Ford was able to avoid lengthy and complicated homologation procedures with the motorsport licensing body by using their earlier certification; at 1840 cc the engine was already approved, and Ford was able to convince everybody that the squared-off bodyshell was nothing more than a cosmetic change.

With its 88.75 mm bore and 77.62 mm stroke, the oversquare engine was free-revving and sharply responsive, even in detuned road form. With mild camshafts, a lowish 9.0:1 compression ratio and a solitary twin-choke Weber carburettor, the twin-cam, all-aluminium engine produced 115 bhp and 120 lb/ft of torque. These figures could be increased dramatically by upgrading the camshafts, using a pair of twin sidedraught Weber or Dellorto carburettors, installing a set of 10:1 pistons and so forth... beginning to get the picture?

The driveline was tough enough to take the power. It began with an 8.5 in. diameter single-plate clutch, which led to a close-ratio version of the Type B gearbox. At the back of the car was a Timken-type, front-loading axle—again, the same as that of the RS2000—with 3.54:1 standard overall gearing. In standard form, the car would give lively performance: standstill to 60 mph took under nine seconds, while top speed was a little over 110 mph. By varying the final drive gears—ratios were available from a low 5.14:1 right up to 3.11:1—in proportion to the revised power output, the performance of the car could be altered out of all recognition compared to the original stated figures. It was 'The Potent Mix' all over again.

As well as homologating a whole package of engine options, Ford also gained approval for the Rocket gearbox, a tough, almost bulletproof, piece of equipment which gave yet closer ratios whilst still being a four-speed. For the serious mixed-surface rally competitor, there was a five-speed ZF gearbox which gave an overdriven top gear; such a package allowed numerically high final drive gears to be used, with their attendant improvement in engine-to-road response, without too high a penalty being exacted when driving from stage to stage because of the fifth gear facility. More than one road car of the 109 which were built has been equipped with the five-speed unit (or similar boxes from such manufacturers as Quaife) as a means of dramatically increasing the car's maximum speed.

A similar degree of flexibility existed in the suspension and braking areas of the car. In standard form, the RS1800 shared its spring and damper arrangement with the RS2000, which meant that there was a reasonable degree of ride comfort (certainly more than in the RS1600 from the MkI line-up), combined with a natural mild-understeering characteristic. The brakes were the usual solid front discs with rear drums and, again, their dimensions were shared with the RS2000. By dipping into what appeared to be a bottomless pit of spring and damper options, and various brake system packages—all available from your friendly local RS dealership, of which, by that time, there were close to 100—the car could be made into

whatever the owner desired. In-built oversteer, brakes that could be biased front-to-rear, you name it and it could be done.

The interior of the car was substantially similar to that of the RS2000, in that it had the same fascia. The seats, however, were not quite as good as the Recaros of the RS2000—Ford's attitude then, as it is now, was that a driver intending to pursue a competition career in the car would fit aftermarket high-grade seats and harnesses in place of the Ford items. This also saved Ford some money.

Money was also saved by equipping the RS1800 with $5\frac{1}{2} \times 13$ in. steel wheels (with CN36 Pirellis) and by not bothering to make it look much different to any of the mainstream Escorts; some bumper-height Rallye Sport blue striped decals, a vestigial front spoiler, the spongey bootlid aerofoil, and a pair of front quarter-bumpers were the extent to which Ford went when equipping the car's exterior.

Unlike the RS2000, which was built alongside the main production lines at Saarlouis, the RS1800 was produced at Halewood—fully-trimmed bodyshells were taken from the lines and fitted with their sophisticated Cosworth engines in a separate final assembly area. It was only the intentionally-limited numbers in which the car was produced that made such a method of construction possible and practicable; had the car been destined for a wider audience, clearly Ford would have had to make alternative arrangements.

As it was, the RS1800 went straight from conception to a sparkling career as a rally car.

The RS1800's début. In full rally trim and with Timo Makinen's name on the car, the RS1800 featured an overbored engine and full loose-surface suspension package. This particular car is believed to have been subsequently registered as LAR 801P, which went on to win the 1975 Lombard RAC Rally

All of the production engines, although designed by Cosworth, had been built by Holbay Race Engineering, of Martlesham, Ipswich. As part of its service to Ford, that company built a number of special blocks which used machined steel billet crankshafts (the standard item was a casting) complete with twelve-bolt flywheels. It was this specification of engine that was used as the heart of the competition machinery. Although a few of these engines (which were given the number prefix 'HRE') made their way into production examples of the RS1800, by far the majority were tuned to give about 240 bhp and saw service in the works-prepared rally cars.

Ford made much of the fact that anybody could go to their nearest RS dealership and buy a

As well as the authentic RS1800, there was another option available to RS owners in search of radical increases in power; Chris Rout exercised one such option when he had a Holbay dohc 2.4 litre engine inserted into his RS2000. The package was awesomely fast, yet totally reliable and consistent

package of parts which would convert their standard RS1800—or, indeed, their Mexico MkII—into a machine capable of winning rallies, and the works cars proved the point by being a highly successful blend of off-the-shelf parts which were simple, but won events. Over the course of the next half-dozen years, the RS1800 was to win all manner of rallies and race meetings, in the hands of such drivers as Roger Clark, Hannu Mikkola, Ari Vatanen, Timo Makinen, Malcolm Wilson and Russell Brookes. From its début win on the Granite City (with the redoubtable Roger Clark in the hot seat), the car set off on a course which was to lead to several international championships for drivers and a Manufacturers' World Championship for Ford. The record set by the RS1800 formula has, at the time of writing, still to be matched by any other car or manufacturer.

As well as rallying, the car was used in circuit racing and accounted for yet more laurels gained by Ford. Zakspeed, for example, used the basic package as a foundation for some of their radical 'silhouette' race cars prior to the more attention-grabbing Capris. And in the hot rod racing scene,

the RS1800 formula was to prove to be the car that everybody followed for some considerable time.

Given the extensive competition history of the car, and the fact that rallying destroys cars like few other forms of motorsport, it is not surprising to learn that far more than the official 109 cars were built. In fact, it is virtually impossible to gauge exactly how many of these devices have existed for several reasons. The first is that there are no authenticated factory records; the cars came off the line at Halewood as Mexicos, so there is no separate lineage. Secondly, in addition to genuine factory-prepared (or sanctioned) examples, there was a healthy trade in engines from Ford's Motorsport department to all manner of constructors—if Ford could take a Mexico shell and turn it into an RS1800, so could almost anybody with a decent workshop.

To prove the point, only the day before writing this chapter, I spotted a rally car on a trailer. To all intents and purposes, it was a genuine factory car, but, in fact, it was on its third bodyshell and its umpteenth engine and gearbox (this one had the familiar ZF five-speed unit) since it was first acquired by the rally-for-rent team which operated it. So where does authenticity start and finish?

Much of the RS1800's success was attributable to its simplicity; there was little in the car that

A decade after production of the car ceased, the RS1800 was still winning rallies, albeit regional ones. This particular example is a firm favourite amongst rally fans. Much aftermarket hardware is still widely available for the MkII

could not be fixed from a small stock of goodies in the back of a service car. This concept was taken to extremes by the next car to join the RS line-up, the RS Mexico.

The World Cup Rally had been run so long before that the reason behind the name was but a faded memory to the great British motoring public, but the niche which the car had carved for itself was worthwhile enough for the marque to be carried over to the new bodyshell. Anyway, the name had a nice ring to it.

As with the previous car—which had not been sold as an official RS model—the cocktail which Ford served up from January 1976 made use of a

The RS1800 was similar externally to the Mexico, the simple, weight-saving, flat-front bodyshell having dedicated graphics; the Rallye Sport side stripes were officially unique to the model, although at least one dealer chose them to embellish a shed full of Mexicos

The Harrier was a blatant attempt to milk the same cow which had borne the Mexico—a package of Sport mechanicals wrapped up with abundant RS parts and sold as a pseudo-RS car

simple, moderately-powerful engine of 1.6 litres capacity, paired to the same basic package of driveline components as those of the RS2000. Whereas the original Mexico had used a version of the Kent engine, which produced 86 bhp, the new Mexico was powered by the smaller variant of Pinto engine—which gave a more useful 95 bhp.

This was just as well, because although the new bodyshell tipped the scales at a couple of hundred pounds more than its predecessor, Ford had to be

A special for Australia was the Escort Escapee. This was based on the 1600 Sport, dressed to head for the hills in a set of decals in red, yellow and matt black. The colour scheme was based on that of Roger Clark's works car in the Southern Cross Rally of 1976

seen to be making progress in performance terms. As it transpired, the boxier car was able to beat its earlier, more curvaceous stablemate by only a very small margin in terms of both acceleration and maximum speed.

Whereas the original Mexico had been an outstanding success in sales terms, unfortunately, the same did not apply to the MkII version of the car, and part of the apathy with which it was greeted was attributable directly to Ford's low-key marketing of the car. This extended as far as the press fleet, the block of demonstrators retained for testing by magazine and newspaper journalists. The Mexico hardly figured on the fleet, to the point where published road tests are virtually non-existent.

The interior of the car—which, incidentally, retailed at £2090, while the 1600 Sport was £400 less and the RS2000 was £300 more expensive—was basic when compared to the RS2000, the five-clock instrument binnacle being offset by a plain dashboard. Although there was a lid on the glove compartment, there was no in-dash cubby-hole and no centre console. The bucket seats were good looking, but not terribly comfortable and, unlike the RS1800, there was little chance of the owner of an RS Mexico swapping them for a set of moulded competition items.

The British public was staggeringly underwhelmed by the MkII Mexico. So where did it go wrong? With the benefit of hindsight, it is easy to see that Ford had shot itself in the corporate foot by carrying the model over to the new range. The Mexico's performance was far from earth-shattering, and it cost little less to buy and run than an RS2000, and appreciably more than the similarly-powerful 1600 Sport. In the end, customers either went for the two-litre car and ran it in standard form, or bought a 1600 Sport, tuned it by uprating the carburation and exhaust system, and were still in pocket, despite having a car which out-performed the Mexico.

Such marketing mistakes by the world's biggest motor manufacturer are rare, but not unknown. However, the MkII Escort seemed to be beset by more than its fair share of *faux pas*. Perhaps Ford would get it right the next time, when the first of the front-wheel-drive Escorts came along.

What exacerbated the problems of the Mexico was the abundant supply of tuning parts which were available for the RS models in general, and

An official Ford Australia works car, which was campaigned throughout the latter half of the 1970s, and which was still doing battle in 1981 in the hands of Colin Bond. As with most rally cars, it was probably on its third bodyshell and fifth driveline by then

the RS2000 in particular. For example, there was a package for that engine which gave it an appreciable power boost, principally by changing the stock twin-choke carburettor for a pair of 44IDF Webers, the head for a big-valve item, and the camshaft for a more substantial grind. No such similarly-effective package was offered for the Mexico. Then there was the Salisbury limited-slip differential which helped control the rear of the RS2000. Although this would aid that car, it was wasted on a Mexico in standard trim. The top and bottom of it was that the RS2000 positively oozed glamour and street credibility, yet the Mexico—which was only £175 cheaper when the optional four-spoke alloys were specified—was rarely seen as anything other than a poor relation. The car slipped quietly out of production within three years of its launch, leaving the field exclusively to the RS2000.

What nobody appreciated then was that there would be quite a gap in time before there would be a new RS Escort.

RS2000 in Australia. The Globe Volante aluminium-alloy road wheels were an optional extra—the standard items were pressed steel. The car was supplied in knock-down (semi-assembled) form from Europe, and much of the content was sourced locally. There were several differences under the skin between this car and the European examples, such as the bellhousing, exhaust manifold and air intake system

There was one other MkII Escort that came out of the RS programme—at least it gave the impression of having done so. In November 1979, Ford's simple-but-effective RS1800 package had won the Lombard RAC Rally, giving the manufacturer its eighth consecutive win. As had happened more than a decade earlier following the company's World Cup Rally success, the marketing people decided to capitalize on the occasion by producing a celebratory model.

In spirit and in form, the new car—a strictly limited-edition known as the Harrier—was close to the Mexico's format. Power came from the much-proven Kent 1600 crossflow engine which, by this point, was giving 87 bhp and a similar amount of torque (although the brochure's peak torque point of 36,000 rpm was a slip of the typesetting machine, not some new-found turbine ability from the Kent). The rest of the driveline, along with the engine, was taken from the 1.6 Sport, which meant that its acceleration was peppier than that of the MkII Mexico—the 0–60 mph time was ten seconds, and top speed 103 mph.

To set the Harrier closer to the RS cars and further from the Sport model, it was blessed with a set of 13 × 6 in. four-spoke, cast-aluminium wheels, tinted glass, Recaro front seats with fishnet headrests, twin door mirrors (with remote operation on the driver's side) and special decals in the three shades of Motorsport blue. Two body colours were offered, Diamond White and Strato Silver, and these were offset by matt black trim and rear spoiler. Interior trim was in black Beta cloth, and the fascia was that of the Sport rather than the RS models. Only 1500 of the machines were offered for sale, the majority being in white. The basic car sold at £4330, with supplements of £26 for the push-button, three-band radio, £39 for inertia-reel seat belts, and £36 for the silver paint finish.

Intriguingly, a number of counterfeit copies of this car have been produced over the years, presumably because the limited-production status of the machine inferred a greater value. All that it took was a standard Sport 1600 and a few bits from the RS parts bin. Which, after all, was what Ford had done in the first place!

10 Global visionaries

The world car arrives at last. Or does it?

THE TERM 'world car' has a nice ring to it, especially if you happen to be an accountant working for one of the world's leading automobile manufacturers.

To Ford, the notion of producing a single-car family which would be equally well-received in Melbourne, München Gladbach, Mexico City, Middlesbrough, Minneapolis and Milan was irresistible. By standardizing the vast majority of the car's components—and a small car such as the Escort can comprise close to 100,000 parts—it is possible to make dramatic savings in the research and development budgets, and later in the cost of tooling for production.

Ever since the Yom Kippur War, the world had been painfully aware of how much power was held in the Middle East. All that seemed necessary was a wrong move from the West and the oil supplies would start to dry up again. Therefore, it was decided very early on—in 1976, in fact—that the world car concept would have to be a small, frugal machine. Actually, although the people on the top floor of Ford's world headquarters in Dearborn were none too keen on the idea at first, the ideal car would be of similar proportions to the Escort which was such a resounding success in Europe.

The Fiesta, which had been on sale for only a few months at the time work began on the world car, had already proved that an integral part of the new model's conceptual design should be front-wheel-drive. With typical caution, Ford had waited on the sidelines for several years before taking the plunge into producing a compact car which drove through its front wheels—Fiat had adopted the concept some years before with its 127 and 128 models—but, having decided to enter the fray, had been highly successful with the ultra-compact Fiesta model. That car had combined reasonable passenger space within a diminutive bodyshell. It also proved cheap to run during pre-launch trials and its first few months on sale. By stretching that concept, Ford felt that it would have a winner on its hands. It was right.

The Fiesta used the latest version of the Kent crossflow engine, and for a market which demanded efficient, basic transportation for the masses, this was fine. However, the engine was getting rather long in the tooth, so it was decided, very early on in the Erika programme—Erika was the codename for the world car, following a short-term trend within Ford to give each new model a female name during its gestation period—that there ought to be a completely new family of engines created for what was to be a totally new concept.

Ford's Research and Engineering Center in Dearborn had already started the ball rolling with a radical new design for a single-overhead-camshaft engine which was based around a hemispherical combustion chamber design. However, the American designers had to admit that Ford's European plants were more familiar with the problems of making small engines produce large power outputs efficiently (that is, without burning tremendous amounts of fuel), so the project was handed over to Ford European Automotive Operations at Merkenich and at Dunton to complete the programme.

Ford of Europe—operating between those two centres in Westphalia and Essex—had already been working on the replacement Escort programme for a year or so before Dearborn decided that the concept would become a world car.

Consequently, it was able to integrate the engine programme into the existing research.

The result of those labours was the CVH. The letters are a fairly loose acronym taken from the head's design description—Compound Valve Hemispherical in the USA, and the more complex Compound Valve Angle Hemispherical Chamber in Britain. The design of combustion chamber was state-of-the-art in 1980 when the car first appeared. Interestingly, the head design was changed substantially in 1986 when the Escort MkIII gained its first facelift, but that is another story dealt with in a subsequent chapter.

The block of the new engine was cast in iron, but it was relatively lightweight in spite of this

Many different styling ideas were put up for the Erika programme, with input from both sides of the Atlantic as it was considered to be a world car. These are just some of the concepts, those considered good enough to make it into three-dimensional fibreglass models

material; much computer stress diagnosis had gone into the basic design in Dearborn, and further research had fine-tuned the casting to minimize the wall thicknesses without compromising strength. By varying the bore and stroke dimensions, it proved possible to build engines as small as 1117 cc and as big as 1851 cc, which meant that all possible variants of the new car could be catered for. Power outputs from as low as 45 bhp to as high as 127 bhp could be achieved without recourse to forced induction, and if a turbocharger was bolted on (as it would be towards the end of the MkIII's lifespan), yet more power could be released from the compact engine.

On top of the block sat a cast-aluminium cylinder head. This incorporated a rather neat system of rockers to simulate the behaviour of a twin-cam arrangement and operate the valves, which were inclined on each side of the head, using only a single overhead camshaft. A thin-wall, cast-alloy intake manifold held the carburettor, which could be one of three different types, depending on

Full size glass fibre models of 1976 & 1977 Escort design studies.

Right The CVH (compound valve hemispherical) engine was one of the basic design features handed by Dearborn to the various design teams. By having self-adjusting, overhead-camshaft-driven valves, low maintenance was assured

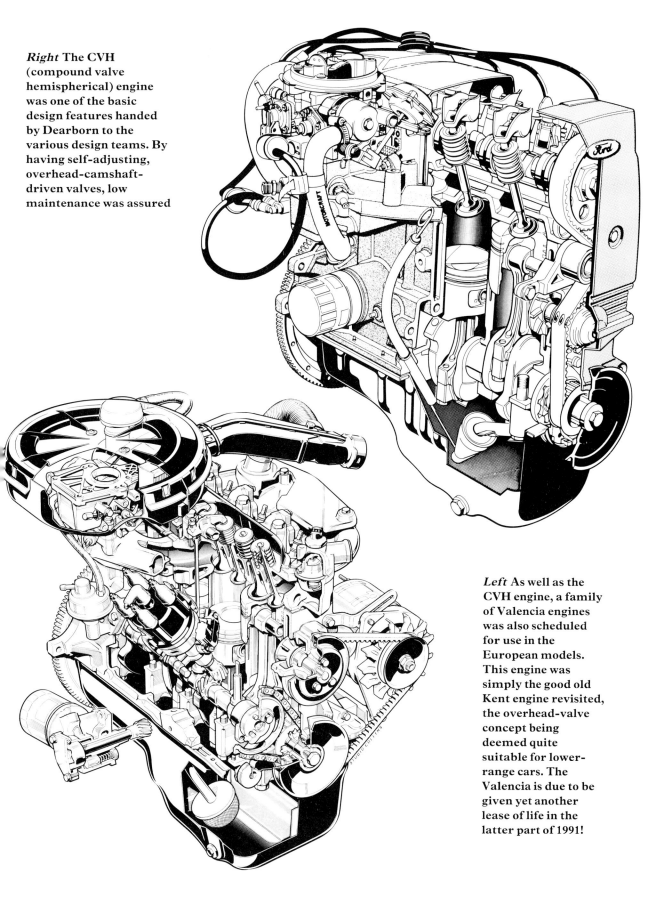

Left As well as the CVH engine, a family of Valencia engines was also scheduled for use in the European models. This engine was simply the good old Kent engine revisited, the overhead-valve concept being deemed quite suitable for lower-range cars. The Valencia is due to be given yet another lease of life in the latter part of 1991!

For the rear suspension of the Escort family (except vans), Ford Dearborn had decided that a fully independent system was essential. This was to prove a major disadvantage to all concerned. Despite several strenuous attempts by the British chassis engineers—who are the best in Ford's world—they could not get the thing to ride and handle well

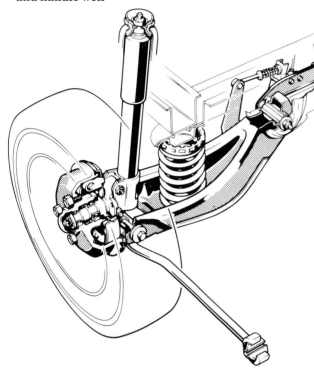

the application; base models (which were built with economy as the prime concern) used a Ford VV (variable venturi) item, whereas the sportier models had a twin-choke Weber. In the USA, the car featured a Weber-Holley twin-choke carburettor.

A 1 in. wide toothed polymer belt drove the camshaft from the crank pulley and also turned the oil pump, which was mounted half-way down the front of the block, along with the water pump, which was adjacent to the oil pump. A lightweight plastic moulding covered the drive belt and its cogged pulleys. The distributor was on the other side of the engine, driven straight from the end of the camshaft, and the fuel pump sat on the rear of the head, again driven by the camshaft.

As with the Fiesta, which had proven the inspiration for Erika, the engine was positioned across the engine bay with a compact four-speed

transmission on its end. A cable-operated clutch engaged the two vital components. Ford made much of the low maintenance requirements of the new drivelines, and to this end, there were such features as self-adjusting hydraulic camshaft followers, a self-adjusting clutch, and a contactless electronic ignition system. Provided the oil, filter and spark plugs were changed at the prescribed intervals, the powertrain ought to be self-sufficient.

No less than 35 of the new ideas which had gone into the CVH engine and its attendant driveline components were patented by Ford Motor Company—but, in time, two of these were to prove more than a little troublesome. The first was a totally new crankcase ventilation system. This used a simple process whereby oil mist was passed through the rocker cover, where it would cool rapidly and condense into oil droplets. These would drain back into the sump and resume their role as a lubricant. Unfortunately, within a couple of years, it would become apparent that this method of reducing unburnt oil fumes would lead to a problem so big that all of the world's major oil refining companies would need to produce special anti-sludging formulae! The other area of trouble was the VV carburettor which, in theory, was a brilliant design; the idea was to have a device which automatically closed its throttle aperture to maintain a high gas velocity and, thus, optimize power delivery. Unfortunately, within a year or so, the automobile emergency services would be attending to thousands of cars which refused to start from hot because the carburettor was pumping in too much fuel and not enough air.

During the design phase of the new model, Ford invested heavily in improving communications between its three main design centres. A land-line computer link was installed between Dunton and Merkenich, and there was a transatlantic link between those two and Dearborn which, at the time, was in the forefront of sub-oceanic cable communications. Fax systems were set up between the centres a decade before they came into common use, and there was a special mail courier service established in conjunction with the Post Office, the Bundespost, and Ford's own intercompany mailing service.

Then there were the work teams. A liaison taskforce (Ford's description), comprising representatives of the Engineering, Manufacturing, Product Planning and Purchasing departments, was assembled with the prime objective of ensuring that everybody concerned knew what everybody else was up to. Engineers crossed the Atlantic

The Research and Engineering Centre at Dunton was the hub of Ford of Britain's involvement in the Erika project. Although the facility has a full-size test track, it is not used for the prime European testing—a more complex facility at Lommel, in Belgium, undertakes that role

frequently to resolve issues which could not be sorted out by the remote communication systems, and quarterly meetings were held between the chief engineers. These rotated between Dearborn, Dunton and Merkenich.

Although the Europeans had started work on the new project before the car was adopted for its world car role, ultimately, it was the Americans, who decided the finished format. They set the target dimensions, the ideal weights and the intended performance levels.

The Escort was to be available in two forms only, a hatchback and an estate car; in both cases, there were to be two- and four-door versions. The original concept called for the five factories that would produce the car—Metuchen, New Jersey, Wayne, Michigan, St Thomas, Ontario, Saarlouis and Halewood—to use common pressings for the bodyshell, to use common engine and transaxle packages, and to use a common suspension arrangement. As it transpired—principally because of the many 'clinics' which Ford held world-wide to gauge market reaction to the proposed new range—only some of the new engine variants and the suspension design made it intact into all versions of the Escort. Everything else was produced locally.

The three-door Escort undergoing endurance testing at Ford's Lommel test track in 1979. Even though Lommel has a very high level of security, Ford took no chances and badged the car with something totally unrelated to the company. This is a common practice to throw the inquisitive off the scent. In all other respects, however, the car is immediately identifiable as a GL, right down to the design of the mirror heads

As is the American way, there were two 'brands' of Escort on sale from the car's launch—the Ford Escort and the Mercury Lynx. The hatchback version was available in two-door form only, whilst the liftback (estate) was offered only with four doors. Two engine sizes were offered: the 80 × 64.5 mm, 1296 cc unit producing 58 bhp, and the 80 × 79.5 mm, 1597 cc engine, which developed 69 bhp. Both were low-compression engines designed to run on lead-free petrol. In addition, each was equipped with a two-way catalytic converter and air pump to minimize toxic emissions.

Two completely new transaxles were offered, one a four-speed manual and the other a three-speed automatic, the ATX. The former was closely modelled on that of the Fiesta, but for the American market, it was built by Toyo Kogyo in Japan—a company better-known for its Mazda cars, and which is partly owned by Ford. The automatic was a split-torque design which, it was claimed, gave 'close to manual transmission' levels of fuel economy by doing away with much of the torque slippage which normally dissipated the power reaching the road surface. This transmission was built at Ford's Batavia, Ohio, transmission plant which had been recently commis-

sioned especially to build the ATX. With 3500 staff and using extensive automation, the plant had a capacity to produce more than 500,000 transaxles a year. This plant alone accounted for some $1100 million of the Escort's budget. For the record, a further $650 million went into rebuilding a substantial chunk of the Rouge River plant in Dearborn to provide CVH engine building facilities, and a further $125 million to ready the Metuchen and Wayne assembly plants.

Part of the car's sales pitch was that it was blessed with fully independent suspension, a distinct rarity on cars of the Escort's size and place in the market as the 1980s dawned. At the front, presumably because it was of European design, was the same arrangement of MacPherson struts, track control arms and forward-running anti-roll bar which had first been seen several decades earlier on such cars as the 100E.

At the rear was a fresh approach for a car of this size. Based on a pair of transverse swinging arms with coil springs mounted part way inboard, the new system used a pair of compression struts running forward to the bodywork, while a pair of vertical strut-type dampers was arranged both to control the suspension and to prevent hub 'climb' under braking action. Ford of America made much of the fact that the new system had been borrowed from costly and larger cars, but some who tried the car in its earliest guises felt that it ought to have stayed there and not been applied to the much smaller and lighter Escort! All of the suspension geometry, front and rear, was preset at the factory—only the toe angle of the front wheels could be readily adjusted. The rear suspension was at its most effective when there was a load on board the car; when it was empty, save for the driver, the rear end would skitter and skip across any mid-bend imperfections in the road surface.

What did merit fulsome praise was the car's steering system. Standard was a manual rack-and-pinion arrangement, while a powered system was an optional fitment. In both cases, the steering was precise, and it enabled the manufacturer to sell the machine as a true driver's car. Brakes, too, came in for praise, the disc (with sliding caliper) and drum arrangement being lightly servo assisted and highly effective.

The genealogy was immediately apparent when looking at the American Escort—the hatchback shared the same 'bustle' styling, the same style of wraparound lights, and, federal-specification bumpers apart, very similar overall dimensions. What did differ tremendously from the European versions of the car were the interior and exterior trim items; it would appear that Mr and Mrs Middle America, although prepared to scale down a size or two and at least look at the cheeky newcomer from Ford (who then, as now, was America's second-biggest manufacturer), were not ready to be weaned off a 'diet' of chrome—lots of it. The bumper bars, the radiator grille, the light surrounds, the window surrounds, the door handles, all around the outside of the car was brightwork. On the inside, there were bright inserts in the four spokes of the steering wheel, chrome bezels around every flat panel, and so forth. Even the instrument cluster, which was totally different to that of the European versions of Escort, was faced with a bright panel. Very 1960s jukebox, and a style of interior decor which Ford's European divisions had outgrown a decade earlier.

On the corners of the car were more examples of American taste—the wheels (which were surrounded by metric European-style radials, a rarity on cars in the USA at the time) left much to be desired; to European eyes, they looked far too brash and glittery.

Despite those Old World reservations, there is no doubting the success of the Escort in the USA. As Ford hoped, it was able to take on the best of the foreign competition which, at that time, were such devices as the Honda Civic, Toyota Corolla and Volkswagen Rabbit (the American name for the

A pre-production, final tooling example of the interior of Erika. This is the lhd GL version, fitted with power windows. The different colours of the components were chosen to highlight the various panels for the benefit of assembly-line personnel

A body in paint on the final assembly line at Saarlouis. This has the wiring loom in place, while the snake pit on the floor inside is actually the seal set ready to be fitted. Once the doors have been hung, the body will meet its driveline before being finished off. The car is a left-hand-drive, five-door GL

Golf). It was also able to catch up with, and soon outsell, such domestic cars as the Chevrolet Chevette and the Plymouth Horizon. By 1982, the car's second full year of sales, it was convincingly ahead of its competition from both the domestic and imported sectors.

In September 1981, a year after the original line-up débuted, Ford North America added a five-door variant to the ranges of both Mercury- and Ford-badged models, and this was a contributory factor in the success of the car. There were also a few new additions to the massive selection of options (when you buy a base model car in America, it is truly basic), the most notable of which was the Handling Suspension Pack. This endowed the car with sharper road reactions at the expense of ride quality.

Another car which also contributed to the success of the range was the EXP, but more of that later.

The 1982 model-year Escorts and Lynxes all benefited from a few detail changes, such as improved fuel systems, the availability of a close-ratio, four-speed transmission, revisions to the shift-points in the automatic gearbox, and the adoption of larger tyres and a longer-range fuel tank. But it would be another year before the real benefits of the international engineering programme began to make themselves known, when multi-port, electronic fuel injection appeared on certain models.

Although, at that point, the engine size was still 1.6 litres, the revised fuel system of the 1983 range was enough to clip a second or more off the 0–60 mph time, despite the fact that power outputs had already been increased recently on the rest of the range when the HO version of the 1600 cc CVH appeared. There was also a new five-speed transmission option, paired to a slightly lower final drive ratio. This, like the injected engine, became a standard feature on the Escort GT and the Lynx RS.

That's right, the Lynx RS. After years of Chevrolet claiming those initials for themselves on the American market, Ford took the plunge and decided to offer an RS version of their compact Mercury model. In keeping with the British RS tradition, the Lynx RS featured alloy wheels, special body treatment, additional aerodynamic aids and bold decalling. Never mind that the four-hole wheels looked like plastic replicas of the German-designed four-hole items that were to be found on the European XR3, they were an improvement on those found on the rest of the range.

Much the same format was applied to the

Bizarre as it might sound, Ford has a team of employees who specialize in producing cutaway cars; they take a car off the line, and then neatly perforate it to show its innards! They go on to chrome or enamel strategic bits of the car to highlight them. This example is a German-market 1.6 GL

equivalent Ford product, the Escort GT. However, its wheels were different and followed a style set earlier by the Mustang GT.

The next major changes to the American range of Escorts—which, by this time, were also being built at Ford's Mexican plant—came with the 1984 model-year line-up, which went on sale in September 1983. In addition to a two-litre diesel option, a turbocharged version of the CVH engine was promised for both Lynx and Escort models. This boosted power to over 100 bhp, and performance figures improved accordingly. The car featured suspension uprated still further from the already-sporty settings of the RS and GT models. It went on sale in mid 1984.

Unfortunately, the euphoria enjoyed by the American buying public was shortlived, for the RS, Turbo RS, and LTS variants of Mercury Lynx were discontinued within a matter of months. The car remained with Ford Escort badging, in both injected and turbocharged forms, but the Mercury equivalents were history. For the 1985 model year, the grilles were redesigned and much attention was paid to improving the overall aerodynamic efficiency by smoothing out the light units, redesigning the huge (by British standards) bumper units, and so forth.

For 1986—when Ford of Europe was producing the MkIV Escort—the range was revised in America, but not nearly so radically. Externally, there was little to distinguish the new cars from the old, unless you looked closely and noticed that there

were 15 in. wheels in place of the previous 13 in. items of the earlier Escort GT. Under the bonnet, though, there was much to shout about, for the CVH had been stroked to give a displacement of 1851 cc. Producing over 120 bhp, the new unit was paired to the five-speed transmission, and there was the option of the three-speed automatic.

Whilst the Ford model of this car was known as the GT, there was a new Mercury which followed the same basic format, but which had a new name that turned a British tradition on its head. Whilst the most powerful Escorts in Britain have traditionally been the RS models, with the XR3 and 3i slotting in beneath them, the opposite seemed to apply in the States. Having dropped the Lynx RS, with its 1600 cc injected engine, Mercury now brought in the tag XR3 for its new flagship sporty saloon!

What was interesting during that first half-dozen years of the world car was that the machine had slowly shed its brightwork, and the later versions of Escort and Lynx were, by comparison, downright subtle. Where once there was chrome, now there was matte black (don't ask me why the

Loaded with options—such as the sunroof, which was an extra—the GL was displayed along with the rest of the range at the car's début in the middle of 1981. Those slotted steel wheels were unique to the trim pack; lesser cars had round holes around the outside edge

Americans add the 'e' to matt—I have no idea), and the interiors had progressively become less and less garish.

Garish was never a word which could have been used to describe the European Escorts.

The cars had appeared at the same time as those in America, having gone on sale throughout Europe in the autumn of 1980. The first example of the new car had rolled off Halewood's production line on 1 September of that year, and by the time that the car appeared at the Motor Show at London's Earls Court, there were plenty of the machines to go around.

Compared to the American cars, the European models, which were shown to an assembled crowd of European motoring journalists in the summer of 1980, were very subtle. Although they were all pre-production models from the pilot line (a sort of practice assembly line used to test production methods), they were exactly the same as the mainstream cars which would be offered for sale. The bodywork, although sharing quite a few common dimensions, was sufficiently different to the North American cars to make it obviously European—edges were slightly sharper and crisper, and there was much use of satin black trim. The bumper bars, for example, were slimline black metal items with wrap-around plastic end pieces, which gave the illusion of a car wider than its 66 in. (or 72.6 in. if you included the door mirrors), and the radiator grille (a dummy, for cooling air was provided by a slot behind the registration plate)

The Ghia interior at the time of the launch. The spindly, four-spoke wheel soon became a little too slippery for comfort. The car is set apart from its lesser brethren by the use of a tachometer—the GL had a clock in that part of the facia

was also finished in black and moulded in plastic.

The wheelbase of the European Escort was nominally longer than that of its transatlantic sister, but the overall driveline format was common to both versions; the same arrangement of swinging arms, inboard coils and outboard struts was featured at the rear of the car, while at the front, there were the same struts, anti-roll bar and steering rack. Spring and damper rates, however, were different—the American settings were considered to be far too soft for European tastes.

Right from Day One, the car was available to European buyers as either a two- or four-door hatchback. Those were soon joined by an estate car (again with two or four doors), and also by a sporty two-door hatchback, the XR3. Eventually, the

range would be extended to encompass a four-door booted saloon, a convertible, a van and a panelled estate known as the Combi—but more of those later.

Naturally, in view of the major investment made in the new CVH engine—the total budget for that powerplant had been put at something approaching a billion US dollars, the major reworking of the Dearborn engine facility being eclipsed by a totally new, purpose-built engine plant on a green-field site at Bridgend, Glamorgan—it featured prominently in the presentation and accompanying literature which formed part of the car's press début. However, although the engine was designed to be produced in sizes from a little over a litre up to two litres, under the bonnet of the 1.1 Escort was not a CVH engine, but the Fiesta-specification, Valencia-built crossflow engine!

When asked about this matter at the time, a Ford spokesman—one of the Public Affairs staff—explained that there was a temporary delay in having the smallest CVH engines built in Bridgend and that, in the fullness of time, the newer engine would find its way into the Escort's engine bay. For the present, he suggested, the crossflow engine was a good, reliable measure for Ford to take. Interestingly, history has proved him completely inaccurate—the crossflow 1.1 was still being offered as standard fare in Escorts produced in the mid 1980s, and by that time it had been joined by a 1927 cc version of the engine.

Moving up a rung, however, the CVH appeared. As with the American versions of the car, two engine sizes were offered: the 1.3 and 1.6 litre models. In standard form, these produced respectable power figures, the 1300 cc engine being rated at 69 bhp, while the taller-blocked 1.6 litre engine gave an extra 10 bhp. All three engines used the same Fiesta-derived transaxle, but gear ratios and final drive ratios varied to suit the power.

The 1.1 engine, for instance, shared its four gearbox ratios (3.58:1 first, 2.04:1 second, 1.35:1 third, and 0.95:1 top) with the 1.3 litre CVH-engined car, but used a 4.06:1 final drive ratio to make the most of the car's 55 bhp. The 1.3, with an additional 25 per cent power, used a much taller 3.84:1 set of final drive gears. The 1600 CVH saloon made use of a less-closely-spaced set of forward gears (3.58:1 first, 1.91:1 second, 1.28:1 third, and 0.95:1 top) in conjunction with a much taller 3.58:1 set of final gears. Of the three variants,

Available with both two and four doors, the Estate offered a good level of accommodation and soon proved successful

the close-geared 1300 cc CVH machine felt the nippiest to drive, although the 1600 offered the benefit of more comfortable motorway cruising behaviour, as the engine was working less hard.

Interestingly, in a move which appeared to totally contradict the world car concept, the front suspension arrangement of the smallest Escort differed from the rest of the line-up by not having an anti-roll bar; location duties were handled by a pair of forward-running compression struts. This gave the car superbly-responsive handling (with torque steer closely controlled), and it would feature on another, far more radical, Escort in time to come. But that is a story for the next chapter.

Following the tradition set by the previous Escort, the new front-wheel-drive machine came in a bewildering array of options. The cheapest model—which retailed at £3375, was the basic 1.1—and basic it was, too. However, it did cost less than the equivalent Fiesta model, so it was acceptable! Vinyl seating, the most basic of fascias (there wasn't even a cigarette lighter) and some extremely inexpensive, felted floor covering were about as much as the buyer got.

Next up from there was the L model, which gained cloth seat covering (with a shade more padding in the seats themselves) and seat backs which reclined, a lid for the glove compartment, a heated rear window, a three-speed heater fan and two-speed wipers.

Then came the GL which, by comparison to the basic model, was positively luxurious. This came

XR3 was, for a while at least, the most powerful example of the Escort available. Earliest development cars ran on the old-style, four-spoke aluminium wheels (from the Fiesta aftermarket range), but by the time that the car actually appeared, the Porsche-style, four-hole rims were in place on each corner

with a decent carpet (just to show how decent, after more than 100,000 miles on the one in my own car, it still comes up like new when it has been treated to a valeting) and with a set of special seat covers in a durable cloth. Headrests came as standard, as did an intermittent-sweep wiper, a lock for the glovebox lid, an instrument panel which featured a clock, a speedo, and fuel level and water temperature gauges. The steering wheel was a cut above those of the basic and L models, while the slightly wider steel road wheels were of a design unique to the GL.

After the GL came the Ghia, which followed the style of the MkII Escort Ghia by providing a 'mini-limousine' environment within the confines of the Escort's modest bodyshell. A tilt-and-slide sunroof with blind (a novelty on that class of car), cropped velour fabric trim, a deep-pile carpet, and even wood fillets set into the door liner panels

featured on the £5400 car which topped the range.

At the time, it was possible to buy most of the models in two- and four-door variants, including the Ghia. However, later, that option was deleted when sales proved that the four-door model outsold the two-door version by a substantial margin. Speaking of options, the range of extras which could be ordered along with the car itself—regardless of model specification—was lengthy. They could also add considerably to the cost of the car.

Examples from the early list include tinted glass at £35, a wash-wipe mechanism for the rear of the car costing £73, a sunroof (standard issue on the Ghia only) at £215, and metallic paint at £74. That was just the tip of the iceberg. There were radio-cassette units, headlamp washers, central locking, opening rear quarter-lights for the two-door models, and so forth. As usual, the Ford list appeared to be extremely comprehensive, but the build policy ensured that the lower down the model scale, the less you could buy, and vice versa.

One option at the bottom of the scale was that of a brake servo; disc brakes featured on all models (solid discs on 1.1 and 1.3 litre models, ventilated discs on 1.6 litre examples), but only the 1300- and 1600-engined models came with servo assistance

A special body kit was developed for the XR3 and went on sale virtually as soon as the car itself appeared in the showrooms. This same kit was to be used throughout the model's lifetime, being fitted to the RS turbo in 1985. This example has the four-spoke RS wheels with Firestone tyres

as standard. The 1100 models (available in only basic and L trim specification) needed an extra £47 spent on them to bring the pedal effort down to what would be considered an acceptable level today.

In addition to the servo booster, the GL and Ghia models also had a 'clean hands' system check arrangement, a bank of five warning lights controlled by a fairly basic computer. These lights monitored oil level, coolant level, washer reservoir contents, fuel tank contents and brake pad wear. Working on the principle that no news is good news, the system was passive; everything was fine while the lights were out. However, the system was to prove notoriously unreliable; our own example of MkIII, a 1981 1.3GL which is still in the family (although now substantially modified), soon developed a habit of crying wolf on a random basis, flashing a warning light every so often. Then it got worse, and one light was always on whilst the engine was running—but never the same light. After a while, I disconnected the brake pad warning light circuit, and the system has worked perfectly ever since. After perhaps 30,000 miles of trouble-free running, I reconnected the brake circuit, and the fault appeared again. What also proved expensive with this system was if the oil

dipstick was dropped; the oil level sensor was a ceramic probe built into the bottom of the dipstick, and this was rather fragile. At the time of writing, it cost more than £40 to replace that component.

That odd aberration aside, the Escort proved a very economical car to run—but that criterion was placed high on Ford's list of objectives for the new car at the very beginning.

Because the Escort was conceived to be all things to all men—and women—a major part of Ford's philosophy was to offer a widely-varied range of cars with equally-varied price-tags, but which had the common theme of economical running costs. Whether the buyer was a private customer who wanted a 1.6 Ghia loaded with as many options as he or she could afford, or a company buying a 1.1 base model for a junior staff member, the car would cost much the same to keep on the road. Naturally, the insurance groupings varied (on the standard scale of one to nine, a base 1.1 would be in Group Two, while a 1.6 Ghia would be in Group Four), but every example of Escort offered low maintenance costs and was also surprisingly frugal on fuel.

In fact, fuel economy was something of a preoccupation at Ford—and at every other manufacturer—during the later part of the 1970s. The Escort was light in weight (between 790 and 900 kg), which meant that the engine was as understressed as possible. This had been achieved by using much plastic and aluminium alloy in its construction. Furthermore, the engines were tuned to give the maximum number of miles to every gallon of fuel. Then there was the body-styling, which was angular and low in line to

The interior of the XR3 was in line with the rest of the range, but it had a special steering wheel and the up-market instrumentation. Earlier cars had the four-speed transaxle, but a five-speed unit was introduced in 1982.

present as little resistance to the air as possible.

The wedge-shaped nose of the car helped split the air above and below the car, and the vestigial front spoiler played its part in directing the air around the bodywork. A sharply-raked screen helped reduce wind resistance still further, while the neat bustle-like design of the bodyshell minimized rear drag, cleaning up what has always been considered a 'dirty' area in car body design. Much fine-tuning of the initial concepts went into the design process, Ford's staff hiring a number of wind tunnels throughout Europe to confirm the efficiency of every change. Indicating a cross-industry level of co-operation which is often concealed beneath apparent rivalries, Ford's staff were to be found in such facilities as the Mercedes-Benz tunnel in Stuttgart and Volkswagen's Research and Development facility.

The net result of Ford's labours—most of which were carried out under the supervision of Uwe Bahnsen—was that the 1980 Escort was able to lay claim to a drag coefficient that was a shade under 0.385, a considerable improvement on that of its predecessor. This is also a better figure than the American version of the 'same' car could give, due in no small part to that car's substantial—and mandatory—bumper bars.

Of great interest is that, right from the beginning, the brief which had been given to the design teams specified a hatchback, an estate car *and* a conventional saloon. So how long was Orion in the background before it appeared? We'll return to that later.

Also interesting is that there appear to have been no great fundamental changes of the Escort bodyshell since it was first conceived as a sketch in one of Ford's styling studios; the angled nose with its low bonnet line, the rake of the screen and the low waistline of the car all appear to have been common themes from its inception. Only the bustle-like back came later, when it proved to offer a number of aerodynamic advantages over a conventional fastback which is cut off at the trailing edge of the rear screen. That 'bustleback', Ford claimed at the time of the car's launch, would also keep the rear windscreen cleaner than other designs. Whether this remained their attitude after they started to fit rear wash-and-wipe mechanisms to the majority of their European Escorts is not known.

In terms of economy, using the formulae set down by the Passenger Car Fuel Consumption

Order 1983—by which time, the majority of Escorts came as standard with a five-speed gearbox offering a second overdrive gear—the fuel economy of a 1.1 three-door was 42.2 mpg in the Simulated Urban Cycle, while the 1.3 three-door gave 33.2 mpg. A 1.6 saloon gave 33.2 mpg, as well. Magazine tests from the time of the car's launch proved to be little different from those later figures.

Speaking of magazine tests, the car was extremely well received by most, and slated by few.

Car magazine described the Escort as a 'Super Ford', and went on to praise its handling, road-holding and overall packaging. However, it did harbour a slight reservation concerning the car's ride quality. In fact, it was the ride quality that led to most of the early negative press which the car elicited; Ford had tuned the package by its usual method of loading the prototypes with either three adult passengers or ballast to simulate their presence, but when the car was weighted down with the driver alone and no luggage, it became choppy and skittish.

Autocar's John Miles appeared disappointed with his test example of the new Escort, feeling that the damper rates were ill-chosen, even though the springing felt right. The car was floaty—as were examples I tested back then—and this was taken very seriously by Ford's chassis engineers who endeavoured to make some eleventh-hour changes to the specification of the damper rates. Unfortunately, the problem ran much deeper than simply the compression and rebound rates of the damper units (despite protestations to the contrary by Ford), and this was to be confirmed a couple of years on when major revisions to the rear suspension geometry were made.

Despite this problem, the car had much to commend it, for within a couple of months of going on sale in Britain, it was voted European Car of the Year by an international jury of motoring writers. The following summer, the car gained the coveted Design Council Award in Britain.

Spurred on, no doubt, by those two successes and, for the most part, ignorant of what the press was saying about the car's questionable ride quality, the customers kept rolling into the showrooms and driving out in new Escorts. Within a couple of years, the millionth Escort had rolled off the production line (at Halewood, a plant which seemed to enjoy more than its fair share of milestones!) and into a showroom.

What made the car a success was the same basic formula that had ensured the success of its prede-cessors; it offered a civilized level of accommod-ation, a flexible choice of drivelines, good looks, and good old Ford reliability.

But lacking from the initial line-up was a sporty version. We journalists had already seen it, but the general public had to wait a few months before they got their hands on the XR3. Most felt that it had been worth the wait—the only disappointed faces belonged to those who were looking to trade in their MkII Escort RS model on its replacement from the new generation.

In the classic Ford tradition, XR3 was a *mélange* of existing mechanical components, carefully breathed upon and combined with new, specially-developed items. The engine, for instance, was the basic 1600 cc CVH powerplant, which had been treated to a Weber 32DFT carburettor (the other 1.6 models used the dreadful Ford VV) and a better exhaust manifold, along with one or two other, minor, alterations which, between them, contributed to a substantial 17 bhp increase—the XR3 was able to boast 96 bhp. A camshaft with longer overlap also contributed to this power gain, but the main improvement came from the new induction system. This engine was paired with the same four-speed transmission as that of the 1.6 litre saloons, but in an effort to improve acceler-ation, the final drive ratio was dropped from the usual 3.58:1 to 3.84:1.

The fuel-injected version of the XR3 was introduced in 1982; this example is being pre-launch tested at Lommel. Note the Capri 2.8i-style wheels which are fitted to this car. Although considered for use on the model, the wheels proved too expensive, as they were bought in from Wolfrace. Instead, the four-hole XR3 wheels were made to Ford's own design by Ronal in West Germany

The braking system was the same as that of the 1.6 litre saloons, but the suspension system was improved and uprated to give crisper and more sporty handling; the rear springs were rising-rate items with a maximum poundage of 220 lb, although at their lowest pressure, they were a modest 128 lb. Such a design enables the car to absorb small bumps and thumps from the road surface, and also to roll gently, but to a carefully-controlled angle. In consequence, the ride quality of the sporting version of the Escort III was better than its more mundane stablemates!

At the front end of the car, the springs were a modest 98 lb, and it also had the same 22 mm diameter anti-roll bar as that which was used on the rest of the range. The vital difference with the XR3 was in the damping. The rest of the range used conventional twin-tube, fluid-filled dampers to control the road springs, but such a system would be inadequate on a sporty model. Therefore, Ford turned to the esteemed German company, Bilstein, who came up with a package of gas-filled monotube units which would withstand continuous rapid action without losing their effectiveness.

Being based upon a simple two-door version of the Escort bodyshell, it was essential that the XR3 stood out from the crowd, that it looked every bit as sporty as its specification suggested. Back to the wind tunnel.

Part of XR3's problem, as seen by the design team charged with improving its image compared

The RS marketing programme for accessories rolled on; in 1982 the range had been extended to include these pleasing seven-spoke, cast-aluminium wheels (again made to Ford's design by Ronal). This particular example of the XR3i (shown in 1984) is made to look even more different by colour-keying the body kit and by making use of the three-bar Orion grille

to the ordinary Escort two-door, was that it would come with 14 × 6 in. wheels shod with substantial 185/60 tyres. These protruded beyond the normal bodyline, so they needed to be shrouded which, in turn, meant greater face area and, thus, greater wind resistance. Eventually, after much work, a set of moulded ABS spats was designed for the car which guided the air around the tyres. At the rear of the car, as much for image as for effectiveness, a substantial rear spoiler was designed. After the style of the whale-tail spoilers used by Porsche on its 911 models, the XR3's item was considered, by some, to be a shade over the top. Those critics would be silenced when the RS1600i arrived, for that car's spoiler was yet more radical.

Also influenced by Porsche were the wheels, which would be offered as optional extras on the car. The 928 series had been introduced at much the same time as development work on the XR3 was in progress, and the former car's rims were light alloy castings with 'telephone dial' holes radiating from the centre. Much the same format of design was used for the XR3, although the number of holes was reduced to four for the 14 in. Ford items.

Surprisingly, the steering rack of the XR3 was carried over from the rest of the Escort range, which meant that it took almost 3.7 turns to get from one lock to the other—yet for all that, it was still heavy to use at parking speeds. The turning circle of the car, never a strong point of the ordinary Escort III range, was impeded still further by the need to put stops on each end of the steering rack to ensure that the wide-section tyres did not make contact with the suspension or bodywork.

The car's interior continued the sporty theme of the exterior. Bucket seats, styled after those manufactured by Recaro, were provided for both front occupants. Along with the rear bench, they were trimmed in a pleasing striped fabric, officially named Laser. The door liners were the familiar vinyl items found on other, lesser, models of Escort. Indeed, much of the interior trim was carried over from the mainstream models. However, there were one or two slight differences, such as the speedometer and tachometer, which read to 140 mph and 7000 rpm respectively—higher limits than those of the normal Escort range. The steering wheel was all new, a thick-rimmed device with 'Citroën-esque' spokes in a deep, inverted V-format.

As is still the case today, the basic car *was* reasonably basic; to bring it up to the usual

With its pseudo-big-car grille and abundant chrome, the North American Escort looked garish. It would be unfair to blame the stylists for this; they were simply responding to market forces, and at that time Mr & Mrs Middle America wanted brightwork. The appearance of the car was not aided in the slightest by the use of cheap-and-nasty-looking wheels

standard of equipment which most existing examples of the early XR3 display, purchasers needed to raid the options list—and pay accordingly. The sunroof and a pair of round driving lamps were the most popular options, followed closely by central locking and power window lifters, the latter items' control switch packs being integrated into the door pull handle/stowage bin assembly. Such options were not cheap, and adding those four items to a basic XR3 would increase the purchase price of the car from £5123 to almost £5700. By the time that delivery charges and the usual other bits, such as number plates and road fund licence, had been added, the price would rise to more than £6000.

To those who viewed the XR3 as a replacement for the RS2000, this was a lot of money. To compare that sporting version of the previous Escort with the new front-wheel-drive sports saloon was a natural reaction, especially considering that both Ford Motor Company and its dealership network were pushing the car as just that. But the XR3 had not been conceived as an RS model—in fact, it was the new range equivalent to the old Sport model—but politics determined that

Ford could not admit that the 'new generation' RS2000 was still a couple of years away, so had to go along with the RS/XR comparison.

If the basic range of Escorts had been catching flak for its dubious ride quality, the XR3 was the subject of intense anti-aircraft fire because its ride was still harder, especially at the rear. On smooth roads and sweeping curves, the XR3 handled superbly, offering a precision and directness which is still good today, a decade on. The rising-rate springs at the rear of the car saw to it that body roll never became excessive, and the somewhat strange-looking negative-camber front, positive-camber rear attitudes of the wheels worked well to maintain optimum contact between the tyres and the road.

Unfortunately, on less-than-perfect surfaces, the combination of stiff springs and firm dampers colluded with the low-compliance tyres to ensure that every bump and thump found its way back through the car to the occupants' dental fillings. The other main gripes—and I must confess that I was one of the critics—were that the low overall gearing made the engine feel a little strained on the illegal side of the national speed limit and that it ought to have had a little more power. All three of these areas would be addressed within the next 18 months.

Even as the first examples of the Escort range were rolling off the production lines at Halewood and Saarlouis (production did not start at the Lisbon plant in Spain until later), Mazda had already been asked to explore the potential of adding a fifth gear to the transmission which it

Total performance was the byword in the 1960s, but by the beginning of the 1980s, total badge engineering was more lucrative. This is the Mercury Lynx, a variation on the Erika theme sold through Lincoln Mercury dealerships

had designed for the Escort. The result of its labours was announced in the spring of 1982, when a developed version of the transmission was introduced as standard fare for the XR3, and as an option on all other CVH-engined Escorts.

The original four ratios of the bigger, 1600 cc-specification, transmission remained unchanged, but a fifth gear which, at 0.756:1, was seriously overdriven was the main feature of the new unit. This prevented the frantic under-bonnet noises when cruising, but to make the most of the car, it was necessary to consider the five-speed as a four-plus-one gearbox. That was the good news. The bad news was that gearchange quality suffered a little and that prices increased. Shortly after its appearance, the five-speed unit—which was built at Halewood—became standard issue on all 1600 cc Escorts, the additional cost being disguised within a wholesale restructuring of the 'menu' in a bid to show added value. Another reason was to discourage buyers from crossing the Channel and making a personal-import purchase; at that time, the concept of buying a car from abroad was extremely popular, and if the buyer was streetwise, substantial savings could be made—the price differential could be as much as 20 per cent. To compound matters further, a full-scale price war was going on in Britain, with all major manufacturers trying their best to discourage personal imports from the Continent by offering 'added value' packages at discounted prices.

In fairness to Ford, much of the reason why it had to charge more for the five-gear car was attributable to the vast amount of re-engineering

which the fifth gear had required. The transmission casing itself was different, being slightly longer to accommodate the additional cluster. This, in turn, meant that the entire engine and transaxle assembly needed to be relocated by almost $\frac{1}{2}$ in. to the offside. To achieve this move, the offside inner wing was reworked, involving new pressings—which, invariably, is an expensive proposition—and a new set of cast-aluminium engine mountings was required. Finally, the entire gearchange mechanism needed to be changed to allow operation of the extended box.

The resulting 20 per cent drop in revs needed to sustain a given cruising speed improved passenger comfort considerably; although capable of good power outputs per litre, the CVH engine was noisy when extended, even though the hydraulic cam follower arrangement was meant to reduce noise levels as well as maintenance times. But that still left the problem of ride quality.

Eventually, this was dealt with by a total reappraisal of the angles under which the rear trailing arms were forced to operate. By moving the pivot point of each trailing arm downwards by 12 mm, and relocating the tie-bars further down by a proportional amount, several objectives were achieved. The most obvious of these was a considerable reduction of the positive camber of the rear wheels. What was less apparent, but more important, was that the wheels could now move up and down in a less restrictive arc with a corresponding reduction in stiction. Damper rates were revised, and the car's ride improved dramatically.

At the same time as these modifications to the rear suspension were introduced, which was in May 1983, the front suspension was treated to a similar, if less radical, overhaul. Firstly, the top mounts of the struts were redesigned to reduce turning friction and to offer a more upright attitude for the road wheels. The compression strut of the 1.1 litre models was dropped at this point, as part of a rationalization programme, and that model gained the same anti-roll bar location as the rest of the range. The new strut top mounts required new inner wing turret pressings—the two can be distinguished easily because the early cars used two bolts to mount each strut, whereas the later models had a single central nut. This added yet more to the production cost of the Escort.

The entire programme had been instigated from two opposite directions, but as an indication of Ford's teamwork ability, there had been an early meshing of skills. On one side were the chassis engineers who wanted to improve the car's ride, whilst on the other were the engine people who were charged with altering the car to take a 1.6 litre diesel powerplant.

Although, traditionally, the diesel engine was viewed as a truck item by the average British motorist, in mainland Europe it had long been favoured as a car powerplant; economy of operation combined with low levels of maintenance ensured that just about every worthwhile car manufacturer in Europe could offer a variety of diesel-engined cars alongside its petrol-fuelled models. Ford could not afford to miss out on this opportunity to sell more examples of Escort, so a new diesel engine was designed and made expressly for front-wheel-drive applications.

Built at Ford's massive Dagenham plant in Essex, the new engine went into production in late 1983. A cast-iron block and head assembly of new design was featured (although, at the time, Ford said that certain of the Kent engine's block design features had been incorporated into the new engine) and, in common with other diesel engines, it came with a very high compression ratio of 21.5:1. The Bosch rotary fuel injection pump was driven from a gear that meshed with the crankshaft (thus, promising permanently accurate injection timing), and the head featured a design of chamber known as the Comet Vb Ricardo combustion chamber, which optimized the fuel ignition process.

Bore and stroke were square, each measuring 80 mm, and the unit had an overhead-camshaft arrangement. This allowed the engine to spin freely and quickly, breaking with earlier diesel engine conventions accordingly. The power output of the engine was respectable—54 bhp at a high (for diesel engines) 4800 rpm—while torque was even more impressive at 70 lb/ft at a usable 3000 rpm. These power levels would enable Ford to claim an honest 51.4 miles to every gallon of fuel.

Reaction to the new engine was very favourable, and it is fair to say that the Escort diesel models were instrumental in causing a serious shift in attitudes towards that form of engine by the British public. The mainland Europeans needed no such encouragement, but took to the machine straight away. A diesel option has featured in the Escort line-up ever since, and the indications are that it will continue to do so indefinitely. Much of the engine design time had gone into the area of noise suppression, which paid off when the car went on sale because, apart from sounding a little like a taxi whilst idling, the unit was quiet, efficient and smoke-free. From those concerned primarily

with economical motoring, the diesel Escort proved attractive and worth the price premium when buying new—a diesel engine adds perhaps ten per cent to the cost of a smaller-engined Escort which would give similar (sub-100 mph maximum speed) performance levels.

Ford had spent several years developing its new diesel engine and readying it for production. Another programme had been started at much the same time, but this focused on the other end of the range and came to fruition earlier. On display at the British Motor Show in October 1982 was the XR3i, the first mainstream Escort to be offered with electronic fuel injection.

Right from the time that the XR3 went on sale, Ford had been painfully aware that although it was selling well, it could have done better if more power had been available. Volkswagen had already proved the effectiveness of electronic fuel injection on their Golf GTI, a machine which had evolved from the mainstream Golf range and which had been on sale in Germany since the summer of 1976. By the time that the XR3 had gone on sale, more than 150,000 GTI Golfs had been sold throughout Europe (although only a tiny number had made it into Britain due to the need for right-hand-drive models). This had taken everybody by surprise, for Volkswagen had obviously mined a rich new seam of the car-buying public. And a considerable part of the GTI's appeal was rooted

The station wagon is an integral part of the model line-up in America. The Mercury Lynx version with its cheesegrater grille had been a consistently good seller, helping to put the Escort/Lynx model at the top of the American sales charts

in the fact that not only did it perform well, but also that it could offer the cachet of having fuel injection.

The word went down from Ford of Europe's Product Planning Department to the Special Vehicle Engineering Department in Dunton that it would be a good idea if SVE explored the possibilities of injecting a burst of new vigour into the XR3.

Special Vehicle Engineering was a relatively new operation at that time—formed in 1980 as part of the Product Development Group, Ford of Europe—and the XR3i was to be its third project, following on from the Capri 2.8 injection and the XR2 Fiesta. Under the leadership of Rod Mansfield, the SVE team had already garnered a substantial amount of expertise in fuel injection systems from the Capri project, so it was able to cover the groundwork in leaps and bounds. As with the Capri, the system came from the German company, Bosch. It was their excellent K-Jetronic continuously-metered system.

Electronic fuel injection was introduced to the Escort line-up in North America in 1982. Over the years, the powerplant rose in size and power output, until eventually the 1.9 litre version was to be found in the sportier models

To install the Bosch hardware on the engine, a completely new, cast-aluminium inlet manifold was designed, as was a larger-bore, cast-iron exhaust manifold for the other side of the cylinder head. The rest of the engine specification was the same as that of the carburated XR3 in the interest of keeping production costs to a minimum at Ford's Bridgend engine plant. However, a few changes were required to the Escort itself to allow it to use fuel injection in place of the carburettor.

The first of these was to install an ultra-high-pressure electrical fuel pump as closely as possible to the fuel tank; at that time, the XR3 stood alone in the Escort ranks with a 47 litre fuel tank (10 litres bigger than the rest of the range). To allow for the maximum 80 psi fuel pressure which the K-Jetronic system demanded, the fuel lines were replaced with proportionally tougher items, and a return line was added to dump surplus fuel back into the tank. An accumulator tank was provided to ensure that the car would burst into life immediately the starter was turned, rather than having to wait for fuel to make its way from the main tank, and a cold-air device was added to ensure stable running at high speeds. Finally, the alternator was uprated to ensure that sufficient current was generated to run the system as well as the rest of the car's functions.

The Lynx RS was that range's equivalent to the Escort GT. By European standards (which were appreciably more subtle), the car was garish and brash. It was certainly understated by American standards, though

With this package of parts in place, SVE was able to boast a 9 bhp advantage over the carburated engine, and a similar boost in torque output. At 105 bhp, the XR3i still trailed the 110 claimed by Volkswagen for their GTI, but perhaps what was more important was that the XR could give 105 lb/ft of torque, 14 lb/ft more than the VW product.

To make the most of the revised car's acceleration potential, and in view of the fact that now there was a five-speed transmission in the XR3, SVE altered the overall final drive ratio of the injected Escort to 4.27:1 (the ratio that was being used in the Escort van) from its previous 3.84:1. The overall engine cruising speed was still better than it had been previously, thanks to the overdrive ratio of fifth gear, but acceleration was quite sharp because of the shorter range of the interim gears. In practical terms, the XR3i was capable of the benchmark 0–60 mph sprint in nine seconds (which compared favourably with the previous car's 9.75 seconds), while maximum speed was virtually unchanged at 111 mph. Even more important was that the XR3i felt appreciably quicker than its predecessor, and that it could hold its own against the Golf GTI.

Production of the XR3i began at Saarlouis, in October 1982 (the sporting Escort was not a Halewood product in any form until the following

winter), in both left- and right-hand-drive formats. It was an immediate sales success, helping to give the model a five-per-cent increase in sales—in its first year on sale, the carburated XR3 had accounted for just over nine per cent of Escort sales; by the end of the second year, it was responsible for 14 out of every 100 Escorts sold.

The next major change to the XR3i came in May 1983, when it gained the suspension redesign which was applied to the rest of the European models. Since that time, the XR3i has been a consistently good seller for Ford.

Another model which Ford was keen to carry over from the MkII Escort was the van variant. Right from the days of the Anglia—indeed, from before then with the 100E—Ford had dominated the small van sector of the market, providing transport for thousands and thousands of small businesses. There was no way that the company was prepared to sacrifice that lucrative market simply because the Escort range was changing to front-wheel-drive.

When it arrived a few months after the saloon range, the new van followed the familiar format by sharing its nose, interior and running gear with the saloon, but behind the seats it offered as much space as most small businesses were ever likely to need in a delivery van. As previously, two variants were offered, the 35 and 55, but there were three engine options: the basic 1100 cc Valencia engine with its 55 bhp output, the 1300 cc CVH, and the 1600 cc CVH—and the last two came with the same power levels as their saloon equivalents. The four-speed transaxle was combined with the same front suspension and braking arrangement as the saloon models, but from the doors back, everything on the van was unique.

Although Ford was happy with the tranverse swinging-arm arrangement of the saloons, this was dispensed with for the commercial application. In its place was a simple, cart-sprung, tubular 'dead' axle which also allowed a slight extension of the wheelbase to 98.4 in. The revised rear suspension arrangement allowed a wide, flat floor area, with only minimal intrusion from the wheelarches; the fuel tank and spare wheel/tyre were mounted beneath the floor, the latter item being released by undoing a bolt from inside the load area. The rest of the van's sheetmetal was a neat extension of the front panelwork, following the same swage lines along the waist.

A higher roofline than that of the previous van was integrated into the design, while at the rear, there were the familiar twin doors which had been a feature of Ford vans since the 1950s. In a bid to improve sideways vision when emerging from junctions, Ford had thoughtfully provided the occupants with an extra pair of slim windows just astern of the doors.

The van was an immediate success and carried on the trend by carving a sizeable lead over the products of other makers in Europe. In time, its market share would increase still further when the diesel-engined version was added to the roster.

One other application which was considered—and which I was fortunate enough to be able to test in the early 1980s—was a Sportsvan version, the brainchild of Uwe Bahnsen. The idea of the leisure vehicle based on a commercial model was a major growth market in the United States of America,

As the range aged, the more subtle it became—American tastes were changing and Ford North American Operations decided to lead a little, rather than being led. The 1986 Escort GT was wholly acceptable, even by European standards

and Herr Bahnsen felt that there could be a similar potential in Europe. Therefore, he commissioned an exercise based on a standard van bodyshell, but in place of the usual running gear were a full-specification XR3 engine and transmission unit (still the carburated engine and four-speed box at that juncture) with an uprated suspension system, the XR3 braking system (which utilized the van's bigger rear drums anyway) and a full XR3 interior.

I still have fond memories of that test, in particular the expression of surprise on the faces of other drivers when I was able to hurtle past them towards the horizon at speeds which were just silly in a light commercial vehicle. Unfortunately, few people shared Herr Bahnsen's interest in that particular project, and the XRV (as it was christened) never came to anything. Interestingly, it seems as though the idea could be reborn in the 1991 generation of Escort, but only time will tell.

With the line-up completed by the van, and with the engine and suspension ranges tidied up neatly by 1983, the mainstream Escort range continued on an even course, with few changes, right through until the winter of 1985–6. As with the previous model of Escort, a Popular model had been introduced along the way as a 'loss leader', while a Laser model had also been inserted into the range between the L and the GL as an 'added value' package. Those additions aside, the basic range changed little. Inflation, of course, had taken its toll, and by December 1985, a 1.1 Popular cost £4750, whilst a 1.6 Ghia five-door (the three-door variant had been dropped in 1984 due to a lack of demand) was costing £7330. An XR3i with alloy wheels, central locking, driving lamps, metallic paintwork, tinted glass, power windows, sunroof and the rest of the usual extras would tip the price to the wrong side of £8850.

But there was more to the Escort range in the first half of the 1980s than the mainstream models. Much more . . .

11 Variations

Different strokes for different folks

ALTHOUGH the whole idea of the front-wheel-drive Escort was that it would be a world car with a global appeal and attraction, it soon became apparent to Ford's satellite operations that there was a need which extended beyond the regional variations on the theme already mentioned in the last chapter. This would seem to be a good point at which to look more closely at the special models that appeared as offshoots of the same family.

The styling of the early EXP (and its Mercury stablemate, LN7) was pleasing, apart from the 'bug-eye' headlamps. Early styling sketches called for pop-up lamp clusters, which would lie flush when not illuminated, but the cost ruled these out

As Dearborn was the hub of the Ford empire, it is the logical place to start.

The Americans have had a thing about coupé versions of cars for years; back in the 1920s there were two-seater examples of the Model A Ford (and the equivalent model from arch-rival Chevrolet), so for Ford North America to carry out a similar operation in the early 1980s on the Escort was not surprising. The car burst on to the scene in the 1982 model year, which meant September of the previous year, and in true FNA style, there were two versions; the Ford model was known as the EXP (an allusion to experimental), while the Mercury equivalent was the LN7.

Although the model's styling was hampered by its substantial federal-specification bumper bars,

With accommodation that is best-described as 'two-crush-two', the EXP/LN7 models were really the Erika range response to a continued demand for closed coupés. A liftback design allowed access to the capacious luggage area. Engine range over the machine's lifetime has varied from 1.6 CVH right up to 1.9 EFi, and even a turbocharged derivative

its overall appearance was pleasing, save for the 'bug eye' headlamps which jarred the otherwise flowing lines of the car. Although based on the floorpan of the Escort range, the EXP/LN7 shared no body panels with its less-glamorous stablemate. A definite two-seater, the car was an outright sportster in appearance, but it failed to deliver the goods in terms of performance; even the 1600 cc version could only just manage to top the 100 mph mark on its speedometer. Ford claimed a very low drag coefficient of only 0.354 for the model, but this was met with the occasional raised eyebrow by seasoned observers, especially those familiar with the more technical aspects of wind resistance.

According to one of the styling team, the original concept sketches called for pop-up headlamps, of the type favoured by European sportscar manufacturers, but these were ruled out during the car's gestation period on the grounds of cost. Having lamps which lay flush with the nose of the car when not in use would have given a distinct advantage in reducing wind resistance, and also made a dramatic improvement to the car's daytime appearance. As it transpired, the accountants

within Ford (I have a mental picture of great battalions of grey men in grey suits who look at an idea, shake their heads and walk away) decided that the car would have to have fixed lights, even if it did mean that styling and efficiency would suffer.

Partly because of its lack of performance, and partly because of its lack of visual appeal, the Escort coupé never sold in any great numbers, despite several attempts to revive its fortunes by adding the turbocharger system from the Lynx RST, fuel injection, and so forth. In April 1985, the car quietly slipped out of production, almost unnoticed.

Yet, obviously, somebody at Ford loved the project, because a year later, it was back. This time around, the styling had been tidied up considerably, the dreadful bug-eye lights having been dispensed with, along with the dropped centre grille. The 1986½ car had been renamed Escort EXP (no Mercury model), and the lineage was far more pronounced because the front end of the car was shared with the sporting Escort. Under the revised sheetmetal was an opened-out version of the CVH engine which was rated at 1.9 litres, was fuel injected and, despite being hampered by full emission control equipment, was able to put out more than 120 bhp gross, 108 bhp net. For the fainthearted, those who merely pose rather than posing a threat to society, there was also a lower-powered version of the same engine, which was carburated and gave a net 86 bhp.

In common with the mainstream North American Escorts, EXP was available with either the five-speed manual transaxle or three-speed automatic, and the overall gearing was set deliberately high to optimize fuel economy. Ford was keen to offer the highest-ranking two-seater in the annual chart produced by the Environmental Protection Agency (EPA) which details the 'gas mileage' of every car on sale in the USA during the year.

In keeping with the mainstream models, the equipment levels of the various EXP/LN7 derivatives over the years rarely rose above fundamental. There were bucket seats on the inside, while externally, the Sport (the injected version) gained a set of light alloy wheels in place of the usual steel items by the time of its $1986\frac{1}{2}$ reincarnation, along with such mechanical details as power steering, dual electrically-operated door mirrors and a centre console with graphic functions display. However, the owner of either model would have to dip into a lengthy list of options for such features as a rear screen heater, tinted glass, a sunroof, or even a delay-sweep wiper.

Interestingly, although it was conceived by Ford North America for its home market, the EXP was considered for a wider audience; the capacity was available at Saarlouis and at Halewood to allow it to be built for a European market. What stopped it ever appearing in showrooms on this side of the Atlantic was a reduction in the overall market for sports coupés, which was already becoming apparent through a drop in Capri sales. Ford is a volume car maker, and anything which sells less than, perhaps, 150,000 units per year is just not worth dealing with. When the Capri had first appeared, it had the marketplace virtually to itself, but over the years, Vauxhall-Opel, Renault and Fiat had all joined the fray, and by the mid 1980s the Japanese were also producing highly successful coupé models. It was this erosion of the market share which convinced Ford that it ought to leave that area alone, so EXP never made it to Europe. With the benefit of hindsight, it is possible to surmise that the overall scene, as viewed by Ford, might have been substantially rosier had the company been prepared to re-engineer the Capri. By endowing it with small, fuel-efficient, but high-powered, engines, independent rear suspension and more contemporary bodywork, Ford might have been able to reverse its decline in the coupé market. As it was, the EXP and the Capri were allowed to slip into history. By 1989, the only small sports coupé which Ford offered for sale in the North American marketplace was the Probe, built at Mazda USA's Blackrock, Michigan, plant.

However, we in Europe received something that the Americans were never offered, and that was a true convertible Escort. Ralph Nader's book on automotive safety, *Unsafe At Any Speed*, created shock-waves throughout the American motor industry for many years after its publication in 1961. One near-casualty of the paranoia brought on by Nader's crusades was the open-topped car. Contrary to expectations, the convertible was not killed off by legislation in the 1970s, but instead found new favour, particularly in Europe.

As with the XR3i, at least part of the inspiration for the car came from Wolfsburg, where Volkswagen produces its range of Golfs. Part of the line-up was an attractive, open-topped version of the car, a machine specially produced by Karmann coachbuilders in Osnabrück. This had been a resounding success and had found particular favour among the young and upwardly-mobile. Ever keen to seize on a marketing opportunity, it occurred to Ford that an equivalent Escort model might be a worthwhile project. In 1990, the 100,000th example of the Escort Cabriolet (derived from the French name for a lightweight, horsedrawn chaise) was registered, proof enough of Ford's endorsement of the concept.

As with the XR3i, Ford's Director of Engineering, Clive Ennos, passed the development work to

In later life, those unfortunate headlamps were dispensed with, and the EXP gained the nose cone of the equivalent Escort model. This was not only easier on the eye, but also on the balance sheet—commonality of panels saves money! By this time, the Mercury model had been dropped. At one point, the EXP was considered as a Capri replacement in Europe, but overall financial considerations stopped the idea

Special Vehicle Engineering at Dunton—although all production would be handled by Karmann, where the car would be built alongside the Volkswagen GTI Cabriolet.

Because the Escort has a monocoque bodyshell, it relies on its overall shape for strength, and removing any single part of the structure weakens the car considerably; cutting out the roof section would immediately result in the floorpan folding, the doors dropping in their frames, and a host of other similar problems. Therefore, it follows that there was much more to the project than simply trading in a solid roof panel for a folding cloth item.

The first move was to forget all about using the hatchback's bodyshell as the basis for the conversion and, instead, to develop the new model around the two-door estate (or wagon, in Ford's corporate vernacular) which would minimize the amount of development work in such areas as the rear quarters, rear lamp clusters and so forth.

If you slice the top off a boiled egg's shell, the remaining lower portion becomes extremely weak, and the same applies to a monocoque bodyshell. To be quite certain that a similar fate would not befall the development bodyshell the first time that the zipsaw cut into it, the SVE team began by adding a pair of longitudinal beams to the floorpan's underside, just inboard of the rocker panel sills. This would effectively counter any lengthways crumpling of the floor.

A new sheetmetal section was designed to fit between the rear damper turrets. This would serve two purposes; the first was to offer additional structural rigidity by holding the turrets in position, while the second was to form a shelf which would accommodate the folding hood assembly and seal off the luggage area from the outside world. Moving forward, an elliptically-sectioned hoop was installed, being mated to the floorpan at its open ends and running across the car laterally at roof height, immediately astern of the door shut line. Again, this serves two purposes, combining additional structural stiffening with a good degree of occupant protection in the event of the car turning turtle.

The front bulkhead was stiffened appreciably by adding additional lateral bracing, while the door front posts were reinforced to preclude any risk of the scuttle twisting and of the doors dropping on their hinges. The doors themselves called for additional attention; whilst the Escort range uses a common frame design to support the door glass, such an arrangement would be inconsistent with

Right and below right **With the roof up or down, the lines of the Cabriolet were pleasing. This XR3i specimen shared its wheels, external trim and internal trim with the hardtop XR3i**

the open-air appeal of the car. Therefore, the top rail of the frame was cut off at the point where it meets the top of the windscreen surround, and a vertical quarterlight strut was inserted to brace what would otherwise be a floppy strip of metal; the Cabriolet became the only Escort model to have two-piece door lights, the quarterlight being fixed closed. The top rail of the windscreen surround was stiffened by inserting yet more metal, which would also provide an anchor for the front retaining catches of the double-skinned, folding hood.

The hood mechanism of the Golf took up a substantial amount of luggage space when the roof was folded open, but Ford was keen not to have to make such a sacrifice. Therefore, the hood of the Escort was of the 'half in, half out' style, the uppermost section being stowed above the bodyline. A substantial steel framework, with a simple locking mechanism, ensured that the hood could be raised and lowered quickly and easily, while the weatherproof, canvas outer covering was matched by a soft inner headlining. None of the main mechanism was on display, only the loop-grip lock mechanism and the folding brace bars were visible on each side of the car's interior.

Although following the general styling of the rest of the Escort range, the rear panelling—the two side panels and the bootlid—was unique to this model. Actual construction at Osnabrück followed a sort of hybrid KD kit form, pre-assembled floorpans, complete with inner wings, being delivered to Karmann, along with all of the other common bodyshell parts. The cars were then built virtually by hand, gaining their special reinforcements, their unique rear panelwork and the specially-modified doors before having their mechanical components and interior trim installed. It was this aspect of the car which led to the model commanding a premium of some 20 per cent over the price of the saloon equivalent. £7350

The Cabriolet was developed by Ford Special Vehicle Engineering at Dunton, in conjunction with Wilhelm Karmann of Osnabrück. Initially, the car was available in three different trim packages: the GL shown here, the Ghia, and the XR3i. Launched in 1983, the Cabrio went on to clock up 100,000 sales by the end of the decade

At the helm of Ford Special Vehicle Engineering, the team responsible for the engineering of the Cabriolet, was Rod Mansfield. A founding member of the AVO operation, Rod headed SVE from its creation in 1980 through to 1990, when he was moved to Ford's subsidiary, Aston Martin, as head of chassis engineering

would get you a 1.3, whilst the 1.6i model cost a whisker under £8000.

Initially, there were three different driveline options, 1300 cc and 1600 cc carburated models being headed up by a 1.6 fuel injected variant. The car went on sale in August 1983 and was an immediate success. What it lacked dynamically (despite the substantial stiffening and reinforcement of the bodyshell, it would still twist when being pressed hard through bends, and because of

On sale in South Africa was the Escort Sport, a combination of the basic three-door bodyshell, GL interior trim pack, and the XR3 carburated engine. The car was built from a knock-down kit supplied by the Halewood plant and shipped via KDO at Dagenham

the 100 lb weight penalty, model for model, it was slower than the equivalent 'tin-top' Escort), it more than made up for in image.

Provided it was not taken seriously as a competition machine, the Cabriolet was good value in terms of enjoyment, although it was a lucky buyer whose example did not let in water from the screen header rail when it was raining—it took several redesigns of seal assembly before one was settled upon which was truly weatherproof. That was the only complaint about the hood, for in all other respects it was excellent and offered minimal buffeting at even high speeds, thanks to its double-skinned design.

Visibility from within the car was reasonable, if restricted when compared to the two-door hardtop Escort; with the hood up, there were wide blind spots in the rear three-quarter position, and the additional width of the central hoop increased the blind spots on the B-pillars. Ford had specified a glass rear window rather than the usual clear plastic one, in the interests of durability; plastic invariably faded and yellowed, gradually becoming opaque. By having a glass rear light, Ford was able to prevent such problems for Escort Cabriolet owners. However, because of the hood's folding mechanism, the glass area was appreciably smaller than that of a hardtop. One other advantage of the use of a glass window was that a heater element could be inserted, and this was a standard feature of the car.

When the roof was opened, the section of the hood which was proud of the bodywork could be covered with a neat tonneau cover which tidied everything up nicely. However, it protruded some 6 in. above the bodyline, so it had to be peered around when attempting to reverse into a parking space. Although it was possible to drop the door windows down to the level of the door tops, the small pair of windows behind the B-pillars would only drop by two thirds of their full height, which meant that there was always a bit of glass sticking up on each side.

As with all Escorts of the time, the 1983 Escort Cabriolet came with an extensive list of extras and options, such as alloy wheels, power windows and the like—and as with the rest of the range, there was the hands-free, systems-monitoring battery of warning lights. As befitted the two different options, Ghia and injection, there were two types of trim; the Ghia was heavily soundproofed, had wide Ghia-style seats in the front, and came with a deep velour carpet. The 1.6i variant had a set of the sports seats from the XR3i, a sportier steering

The carburated XR3 engine produced 96 bhp, enough to give acceptable, if not exactly 'ball of fire', levels of performance. The Bridgend-built engines proved able to run well, even on the sometimes dubious fuel octane levels available in South Africa

wheel and the same Monza trim fabric as that used inside the XR3i. Both trim packages included a locking glove compartment (with light) and manually-adjustable, remote-operation door mirrors. Externally, the cars were immediately set apart because the Ghia variant had the abundant chrome trim which featured on the saloon equivalent, whereas the Cabriolet 1.6i shared the wheel-arch spats (and usually the optional aluminium-alloy wheels) of the XR3i, along with the matt black trim.

Of the three variants, the 1300 cc model was by far the least popular, and this was quietly dropped from the line-up in October 1984 as part of the overall range rationalization mentioned in the previous chapter. The remaining two versions of Cabriolet were upgraded at the same time, several former extras (such as the light-alloy wheels of the XR3i) being integrated into the standard package. By the end of 1985, the prices of the two remaining open-topped Escorts had climbed to £8400 for the Ghia, and £9585 for the injected version.

Meanwhile, the Escort continued to spread its wings, special versions being built for localized

markets. For some inexplicable reason, Brazil's car manufacturing industry has always been far more closely aligned to that of Europe than to North America's, and this tradition extended to the Escort, which went into production in Brazil in July 1983. The small selection of 1100 cc and 1300 cc saloons and estate cars which went on sale in that republic were European engineered and drew nothing from the Dearborn cars.

Whilst some of the tooling for those cars was shipped in from Germany and from Great Britain, the majority was made locally from designs and blueprints sent from Europe and accompanied by appropriately-skilled, specialist staff.

In South Africa, the Escorts were made from KD (knock-down) kits of parts. As with the earlier Escorts which were shipped to the Cape, they comprised partly-built bodyshells from Halewood which were teamed with the rest of the main driveline components at Dagenham before being loaded on to a ship bound for the plant in Port Elizabeth.

The Escort Sport was the most interesting of the finished products, combining the three-door bodyshell with the old, carburated XR3 engine. With 96 bhp, the machine was no ball of fire, but then it didn't pretend to be; there were no trick wheels or aerodynamic aids, save for a vestigial pair of front wheelarch spats and a small rear spoiler which looked as though it had come from Halfords.

The interior of the car was equipped with the same trim package as that within the home-grown GL Escort, but there were special—presumably local—fabrics. Also local were the wheels—pressed-steel, five-spoke items which came as standard with 175/70 × 13 in. tyres. Only a discreet Sport badge on the tailgate and the use of the original-pattern XR3 steering wheel indicated that this was more than a standard 1300 three-door Escort. As tends to happen, the suspension settings were decided locally, and by European standards, they were very soft and bouncy. This was a response to the need for cars which could deal with compacted dirt roads as easily as tarmac surfaces.

Also produced in South Africa were local variants of the base-model Escort and of the Ghia five-door saloon. A small number of estate models were also built for consumption by the South Africans.

But what about the Far East, the cars for the Australian marketplace? The answer is that Ford was shipping out crateloads of their familiar blue oval badges for appending to Mazdas. The Escort, as such, no longer existed for the Australians.

Ford's decision to move over to the Lazer from the Escort was based on sound financial groundwork. The company already owned a sizeable slice of Toyo Kogyo, the holding company which encompasses Mazda Cars, and had colluded with them on the transaxles for the front-wheel-drive Escorts; all tooling for production world-wide had emanated from Mazda's plant in Japan. Ford had muscled in on Mazda when that company ran into

serious financial difficulties in the late 1970s after attempting to make the quantum leap in replacing its aged, and unimaginative, small car, the rear-wheel-drive 323, with an all-new, front-driven model. In addition to finance, Ford undertook to provide Toyo Kogyo with an information and technology service. The result of this was that when the new 323 emerged to critical acclaim in 1980, it could honestly be described as a first cousin to the Escort. Not quite a world car variant, but close enough for comfort.

Part of Ford's problems in the Far East had concerned the outrageous cost (in accountancy terms) of shipping knock-down kits to Australia for what was, in global terms, a small market sector; it was uneconomical to ship more kits to New South Wales, but until a more cost-effective way of increasing the numbers of cars available in that small market segment could be achieved, Ford's slice of the action would be frozen. Mazda already had a substantial foothold in that part of the world, and by co-operating on an entire car programme, both parties could benefit. This is the sort of thing that brings a smile to the face of a corporate accountant.

The overall dimensions of the Lazer were similar to those of the Escort, and the car was available with a choice of two engines, 1300 cc and 1500 cc. Of overhead-camshaft design, these powerplants were loosely related to the CVH—and by the time that specially-stamped rocker covers had been appended to their top ends, nobody would really question the status of either engine. Stick the Ford badge on it and it becomes a Ford.

The tactic worked. Ford's market share in the Escort class has gained year on year since the programme was inaugurated. The original three-door bodyshell was joined by a five-door variant, then by a four-door conventional saloon. Sporty drivers were catered for by the Lazer Sport, which featured twin carburation (and later fuel injection) and which provided similar performance levels to those of the European XR3i.

Ford also managed to steal the march on its arch-rival, General Motors, with the Mazda connection, for GM had been working on improving its slice of the small car market by buying up Isuzu. That company has never been able to gain anything like the market share enjoyed—relished even—by Ford-Mazda. Ford was so impressed by the venture with the 323 Lazer that later it was to repeat the move one size up, with the Telstar. But that is another story.

By the time that this book is published, the third

For the Australian market, Ford opted not to use the Escort, which the rest of the world had, but instead to make use of the technology available in Japan. The Laser was effectively a re-badged Mazda 323 and was launched on to the market in March 1981. Rather surprisingly, Mazda used a flat-faced front for the car, rather than the wedge section favoured elsewhere

generation of 323-based Australasian small car will be close to appearing, and it will have driven the last nail into the coffin lid of Ford's world car concept. The company's philosophy of being market leaders rather than market led will have died with its appearance; despite how Dearborn would like it to be, the fact remains that local markets determine local products—especially in the small car sector.

By making the entire new Escort range hatchbacks, Ford had taken a major gamble. Fortunately, the buying public world-wide had taken to the concept, and the model became extraordinarily successful; it has become Ford's biggest selling nameplate ever.

Yet there were still those who preferred the conventional booted saloon.

By the time that the Escort appeared on the scene, the final tooling was already being made for the replacement models for both Cortina/Taunus mid-sized, and Granada large-sized cars. Both of these were also destined to be hatchback models. By the time that the sub-compact Fiesta was brought into the equation, it was obvious that by the mid 1980s all of Ford's European car range would be either hatchback saloons or estate cars;

The latest generation of TX3, introduced in 1990, has grown into a longer car, which looks much more like the American-designed CT-20 Escort than its predecessors. This comes as no surprise, as the two models were being developed simultaneously. Such touches as the pillar-mounted radio antenna are classically Japanese in concept

Released in 1985 was the TX3 Laser. This had its own unique dual rear spoiler arrangement, special aluminium wheels and smooth overall appearance

A car which would not have happened, had it not been for British Ford man Sam Toy, was the Orion. Based on the same floorpan (to the rear axle line) as the Escort, the Orion was perceived as a more up-market car than the hatchback. For this reason, it was available only in the more luxurious trim packages

there would not be a booted saloon in sight. Was Ford sticking its corporate neck out a little too far? Somebody in Ford of Europe's senior management obviously thought so.

Once again, it was Ford's arch-rival in Germany who lit the fuse, for in 1979, VW introduced the Jetta—a slightly extended saloon version of the stunningly successful Golf model. This confirmed to Ford's senior management in general—and Sam Toy (who was about to become Ford of Britain's Chairman and Managing Director) in particular— that the concept was worth following. A Ford man since 1948, Sam Toy had been instrumental in Ford's British-market consolidation, and he knew just how important the Cortina had been in finally putting Ford at the top of the tree. The order was put out that work was to begin on developing a saloon version of Erika to join the rest of the line-up at the earliest opportunity.

The most memorable quote that I can recall from the Orion's launch in July 1983 came from

Sam who, in a stage aside, mentioned casually that he would kill anybody who called the car a 'Dagenham Dustbin'. It said much about the role which the Orion would be playing for Ford, for in addition to being an alternative for the Escort buyer, it also served to accommodate some of those who had expressed dismay that the Cortina's replacement, the Sierra, had been available only in hatchback and estate car form.

Although it was evolved directly from the Erika programme, the Orion was to have its own identity, and from its inception, it was given its own entry in the sale charts—usually coming seventh or eighth in the top ten. Although the car followed the rest of the programme for the front-wheel-drive Escort, it says much for the design teams in Merkenich and Dunton—who both became involved in the project—that the styling of the car so neatly integrates into the rest of the line-up, yet at the same time is able to hold its own identity.

Apart from the front grille and the wheeltrims on certain models, the Orion and Escort were identical to as far back as the central B-pillar. The Orion used the slightly longer floorpan of the Escort estate car to increase the available boot space, and because of its introduction date (it went on sale in September 1983), all of the updates to the suspension introduced on the Escort range were integrated into the Orion from the

The Orion's wraparound rear window, its slim pillars and its raised rear deck level conspired to set it apart from the Escort. The grille was unique to the model, with three rather than five cross-runners

beginning—although it was rumoured that a few pre-update floorpans were produced for sale, apparently this is untrue.

The Orion's roofline shared a common height with that of the Escort—rear seat passenger accommodation was a prime design parameter—but ended sharply just behind the rear seat line, rejoining the main bodyshell by means of a pair of relatively slim pillars. As with the Escort, the rear door windows were two-piece, with fixed rear quarterlights. The rear window was of wraparound design and had a profile angle of about 40 degrees from the vertical. The rear wings, back panel and bootlid were all unique to the model and followed a top-line profile higher than that of the side glass to optimize luggage capacity. An impressive 0.37 cd figure was claimed, which was better than that of the Escort!

The running gear of the Orion was shared with the Escort, and the original launch line-up comprised 1300 cc and 1600 cc carburated engines together with the XR3i's 1600 cc Bosch fuel injected powerplant. From the outset, the car was available only with the five-speed transaxle, or with the automatic option. Because the car was intended to assume a more upmarket stance from Day One, the Orion was launched in only GL and Ghia trim, the injected engine being available only with the latter trim option. That car, the 1.6i Ghia,

was also treated to a rear anti-roll bar and proportionally softer rear springs, but it shared the rest of its suspension settings with the XR3i.

The fuel injected Orion was an immediate success because of the level of performance that it offered—the car had 3.84:1 overall gearing rather than the XR3i's 4.27:1, and this made for a car which was as quick in terms of acceleration, and faster in terms of top speed, than the similarly-engined Escort. It was also quiet and comfortable, thanks to its Ghia trim and soundproofing package.

A rather neat innovation found on the Orion was the rear seat back arrangement; rather than being

Thanks to its extended rear floor area, the Orion was blessed with a good sized boot that could swallow up surprising amounts of luggage—although the hinges needed to be allowed for when packing, as they intruded into the load area

fixed, as it had always been in previous Ford saloons, it was hinged and was also split two-thirds of the way across its width. By folding the seat back forward, it was possible to accommodate longer loads than would fit in the boot alone, while the split-back arrangement meant that owners could carry one rear seat passenger and a long load.

Another, less conspicuous, benefit which Orion owners gained was that the sound quality from the standard stereo radio-cassette player was better than that experienced in the Escort; the fixed parcel shelf of the saloon allowed the adoption of bigger speakers than those which were fitted into the Escort's rear quarters. Then, as now, the actual stereo fitted to the car varied, depending upon the

trim level and whether or not the new owner paid a premium for a better unit from the factory options list.

Speaking of options, the Orion owner needed to spend less on his or her car because a number of items which were available for the Escort as extras were issued as standard with the Orion; the aluminium-alloy wheels (shod with $175/70 \times 13$ in. tyres) were typical, as these were standard issue on the injected model whereas, at that time, the Escort XR3i buyer was expected to pay extra for them. In time, the alloys would be integrated into the price of the Escort.

Throughout its life, the MkI Orion (now there are three generations in existence) benefited from all of the detail changes which were executed in the main Escort range. This has helped the car to maintain its status as a part of Ford's small car family.

The updating of the mainstream range will be dealt with in due course, but in a bid to hang on to the chronological thread that I had in mind when I first sat down to write this book, it is perhaps wise now to take a look at the RS Escorts for the 1980s.

The inside story on the Orion Ghia; sharp eyes will not miss the additional interior lights on the centre console, the tape rack, the rheostat for the wiper delay speed, and the sports-style seats. The MkI Ghia injection has since gained appreciation for its good blend of packaging and, thus, has become something of a collector's item

12 Deviations

The RS models for the early 1980s

WHEN PRESSED, the team at Ford's Public Affairs (then headed by the gregarious John Southgate) conceded that the XR3 which we were shown at Erika's launch in 1980 was not, in fact, a replacement for the RS2000, but was more of a Sport model. When asked if we would see another RS Escort, however, a coy silence ensued. However, one of the engineering team present at Birmingham that day did let slip that eventually there would be a front-wheel-drive RS model.

It arrived in October 1982 and was called the RS1600i.

Developed by Ford Motorsport and intended as a homologated competition machine, the 1600i was based on the XR3i, as might have been expected, but scratching the surface revealed a host of vital—if sometimes small—differences between the two cars. Although previous RS models had been built with stronger bodyshells, such was the integrity of the three-door hatchback body of the new model that standard shells were used to create the RS1600i.

As its nomenclature hints, the powerplant of the car was based on the same cylinder block as that found in all 1600 cc Escorts. The crankshaft assembly of the CVH block was tough, so it was left standard. However, the 9.5:1 pistons of the XR3i were changed for a set which gave a compression ratio of 9.9:1—more compression makes more power. To improve the feed of fuel and air into the engine, the cylinder head was revised by installing a more radical camshaft which increased valve lift. On the standard Escort, the valve operation was taken care of by hydraulic followers which automatically adjusted clearances, to reduce noise levels and minimize maintenance. However, such

devices also act as an engine speed limiter, effectively preventing the unit from spinning at anything beyond about 6250 rpm. Competition vehicles need appreciably more than this—8000 rpm is nothing unusual—and to allow the engine to spin much higher, a set of solid cam followers was installed. These were manually adjustable (using a special tool which required the dexterity of an octopus and the strength of a gorilla to operate), but brought with them a problem—noise levels from the camshaft assembly were conspicuously higher on the new powerplant. To dampen them, a ribbed, aluminium-alloy casting was designed to fit in place of the usual pressed-steel rocker cover. Apart from its practical application, the new cover looked extremely competition orientated—subsequently, a sizeable number of extra covers were sold to XR3i owners seeking to improve the image of their cars!

Although in pre-production, the existence of the injected version of the XR3 was not common knowledge at the time of the RS1600i's appearance, so to the outsider, the adoption of the Bosch K-Jetronic fuel feed system was a major advantage of the RS1600i. To make the most of this, the exhaust system was matched in flow capacity by increasing the bore of the cast-iron manifold and the overall diameter of the system. Finally, the ignition system was changed to a twin-coil, distributorless unit which used a flywheel trigger to control spark timing. The net result of the modifications was that the RS1600i engine could produce 115 bhp at 6000 rpm, and 109 lb/ft of torque at 5250 rpm. As with previous RS models from Ford, these figures were merely a starting point, and appreciably more power could be released from the engine quite easily. For example, bigger valves and matched ports in the cylinder head could release another 20 bhp, and isolating the 6500 rpm rev-limiter in the ignition system would allow higher engine speeds to be reached, again, releasing more power. In full racing trim, the car could produce over 150 bhp.

To back up the engine, the clutch (which had a 200 mm driven plate, just like all other 1600 cc Escorts in Europe at the time) fed the power to what was, essentially, a standard 1600 cc Escort transaxle; the first four forward gears were the same as those of the XR3, but fifth was lowered slightly to 0.83:1 from 0.76:1. Ford Motorsport desired a transmission with closer ratios overall, and felt that the heavily overdriven top gear was not in keeping with the projected performance of the RS1600i. However, it was decided that the XR3i's final drive ratio of 4.27:1 was too low, so the 3.84:1 gearing was specified. A further small increase in gearing was achieved by using new seven-spoked Ronal aluminium-alloy wheels (cast to a Ford design), in a size of 15 × 6 in. For the German and French markets, these were shod with Phoenix tyres, but the British cars were supplied with Dunlop D4 tyres.

The mainstream suspension changes, which were due for release in May 1983, were by no means sorted when the RS1600i was being planned, so a substantial amount of work was put

The RS1600i followed the mainstream range of MkIII Escorts some two years later. It was conceived, as were most RS models, to be essentially a competition machine, hence its substantially wider wheels and an engine which featured electronic fuel injection

into making the best of what they already had. The first move made by Motorsport was to recruit Koni, the esteemed Eberhan-based damper manufacturer, to develop a set of struts which would work with the revised spring rates; the unspectacular front springs were at 150 lb, not far removed from those of the XR3, but the rising-rate rears, at about 340 lb, were substantially stiffer than any other Escort's.

Torque steer has always been a problem with the front-wheel-drive Escorts, and it was not properly tamed until 1990, when the Fiesta-style bottom links were introduced. Motorsport, however, made a game attempt at curbing the excesses of the front wheels by designing a completely new method of locating the lower ends of the struts. Whereas the standard Escort range used the anti-roll bar to locate the struts, the 1600i had a new pair of compression links which ran from the struts to the front frame rails; in principle, the arrangement was similar to that of the earlier 1100 cc Escorts, but in practice, they were appreciably tougher and more businesslike. This freed the anti-roll bar to do its job of augmenting the springs. It was affixed to the bodywork by means of a specially developed, cast-aluminium crossmember. At the rear of the car, the basic geometry of the rest of the Escorts was carried over to the new RS model, and according to the literature which came with the new car, this was also supposed to feature an anti-roll bar. However, there has never been any evidence to support such an installation—without exception, every RS1600i of which I have heard with the rear bar fitted has been thus equipped *after* it came off the Saarlouis production line.

The chassis on the early cars was never good, however; the extreme angles which the rear suspension system adopted when running at high speed into curves led immediately to the car steering itself from the rear and, thus, to totally unpredictable road behaviour. There were great sighs of relief all round when the revised mounting points for the trailing arms were introduced in May 1983.

Also causing concern was the braking action of the right-hand-drive examples of the RS1600i. As the car had been conceived for European, rather than British, consumption, it had to be converted from left-hand-drive to right-hand-drive—completely opposite to all previous RS Escorts. Because of the rather complex plumbing of the injection system, it was not possible to use the regular servo arrangement found on all other

The interior of the RS1600i was appreciably more up-market than its stablemates, with high-quality sports seats (by ASS of Germany), a Ford Motorsport four-spoke steering wheel, a leather-trimmed gearknob, deep-pile carpeting (with extra soundproofing pads), and subtle grey velour fabric trim. Power windows and central locking feature on this particular example, although they were available as optional extras for certain markets

Below That special rocker cover, cast from aluminium, not only looked sporty, but also suppressed the additional noise from the manually-adjusted cam followers. They were used to allow a higher rev limit for competition work and required the dexterity of an octopus with the strength of a gorilla to adjust. The fuel injection system was a Bosch package. Surprisingly, the RS1600i was not a Dunton SVE project, but it was developed at Merkenich

Escorts. Instead, a cross-shaft and rocker was provided to operate the left-hand-drive model's servo unit. The rest of the system was taken straight from the XR3 parts bin (although 1 in. larger diameter rear drums could be obtained via the RS dealership network) and, on paper, the system ought to have been satisfactory. In practice, however, much of the driver's pedal action was absorbed by the linkage, which would twist against the bulkhead to which it was mounted. The result would be a distinctly poor pedal action and braking which would stop the heart before it would stop the car.

The level of interior trim with which the car was issued was impressive, and suitably distinguishable from lesser Escorts. Although the fascia panel was the same as that of the XR3—and, in turn, much the same as that of all better-equipped Escorts—the RS1600i's was set apart by the adoption of a Ford Motorsport four-spoke, leather-rimmed steering wheel with matching gearknob. The front seats were deep and wonderfully supportive, reclining items made by ASS of West Germany, which were trimmed in a tasteful mid-grey velour fabric to match the finish of the door liner panels and the back seat. A full centre console featured in the car, as did a deep-pile carpet and a degree of extra soundproofing.

Externally, the car was very distinctive. A deep 'snowplough-style' front spoiler, in moulded ABS, wrapped right around to the sides, climbing up to above bumper height on the front arches, whilst at the back of the car, there was a new aerofoil. The latter item was responsible for some of the delays in the RS1600i's début. The Motorsport people wanted an effective spoiler which would make the car look suitably different, yet the designers had great difficulty in coming up with one which would outperform that already to be found on the back of the XR3.

The work carried out by tuning specialists Turbo Technics on the Escort XR3 powerplant was to prove instrumental in the development of the first Ford Escort Turbo. This particular car, a Turbo Technics demonstrator, displayed phenomenal acceleration, but with less-than-perfect road manners on normal surfaces

To complete the image of the car, there was a set of special striped decals on the bonnet forward centre-section and on each side of the car below the rubbing strake. At the rear, a simple decal bearing the legend 'RS1600i' completed the appearance.

The majority of the cars came with such items as a sunroof, power windows and central locking as standard, although these were officially listed as extras; it was basically a matter of confronting dealers with a *fait accompli*. Other extras available on the RS1600i were driving lamps and upgraded stereo equipment.

The original plan had been to build 5000 RS1600is, just enough to allow the model to compete in international motorsport. However, the demand for the car took everybody by surprise, and eventually more than 8500 examples were built, of which some 2500 were produced in right-hand-drive for the British market.

At the same time as the suspension updates were introduced on the car, a number of other detail changes were introduced; post-May 1983 cars have smooth, rather than crushed, velour fabric trim, a different gearknob and a larger fuel tank for improved cruising. The last item precluded the installation of a rear anti-roll bar.

The car was well received for road use, but in competition, it was a different matter because it proved extremely difficult to set up and use competitively; although figures of up to 180 bhp had been mentioned as being extractable from the engine, the realistic maximum output proved to be nearer 150 bhp. Thus, it was not really competitive. It wasn't as if the chassis could compensate either—established racing teams, such as Abbott Racing of Wix, later to be so successful along with

Turbo Technics' Geoff Kershaw, whose knowledge of forced-induction systems for the CVH engine was heavily tapped by Ford Special Vehicle Engineering. Formerly a director of Garrett AiResearch, Kershaw established Turbo Technics in 1980. Amongst the cars to his credit have been the Saab 99 Turbo, the Capri Turbo and the Fiesta XR2 Turbo

television presenter Mike Smith, found it fiendishly difficult to set up the car accurately. The Abbott brothers, Lionel and Ed, have since gone on to achieve much success in tuning the hot Ford models, and sorting out errant RS1600is is a major part of their business. With the benefit of their racing expertise and subsequent experience of road cars, they are now able to produce cars which have far better road manners than the original production vehicles, but it took years to achieve—years during which Ford's research and development staff had moved on to projects new.

The key to the RS1600i's appeal had been that it was exciting to drive; it left a tingle in that special way which had always typified Rallye Sport cars, even if its dynamics were distinctly suspect. Ford had proved yet again that the sub-marque of RS was alive and kicking—and for the later part of the Mk III Escort's life, it had a car ready which would totally eclipse the first front-wheel-drive RS.

The original launch brochure had the line 'White Hot' writ large over the bonnet of the Escort RS Turbo—and hot stuff, it was. It was also

white—all of it, save for the wheels, tyres, driving lamps and decals, was finished in Diamond white.

Ford had been experimenting with turbocharged Escorts since the latter part of 1981, when Motorsport at Boreham got its hands on a newly-converted XR3 that had been put together by the then-fledgling company Turbo Technics. Headed by a former director of Garrett AiResearch, Geoff Kershaw, Turbo Technics had responded to market demand by developing a forced-induction system for the XR3 which used a compact and efficient T.03 turbocharger blowing through the sealed and specially-adapted standard XR3 carburettor. The conversion boosted the car's standard 96 bhp to about 120 bhp, but more importantly, it transformed its performance, making it positively exhilarating to drive; a turbocharged car always has a great deal more top-end surge than all but the best-designed normally-aspirated engines.

However, there were a few aspects of the car about which the Motorsport team was unhappy. One was that the fuel economy was not great because the carburettor was not ideal for forced-induction duties. Another was that the additional power exaggerated the torque-steering characteristics of the original XR3. The team was sufficiently impressed, however, to retain Geoff Kershaw's services as a consultant (few people have as much experience of turbocharging as he has—one of his earlier projects had been to mastermind the system used with such success by Saab on their 99 and subsequent model ranges) and to put together a car for evaluation by senior management.

The first phase of the project was to offer a factory-supplied turbocharger kit for the Escort, this being assembled and marketed by the Boreham team, working under Bill Meade. But bigger things were to come.

The concept of a complete, limited-production, turbocharged car was an appealing one, if only because it would encourage more showroom interest—and more people in showrooms meant more people leaving them with new Escorts. Even if their purchases were further down the list than the XR3, they would still be buying Ford cars.

The development programme moved from Boreham to Dunton and came under the wing of Rod Mansfield—a number of Boreham's staff were seconded to Dunton, too. There were also moves much further up the ladder at Ford, the most important of which for the Turbo programme was Stuart Turner's arrival at the helm of Motorsport. Keen to turn around Ford's flagging competitions record, Turner had cancelled a couple of projects—about which more later—but was a firm devotee of the idea of a turbocharged Escort. Product Planning became involved, and the die was cast to start the RS Turbo programme.

As the RS1600i programme had already proved, it was necessary to produce a package able to develop—and then deliver to the ground—close to 200 bhp. The power delivery was no problem, but getting the chassis to handle it was another matter entirely. The solution lay partly in utilizing the revised suspension bottom link assembly to be found beneath the nose of the RS1600i, but far more so in the viscous coupling which Ford had been experimenting with for several years.

Created by FF Developments—best-known for its four-wheel-drive system for the Jensen Interceptor FF—the viscous coupling was a sophisticated form of slip limiter which utilized fluid

Whereas the early turbocharged Escorts used a blow-through carburation system, by the time that SVE started to develop the RS Turbo as a serious production machine, they had the benefit of Bosch electronic fuel injection. That gave 132 bhp with the Garrett T.03 turbocharger

friction rather than mechanical clutch plates to apportion grip between the two sides of an axle. Tony Rolt of FF Developments had taken his invention to Ford, where it was seen as being of use primarily for motorsport applications, but its relative smoothness when compared to the traditional limited-slip unit made it appeal to Special Vehicle Engineering for use in road cars; whereas the action of a Salisbury LSD is sharp and biting, a viscous coupling (or Viscous Control, as FF prefer to describe it) is far more cushioned in its take-up of wheel slip.

Whereas the early development work on the mainstream cars had to be done using simulations and extrapolations, because the floorpans were not available for testing, with the RS Turbo, development took the more direct form of building test units of whatever component was in question and slotting them into an otherwise standard car. There was also the active competition life of the Escort upon which to fall back, and quite a number of works-supported competitors found themselves involved in testing new components in their cars. Indicative of this was the transmission for the RS Turbo. In standard form, the Escort's transaxle would take up to 150–160 bhp before something

broke. However, as the Motorsport Division planned to campaign the RS Turbo with appreciably more power than that, it was necessary to beef things up somewhat.

The competitors already involved with Ford were able to feed back information that the casings were not very durable and were prone to cracking, even under a modest power load, when the cars were driven over rough surfaces. Therefore, a new casting was developed for the main transaxle case which had substantial ribs built into it to brace the structure. Then there was the problem of the XR3-specification differential unit stripping its gears under hard acceleration when traction was good. This was overcome by installing big and beefy final drive gear and pinion assemblies, which retained virtually the same overall gearing, but which would take the power. Finally, the gearbox bearings were replaced with bigger, stronger items as they were found to be suffering when the power being pushed through them was high.

Speaking of power, the engine was substantially altered to take the new turbocharger installation, starting with the pistons. The standard 9.5:1 compression ratio would have been far too high for a forced-induction system (high compression means a lot of heat, and too much heat wrecks engines), so a new set of forged pistons, with a cr of 8.3:1, was installed. These would keep chamber temperatures to a controllable level, even when the turbine-heated, pressurized air was forced into the cylinders under full boost.

Those early blow-through, carburated, turbocharger installations were good, but far better results could be achieved when the fuel was added to the pressurized air by injection. The turbocharger itself, again a Garrett AiResearch T.03 unit, was mounted to the cylinder head by means of a specially-cast, high-nickel-iron manifold, which also retained the wastegate mechanism that dumped excess air when full operating loads were over-reached. Whereas on the development engines the turbine's intake side blew straight into the carburettor, for the new production car, an air-to-air intercooler was inserted next to the water radiator. Air from the turbocharger was blown through this intercooler, where its temperature was reduced, before making its way to a plenum chamber atop the engine's intake manifolding.

Accurate ignition timing is absolutely essential on any engine if the best is to be gained from it, and in the case of a turbocharger, it is nothing short of crucial; any deviation from the required ignition settings will result in either too little power being

Although it looked as though it shared the rest of its running gear with the RS1600i, in fact, the RS Turbo had slightly different wheels and a different front suspension arrangement. A limited-slip differential—a viscous coupling designed by FF Developments—was used in the car to control excess wheelspin

developed or the onset of pre-detonation. And pre-detonation (also known as pinking) burns holes through the tops of pistons, blows cylinder head gaskets, and suchlike. Therefore, Ford could leave nothing to chance. As this was to be its first series-production, European turbocharged car (Ford North America had already produced a fairly agricultural Mustang 2.3 Turbo, and there had been a limited run of 200 2.8 litre Capris built in Germany), the company could not afford any sort of reliability problems which would lead to a loss of faith on the part of the RS customers.

In the event, electronics were introduced to control not just the ignition mapping, but also the overall boost levels which the turbocharger could achieve before the wastegate interfered. The chosen module, produced by Ford, was christened the ESC-II and utilized a set of pre-stored data references within its microprocessor unit to select the ideal settings—a series of sensors ranged around the engine told it what was going on, and its 'brain' selected the ideal settings. For the production engines, Ford used a modest set of references which allowed the engine to develop 132 bhp at 6000 rpm, with 132 lb/ft of torque at half that speed. For competition vehicles, a relatively simple remapping of the microprocessor unit would allow substantial gains in net power. This has led, in turn, to a healthy aftermarket industry throughout Europe, modifying the management systems of privately-owned road cars to allow

The 'almost RS' title must surely go to the RS1700T. This was conceived as a stopgap measure by the Motorsport people, who were less than enthusiastic about having to create a winning combination whilst hampered by a front-wheel-drive arrangement. In essence, the RS1700T was a state-of-the-art RS1800 arrangement, boosted by a turbocharger and stuffed inside a current Escort bodyshell. The project was axed, quite rightly, by Stuart Turner in 1983

owners to exceed the basic performance levels of their previously-standard purchases. Another case of Ford helping the economy, albeit unwittingly!

Power delivery of the standard car, even with its modest 5 psi or so of maximum boost, was impressive, the turbocharger unit being detectable from low down in the rev range, and the power being delivered in a pleasingly continuous wave, right through to the redline at 6500 rpm. Unfortunately, that redline caused some concern among owners, as at that point, the engine would cut out sharply — if the driver was in mid-bend, the suspension would suddenly unload, causing a loss of control. Then, as the engine speed dropped, the power would reappear and return the car to its previous state. Most unnerving.

The suspension system itself was nicely sorted and, in retrospect, was probably the best of all production Mk III Escorts. A similar arrangement to that found at the front of the RS1600i was utilized on the Turbo model, with compression struts locating the lower ends of the MacPherson strut damper units. The dampers used on the RS1600i were deemed unnecessarily hard for the new model and, as a consequence, the Turbo came with a set of Girling units of similar dimensions to those on the XR3i, but with softer valving. At the rear of the car, the dampers were the same as those on the XR3i, which also provided the front and rear coil spring rates.

As with the 1600i, Ford specified 15 in. wheels for the car and, again, these were of 6 in. width. However, they were not identical to those of the earlier RS, having a slightly different inset and offset — the amount of the wheel which goes in-board and outboard of its hub mounting face. The tyres were also radically different. The RS1600i had shown a tendency to hook on to the central white line (a condition described as 'tramlining') when overtaking which, in part, had been attributed to the tyres. When the RS1600i set-up was tried in conjunction with the limited-slip trans-axle, the problem became worse. Despite trying all of its favoured tyre brands, the team at SVE could not really improve on the car's behaviour — until, one day, the Michelin man walked through the door. Well, not M. Bibendum himself, but the main development engineer for the region.

At that time, Michelin had never been taken that seriously as a performance tyre manufacturer, the company's reputation having been made with a range of extremely durable and reasonably efficient tyres for mainstream applications. Pirelli, Dunlop and Goodyear were the favoured performance rubber makers, but the new tyre which the Michelin engineer showed them was impressive. It had been developed for use on the Renault 25, a large front-wheel-drive saloon, and offered a longer-than-standard footprint when compared to the competition. Fitting the prototype with a set of these proved their worth. Thus, all RS Turbo Escorts were equipped with 195/50 Michelin MXV tyres as standard.

Having caught so much flak for the poor brakes of the RS1600i, Ford was keen that the new Turbo model should stop quickly, safely and effectively — and with as much pedal feel as was physically possible. The answer was simple enough; raid the XR3i parts bin again. This gave the car the braking it needed without recourse to the complicated and energy-absorbing linkages which had caused all the problems on the RS1600i. With ventilated 240 mm front discs and 203 mm rear drums, and full servo assistance, the system was simple, but highly effective. It could also be easily upgraded by Motorsport by altering the hydraulic pressures.

Although the RS Turbo was a homologation special with an intended production run of 5000, the marketing people were keen that it should look appreciably different — the Special Vehicle Engineering people were equally keen to capitalize on the opportunity to improve the overall aerodynamics of the car. The Rallye Sport aftermarket operation (which is totally distinct from RS Motorsport) had already been offering a kit of additional body panels for the XR3i model, which comprised a new front spoiler assembly, a set of side panels which fitted over the sills, and a rear lower apron cover. These improved the stability of the car at higher speeds and also looked extremely sporty. By the time that the RS Turbo was due to hit the market, the facelift, which was on the way for the entire Escort and Orion range, was well under way. Therefore, nobody was particularly keen on the idea of producing a new set of panels to add to a bodyshell which was reaching the end of its working life anyway, so the decision was taken to utilize the RS kit for the Turbo model.

In the interest of expediency, and to give the car an individual personality, the decision was also taken to offer the RS Turbo in any colour you liked, so long as it was Diamond white. With the body kit appended to the car and with everything colour-keyed to match, the device certainly stood out from the crowd—as a finishing touch, the five-

Although the original 'show' car displayed to the press, as an aside to the launch of the MkIIa Granada in 1981 (alongside the preview of the XR2), looked dramatic with its NACA ducts, the few genuine cars that were used on stage rallies dispensed with such ephemera and looked like this. This one was campaigned with moderate success by Simon Nutter of Kendal; the registration plate is genuine

louvre grille of the XR3i was ditched in favour of the three-bar item which had been designed for the Orion. Using the sleight of hand for which it is a legend, Ford had created a distinctive-looking new flagship for the Escort range by simply raiding the body parts bins, thus, there were no additional tooling costs for panelwork!

The interior of the car was also distinctive. A set of Recaro front seats was installed, trimmed in a chic grey velour (Monza, as Ford describes it) and piped in blue. The same material featured on the rear seat and the door liner panels. The steering wheel was changed for a thick-rimmed, three-spoke, soft-feel item, and as might be expected, there was the up-market series fascia, complete with the hands-free warning light system. The stereo was the SRT/32/P, complete with four speakers and joystick balance, and there was the option of a more up-market unit, the all-electronic ECU–1. As the car was developed primarily as a tool for motorsport applications, the expected package of central locking, power windows and sunroof was an optional extra, although tinted glass was standard.

When it arrived in the middle of 1985, the car cost £9250—£1975 more than the XR3i. By the time that the Custom Pack of sunroof, power windows and central locking had been added, and delivery charges paid, there would be little change from £10,000—an awful lot of money for an Escort. Fortunately, the car was extremely well

received by press and public alike; *Performance Car* described the throttle response of the turbocharged 1600 CVH as being 'as good as many unturbocharged engines. Even turbo-haters on the staff were warm in praise for the work carried out by Special Vehicle Engineering'. *Fast Lane* said that the car had 'exceptional roadholding which finally seduces you', concluding that the RS Turbo was the 'best Escort yet'. High praise, indeed, from a pair of magazines not renowned for any form of bias towards Ford.

It had been planned to build 5000 examples of the car, although in fact, slightly more than that number were assembled; once that figure had been reached, the required homologation certificate could be gained from motorsport's governing body and the car could be entered in serious competition.

Competition use had determined the overall gearing of both the RS 1600i and the RS Turbo, and it was the gearing that led to the few complaints that were levelled against the straight-line performance of either car. The high-revving, fuel injected CVH of the earlier car had a very narrow powerband—remember, peak torque was not reached until the tachometer needle was wavering above 5000 rpm—but it had the 3.84:1 final drive gears which meant that the machine had to be revved very hard to get the best from the performance potential. This engine would have benefited from having lower overall gearing of, perhaps, 4.06:1, but that gearing was considered unsuitable for European racetracks. Conversely,

Part of the packaging was this neat method of ensuring adequate airflow for the several oil coolers. This pair provide cooling air for the rear axle (a Porsche item on the prototype, but a Hewland affair on this particular car) and for the engine

the RS Turbo's torquey engine, which had the benefit of much higher top-end performance, thanks to its forced-induction system, was given 4.27:1 final gearing because that was the ratio favoured by rally teams and racing drivers who needed sharp, punchy acceleration out of tight bends and corners. If only the two cars had been given each other's final drive gearing for road use, their respective performance figures would have been even better.

As it is, both cars have their followings; interest in the RS1600i is greater today than it has ever been, and the RS Turbo's has never waned—once the car was replaced by its successor, in 1986, people realized what a tough machine it really was.

But there was a third RS Escort in the early part of the 1980s which few remember—and many within Ford would prefer to forget. That was the RS1700T.

This car shared its bodyshell with the rest of the three-door Escorts, but all similarities ended there. Under the lightweight Kevlar bonnet of the RS1700T lived an inline Cosworth BD–T engine, a turbocharged 1.7 litre development of the trusty old BDA so loved by rally competitors throughout Europe. Whereas the usual Escort arrangement was front-wheel-drive, the RS1700T was a rear-driven machine, utilizing, on the prototype, a Porsche 924 transaxle; for production cars, the intended transmission was a similar assembly made in Britain by Hewland Engineering. A torque tube joined the two items.

The car's *raison d'être* was a need on the part of Boreham, Ford of Britain's motorsport centre, to continue its winning tradition with the new model range—there was no way that a budget could be approved for continued use of the old Mk II bodyshell, highly effective though it was, when the showrooms were full of new front-wheel-drive cars. However, whereas the equivalent German department (which, traditionally, had concentrated on racing activities) felt that it could evolve a good competition machine from the Erika programme, the rally-orientated team at Boreham had no faith whatsoever in front-wheel-drive for its particular branch of motorsport. Thus, it hatched a plot which basically revolved around dropping one of the new bodyshells over a chassis which carried the state-of-the-art in rear-wheel-drive technology. The underlying attitude was that, with a little luck, nobody would really notice, that the public would be hoodwinked into believing that the car really was a close relative of the showroom cars.

And they almost got away with it.

Holding the assembly together was a network of steel tubes, sheetmetal fabrications, and some remnants of the original bodyshell. An essential part of the car's packaging was designed around a need to save weight, so wherever it was possible to replace a piece of steel with a moulded Kevlar lamination this was done. (Kevlar is a material developed by DuPont, which is laid up in much the same way as fibreglass, but it is much stronger.)

The first example was shown to the press in 1982 at Ford's Lommel, Belgium, test facility, as a sideshow to the main business of the day, which was to sample the then-new Granada range. A stunning, brutally-handsome machine, the white RS1700T featured NACA ducts on its bonnet, dramatically widened wheelarches, ventilation slots cut into the rolled pan and rear arches, and serious-looking front and rear spoilers. The car was fully glazed and trimmed, and it was extremely successful at drawing attention to itself; even cynical motoring hacks of the old school were seen to show interest in the project.

However, dramatic in appearance though they may be, such addenda increase the weight of a competition vehicle, and by the time that the RS1700T was undergoing serious testing in Wales, during the following winter, the majority of them had been stripped off; the glazing had been replaced by clear plastic, the bonnet had simple slots cut into it to facilitate cooling, and the sculpted front and rear pans had been removed.

The suspension system was designed to cope with arduous rally stages and consisted of a set of four coil-over-struts located at their top ends by turrets, and at the bottoms by wishbone links. Those last items, incidentally, were nothing more than Sierra items, which showed Boreham's commitment to saving expense by using as many parts-bin pieces as possible. Substantial disc brakes—again, from other models in the Ford range—featured on each corner, and the steering was a suitably-modified fast Escort rack.

The plan was to build 200 of the machines, which would be just enough to homologate it for Group B rallying where it would take on new models which were in the pipeline from Audi and from Lancia. However, therein lay a problem; ever since Ford had closed the doors on the old Aveley site, it had nowhere to build small runs of cars—and 200 examples of a rare beast such as the RS1700T simply could not be put together by Ford on a line alongside the main production runs at any of their European factories. Had the car

Not everything from the RS1700T programme was written off when the car was axed; the turbocharged BDT Cosworth was refined further and eventually used to power the sensational Group B RS200 rally monster

been desirable as a road machine, it might have been possible to justify the costs incurred in having it built by an outside contractor (as was to be done later with the esoteric RS200 4WD machine that retailed at over £50,000), but from the way that the 1700T programme was looking, such a move was out of the question.

As it was, the 180 or so examples of the car, which would be left once the factory Motorsport division had taken what it needed for competition purposes, would be expected at least to match the build quality and trim levels of the XR3i, and any other Escorts which they happened to be alongside in showrooms in Britain and West Germany. Basically, the team at Boreham was not equipped to do that. They are all enthusiasts on the old airfield, and if anyone in Britain can produce world-class rally cars, they can. But production cars? Mention production models at Boreham and watch their eyes glaze over.

The entire budget for the RS1700T was coming out of that allocated to Boreham each year and, as I mentioned, the desire was to build a rally weapon which would carry on where the RS1800 had left off. Left to its own devices, and without the need to build the necessary 200 examples for homologation, the team could have succeeded in doing so because it was dealing with an evolution of its existing studies. Budgeting was a major part of the problem with the car; the cost of producing the moulds for the variety of Kevlar panels alone had already eaten up more than £100,000 worth of the available cash—designing and making special trim panels to conceal the vast number of under-skin

The interior of the RS1700T was purely functional—it was built as a rally weapon, and this was reflected in the spartan and businesslike accommodation for driver and navigator. This particular car is still to be found competing in closed rallies in Britain. It is one of only two which survived the axe in Britain, and they did that by being completed in South Africa

modifications which had gone into the car would surely consume many times that amount of cash.

The marketing people were not interested in the project, so their assistance in persuading the main board of Ford to sanction an adequate budget could not be sought. The sales and marketing people at Ford did not need the RS1700T because they had plenty of scope in selling the rest of the mainstream models; a new car such as the Escort can effectively sell itself if it is good enough, and enough people are made aware of its existence.

But Motorsport soldiered on bravely, in all, making a dozen examples of the machine. As might be expected, the interiors of those cars were, um, fundamental; a pair of lightweight bucket seats, a bank of rally-style instruments and a full roll cage were about the limit. There were not even any opening windows in the accepted sense of the term; the occupants made contact with the outside world by opening up a hinged flap cut into the Lexan door glazing!

Serious testing of the car took place in a variety

of locations, with such drivers as Stig Blomqvist and Ari Vatanen at the helm. The car was incredibly quick—especially when Cosworth turned up the wick so that the diminutive twin-camshaft engine produced about 350 bhp—and its handling was slowly but surely sorted out. However, it would never be competitive because it lacked one vital feature which the upcoming cars from Audi and Lancia could offer—it did not have four-wheel-drive.

Before the car could compete seriously in an official rally, the entire project was axed at a product planning meeting in 1983. The man responsible for the decision was Stuart Turner, who had recently assumed the role of Director of Motorsport, Ford of Europe, when his predecessor, Mike Kranefuss, had moved to Dearborn with Walter Hayes. Turner cancelled the RS1700T project and another major project, the C100 endurance racer, which was at a similar stage of development, but he was castigated for his actions; he was seen by the outside world as somebody throwing his weight about. However, with the benefit of hindsight, it is easy to see that he was right; the RS1700T would never have been truly competitive against the German and Italian rally tools because of its relative lack of traction—and it could never have been described honestly as a close-enough relative of the showrooms cars to justify its existence as a road car.

Interestingly, a number of examples of RS1700T are still in existence; in a dark corner of Boreham there is one beneath a dust sheet, and there is another tucked away at Saarlouis; somebody managed to get the Germans to look at it with a view to production! Of the remainder, at least one was written off during the test sessions, while the rest went to South Africa with Mick Jones, a former Motorsport engineer who had been closely involved in the project, but who left to set up his own speed shop in Africa.

Apparently, two of those cars have made their way back to Britain, and it was the owner of one who was able to furnish me with the anecdote which best sums up the attitude at Boreham to the project a few years on. Simon Nutter, a clubman rally driver, took his car to Boreham in 1989, en route to an event in Kent. As he parked his van outside one of the large hangars at Ford's Motorsport Centre, an engineer strolled out of the door, looked at the RS1700T on the trailer behind Simon's van, then turned to a colleague and said (with just a trace of a smile on his face), 'Grief. I thought we'd seen the last of those bloody things!'

13 Growing pains

Escort and Orion receive a nose job

THE front-wheel-drive Escort range had swept in with the new decade, and even by the end of 1985 was still looking good. In fact, it was still looking very good indeed. However, there is a tradition within Ford which determines that the European models are expected to last for a decade, and they are given a mid-life facelift to sustain customer interest. There may be a deviation from this plan of a year here or six months there, and in between there will be minor adjustments to the mechanical specification or the car's appearance, but as a general rule, the customer can expect to see a 'freshly-laundered set of clothes' every five years.

Nobody, however, was quite prepared for the range of alterations and amendments which Ford of Europe gave to us in January 1986 when the facelifted Mk III Escort range arrived. What was expected to be a simple updating turned out to be radical enough to merit giving the car its own status as Escort Mk IV, or Mk II in the case of the Orion. All of this 'mark' stuff gets a bit confusing, especially when it comes to the Escort and Orion models, and it is something that Ford itself never uses; its records are labelled Escort, Brenda, Erika, Erika–86, Orion, Orion–86 and CE–14. But I digress; back to the plot.

From the outside, the changes were not particularly great. New headlamps were designed to improve the light throw and range, and the sheet-metalwork around them was revised to suit; the front wings gained a slightly more bulbous appearance, and the bonnet was altered so that it dropped down between the light clusters. The strip-style bumpers of the original Erika models had gone, along with the metalwork below their lines. For 1986, the bumpers and lower panels

were moulded in a durable plastic which gave a measure of impact absorption without damage and, it was claimed, decreased the wind resistance by directing the airflow more effectively around the car.

At the rear of the Escort, the tailgate was redesigned to integrate a slight lip (again for aerodynamic reasons) after the fashion of the Orion's bootlid. The rear lamp clusters were also changed; on the Escort, the much-praised, Mercedes-Benz-influenced louvred units were replaced by smooth-faced sets, whilst on the Orion the 'gridded' original set was eschewed in favour of a smooth pair.

From the front, the separate identities of the Escort and Orion were established by slightly different air intake designs; the Escort had a single slot for incoming air, whereas the Orion's grille comprised two full-width slots. Other differences were that the sporty models of Escort came with moulded-in overriders, whereas all of the rest of the range had smooth bumpers. As a final distinction, whereas most of the cars' bumper units came in their natural moulded colour (either grey or brown, depending upon the main body colour), those of the XR3i, Cabriolet and RS Turbo were colour-keyed to match the rest of the bodywork.

The changes continued within the car. As with the previous Escort, there were two series of instrumentation (for the upper and lower ends of the range), both housed in the same standard binnacle; buyers of smaller-engined, down-market cars got a speedometer, flanked on its left by an analogue clock and on the right by a small circular water temperature gauge and a matching fuel tank contents gauge. On the bigger-engined, up-market cars the clock was replaced by a large quadrant tachometer. To the left of the instrument panel, mounted on the proud face of the binnacle, were up to three push-button switches controlling the high-intensity rear lights, the rear window heater element and the Triplex 'Hotscreen' heated front screen. On the right-hand side of the binnacle was a small coin tray. On the fuel injected models of Escort and Orion, this tray could be replaced by a four-function fuel computer.

In the centre of the car's dashboard were to be found the revised heater controls—again with the simple choice of three fan speeds, hot or cold air and an off position, screen or footwell airflow—which were operated by a Saab-style set of rotary controls. Below those lived the radio on the Popular model, or the radio-cassette unit on all up-market models. Underneath the stereo was the ashtray with adjacent cigarette lighter, and below that, on all but the most basic model, some form of centre console; this differed depending on the various grades of trim package. The steering wheel was redesigned to provide two thick spokes and either a 'soft feel' or a thick-grip rim—most models received the former, but the injected cars gained the sportier latter style.

Column switchgear had changed, too. In place of the familiar three stalks of the original Erika models was a pair of stubby switches, the lights being controlled by a rotary boss on the left-hand stalk. In what was viewed as a retrograde step, the horn-push had been moved from the left-hand stalk to the centre of the steering wheel. Stowage space ahead of the driver comprised a small—and not terribly useful—tray close to the outboard knee, but the front passenger fared better, having a lidded glovebox and a dashtop open bin. There were small pockets in each front door and a small, flat, rimmed tray above the central pair of air vents.

A new seat design was to be found on the mainstream models, and the door liner panels were also redesigned. Most of the previous model's fabric choices were replaced by new upholstery materials—another sign that Ford wanted the middle-aged Escort and Orion models to be considered as new cars.

But it was beneath the bonnet that the major

Escort production at Halewood was increasingly robotized over the years. This MkIV has been assembled by a series of machines and welded together neatly, great care being taken to ensure accuracy of assembly

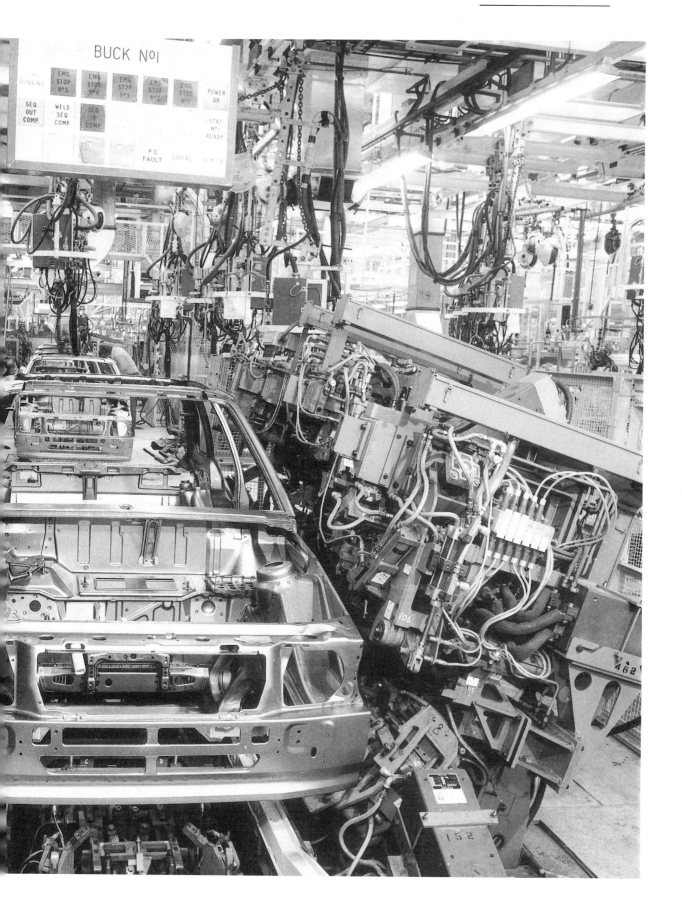

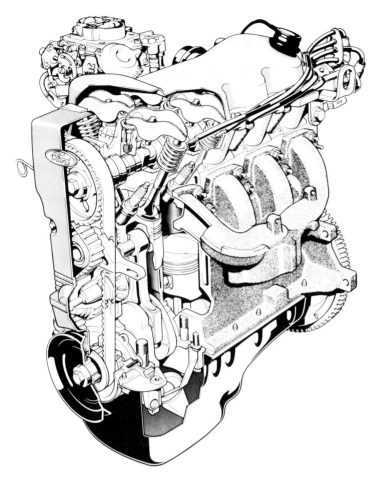

The CVH engine in 1.4 litre form; this was introduced to make the most of EC tax breaks, endowing the Escort and Orion with more power without personal taxation penalties

changes were to be found, the redesigned air filter assemblies of the carburated cars hinting at the altered state of things. The CVH engine sizes had been amended, the 1300 cc size being deleted in favour of a 1.4 litre version which gave a personal taxation advantage. The new size was achieved by combining two totally new dimensions for the bore and stroke—77.24 mm and 74.30 mm respectively. For both this engine and the continued 1600 cc size, the cylinder head design had been changed to one which would increase the squish of the incoming charge, thus allowing it to run on a much leaner mixture of air and fuel. Power output of the new 1400 cc engine was rated at 75 bhp with 80 lb/ft of torque. The 1600 cc engine gained 11 bhp to peak at 90 bhp, and torque rose to almost 100 lb/ft.

More important than the power gains, though, were the revised economy figures; in common with all other major manufacturers, Ford was chasing the best mileage figures possible from each of its engines and, therefore, was well-pleased with the frugal nature of the two CVH lean-burn powerplants. The 1.4 proved to be 11 per cent better than its smaller predecessor, while the 1600 showed a seven per cent gain in economy.

In Ford's view, the move to lean-burn technology was the way forward to improved emission controls without having to resort to the 'gas strangling' catalytic converter. The latter merely filters out and chemically alters undesirable elements in the exhaust gases, whereas a good lean-burn engine will produce far less noxious emissions in the first place, without slowing the gases and, thus, without harming overall performance. A leaner fuel-air mixture means dramatically reduced levels of unburnt hydrocarbons, and applying the technology to the CVH was a sensible step, part of the programme which had been progressively encompassing all of Ford of Europe's engine range.

The concept of lean-burn is based around increasing the squish of the incoming charge, which creates increased turbulence in the combustion chamber and, thus, encourages a more complete ignition process. To achieve this, Ford's engine design team at Dunton—again, working closely with Merkenich—began by redesigning the piston crowns, the final design having been reached after much experimentation with laser-lit test combustion chambers. To make the most of the new piston designs, the cylinder head design was changed from its true hemispherical chamber shape to one which was more heart-shaped. Although the net results of the team's efforts were extremely impressive, the engines still could not meet the requirements of proposed legislation (due to take effect from 1992), so it was necessary to resort to the three-way catalytic converter as a means of cleaning up emissions. The engines first seen in the 1986 Escort and Orion range proved that good emission levels could be achieved together with good economy levels and impressive power outputs. This was to be the last major advance in CVH engine design.

As well as aiming for good emission figures, Ford's major interest (obsession?) was to extract the very best mileage from their engines, and in the pursuit of this the engine range was given electronic breakerless ignition; this move also served to cut maintenance costs by reducing the workload on dealer service personnel at the prescribed servicing intervals. Other moves were to reduce the drag which the pistons experienced when moving against the cylinder walls, and to reduce the power drain created by the lubrication system by fitting low-friction oil pumps.

Both sizes of CVH engine gained new twin-choke Weber carburettors, the 1400 cc version being equipped with a manual-choke DFT, and the 1600 being given a TLD with automatic choke. These, with an array of external pipes and other fittings, ensured an accurate air balance and the nearest-to-ideal induction charge temperature at all times. Naturally, the XR3i and Orion 1.6i continued to make use of the Bosch electronic fuel injection system, but unlike the carburated cars, they showed no net gains in either brake horse-power or torque, despite having been equipped with the same lean-burn, low-drag components as the carburated engines. As well as the CVH engines, the new range was also available with the Dagenham-built 1.6 litre diesel powerplant.

Also, there was a pair of small-displacement, overhead-valve engines, the aged Kent cast-iron crossflow unit having been given a new lease of life some time previously for the Fiesta range; these engines were built in Spain and had been rechristened the Valencia engine. Sharing a common bore of 73.96 mm, but with a choice of either 64.98 mm or 75.48 mm stroke, these engines displaced 1117 cc and 1297 cc respectively, giving an acceptable 50 bhp and 60 bhp accordingly. Add to these the 132 bhp RS Turbo Escort, which followed the main range after a short interval as a mainstream car, and it becomes apparent that the range offered pretty well something for everybody.

Part of the mid-life facelift was the adoption of fresh lamp units, the leading edge of the bonnet being shaped forward and down to suit. Unfortunately, even with a set of driving lamps to catch some of the flak, the bonnet edge is susceptible to stone chips

To aid economy still further, Ford made the five-speed transaxle available on virtually all models. Only the 1100 cc model (which was available in only three-door Escort saloon and estate formats) was limited to four-speed trim for Britain; although, at the time, Ford said that the five-speed 1100 would be available, this was only for certain markets, such as Italy. As an option, Ford offered the '3 + E' four-speed gearbox, which used standard lower gears, but had a very tall top gear—the effect was of a transaxle with no fourth gear!

The five-speed unit became available with several different gear clusters, to suit different engine sizes. Furthermore, the final drive ratios were varied to optimize economy levels. Those of the 1.1 and 1.4 engines were carried over from the earlier 1.1 and 1.3 CVH engines, with a close-ratio set of gears and a 3.84:1 final drive, whilst the 1.3 Valencia and 1.6 CVH engines received a wider-spread set of gears and 3.84:1 or 3.58:1 overall gearing. The Orion 1.6i got 3.84:1 final drive gears, and the XR3i 4.27:1.

Impressive though they undoubtedly were—if only in bringing the range up to the level of the competition's offerings—the engine and transmission changes were soon eclipsed by a major innovation to be found on all of the five-speed CVH-engined variants shown to the press in January 1986. For the first time on a small car, the new Escort and Orion range could be had with anti-lock brakes for a very modest supplementary payment of £400.

Jointly developed by Ford and Lucas Girling—the latter doing most of the work and the former

A similar style of rear lip to that of the Orion boot was adopted for the Escort range, along with smoothed-out rear bumper mouldings and clean-faced rear lamp clusters

claiming the glory—the system was known as SCS (Stop Control System) and was based around a pair of mechanically-driven modulators. Unlike the ABS developed by Alfred Teves and Bosch, the Lucas Girling SCS used no electronics for control, relying on a mechanical inter-reaction instead. Each front wheel drove a modulator unit via a toothed belt, the belts running from teeth machined on to the outer housing of each drive-shaft constant-velocity joint. The modulators were mounted on to each side of the gearbox and were driven at almost three times the speed of the driveshaft. Each was inserted into an otherwise-standard braking system between the master cylinder and the point at which the lines separated front-to-rear. Each modulator controlled its nearest front wheel and the diagonally-opposite rear wheel. The only sources of power for the system were a small pump inside each modulator and the pedal servo pressure.

Within each modulator housing was an integral wheel deceleration sensor and the pressure modulator, as well as the pump assembly. The sensor was a simple device, making use of an overrun flywheel which detected any deceleration greater than 1.2 g, at which times it caused a ball and ramp drive to generate axial movement which, in turn, was linked to a dump valve in the hydraulic pressure line. As soon as this started to function, a cut-off valve isolated the master cylinder (main-

The Orion gained a similar facelift to that of the Escort, although the design of the front bumper/spoiler moulding was slightly different, as it had been in its original form. Running gear was shared with the Escort, although there has never been a turbocharged version

taining pedal pressure), but the wheel which was in danger of locking was allowed to accelerate again until the flywheel speed became synchronized. At that stage, the system either reverted to normal operation or reactivated the anti-locking if the need was still there.

The idea of the system was to offer a half-way house between the standard braking system and the high-specification (and high-cost) electronic anti-locking systems which feature on bigger cars. To prove the worth of the system, Ford unveiled it in Finland, on a frozen lake which had been marked off in lanes. The SCS was effective—although a driver trained in cadence or pulse braking could beat it—and it allowed the driver to retain a good deal of steering control whilst panic-braking.

So effective was the system that it went on to win a host of awards. The first of these was the RAC Dewar Trophy, followed closely by the Archimedes Award from the scientific design journal *Eureka!*, then by the Safety Design Award, jointly presented by the AA and the Society of Motor Manufacturers and Traders. Within a year of being announced, the system had clocked up a further three major awards—from the Dutch Centraal Beheer insurance company, the Worshipful Company of Coachmakers, and finally from Castrol, whose Gold Medal was co-sponsored by the Institute of the Motor Industry. The greatest accolade of all, though, came from Technischer UberwachungVerein Rheinland (TUV) the esteemed (and feared by some!) German testing organization, which carried out a series of controlled tests on SCS-equipped cars. After using 77 test drivers—and making 769 individual tests—TUV declared that the Stop Control System was an important contributor to road safety.

In early 1986, the Escort line-up began at the bottom with the Popular, which was available as a three- or five-door saloon, or a three-door estate, with either the 1100 cc (three-door and estate) or 1300 cc petrol engines, or the 1.6 diesel. For your money—which varied from £5312 to £6785—you received a fairly basic package. As with the rest of the range, the car had the new anti-theft locks, a high-security system jointly developed with Chubb which used a totally unconventional spiky key. The two door mirrors had a fairly basic method of remote operation, which was based around a little plastic handle that extended from the outside to the plate which blanked off the front corner of each front door window. The car benefited from a heated rear window and also from an intermittent-sweep facility on the front wipers—a tailgate wash-wipe mechanism was offered on payment of an additional £122, the only factory-fitted option available for the Popular. The car had a basic AM radio, a grey pressed (rather than woven) carpet, a basic but durable tweedy fabric trim, and not a great deal else. It was conceived as basic transport for the lowest members of a company's staff, and basic it was. Ford reckons that very few Populars are sold new as private cars, most going to the fleet market.

Up from the Popular came the L, a car which was available with the 1.3 Valencia, 1.4 CVH and 1.6 CVH petrol engines, as well as the diesel 1600. Buyers of these cars did appreciably better than Popular owners because they could also specify the five-door saloon and estate bodyshells, as well as the three-door models. They gained a decent set of headrests, a 60/40 split folding rear seatback, a velour carpet, and a slightly more luxurious (but only slightly) quality of trim. The AM radio was replaced by a digital three-band radio with auto-stop tape player and a four-speaker system with joystick sound balancing—to go with the cassette player was a plastic console which accommodated a small selection of your favourite tapes. Does Ford's generosity know no bounds? To show how magnanimous Ford is in Europe, the purchaser of an Escort L was even given a rear wash-wipe facility as standard! Oh, thank you uncle Henry, thank you! How can I ever repay you? By paying between £6441 and £7917, that's how.

The L accounted for the majority of Escort private sales, but a close second to it was the GL. The high-economy, low-powered Valencia engines were not available in this trim level; the customer had a choice of 1.4 or 1.6 CVH petrol engines, or the 1.6 diesel unit. Also unavailable

The LX trim variant was one of the sales successes of the 1980s for Ford, offering the company car user a combination of functional running gear with a reasonable level of equipment

was the three-door bodyshell—the buyer could have either estate or hatchback versions of the GL, but only with four passenger doors. As might be expected, the GL was the L with a few more bits attached. The increase in specification started with the fascia, which was the upmarket series instrumentation complete with tachometer; the clock was a digital unit mounted overhead, above the rearview mirror. There was a degree of extra soundproofing, along with a cut-pile carpet, and yet another new, and plusher still, fabric trim. The centre console was a grade up from that of the L and contained slots for a half-dozen cassette cases. Tinted glass was standard, the radio aerial being incorporated into the rear heater element; this was another security move and was based around a system originally developed by a Manchester company, Bi-Fi, which did away with the radio mast, thus offering one less target for vandals. A few options were available for the GL, such as a sunroof at £350, a pair of power-operated door mirrors (complete with heater elements for rapid de-icing) at £72, central locking (complete with torch key) at £251, an upgraded stereo system at £159 (or £338 with graphic equalizer), and power windows at £218. Add all these to the basic price range of £7433–8125, and it became an expensive car.

The scheme continued in much the same vein with the Ghia, which incorporated the sunroof and central locking, along with a velour trim and yet more soundproofing beneath its velvety carpet, for a total price of £8115 for the five-door 1.4 litre, or £8321 for the five-door 1600. The Ghia was not available in any of the other body variants, such as estate or three door.

The XR3i was the next in line and, again, this was based around the three-door bodyshell. To the basic price of £8437 (or£8776 if the SCS package was ordered), the self-respecting owner needed to add £110 for a pair of driving lamps, £240 for alloy rims (a new design, at last!) and often another £121 for the fuel computer. Then there were the usual extras of sunroof, central locking, powered mirrors and windows, and the Mercury grey or black optional paint colours. A fully-loaded XR3i, complete with the upgraded stereo system, would require a customer to part with about £10,800!

Yet that was not the most expensive of the new line-up; a fully-equipped version of the Cabriolet, in XR3i trim (it was also available in Ghia specification), would cost £12,380.

Generally, the updates were well-received, although there were a few complaints from purchasers of new-model Escorts (including yours truly) concerning some of the equipment which had been deleted from the previous range. In particular, the hands-free monitoring light system was missed, for although it rarely worked completely as intended, the low fuel level, coolant level and washer reservoir contents warning lamps were effective. In the new Escort, it was necessary to revert to visual checks of the latter two items, which meant opening up the bonnet. We were also disappointed, upon receiving our brand-new Ghia (the first black 1.6 model produced at Halewood),

Combining the engine of the XR3i with a mid-ground 3.82:1 final drive ratio, the Orion Ghia trim package, a sports suspension system and a set of dedicated aluminium-alloy wheels, the 1.6i Ghia was a highly successful piece of marketing. It offered a GT variant without recourse to 'go-faster' stripes

to discover that such pleasing details as the wood-effect inserts, rear cabin courtesy light and illuminated vanity mirror, which had been on the earlier Ghia, were no longer there. There wasn't even carpet on the back of the rear seat. The consensus at Chez Foy was that the new car was little-improved in equipment levels from the GL which it replaced, despite an appreciably higher price.

What also affected Ford was that within days of the new range going on sale, there was a full-scale strike at Halewood, resulting in the loss of almost two months' production, at a time when dealers were most keen to have Escorts in their showrooms. Particularly hard hit were those dealers who had ordered special-build cars rather than basic-specification models, because Ford operates what seems, to the outsider, to be a rather bizarre practice of stock and production control. What happens is that each week is given a number, the build details are logged into a computer in advance, and the required parts are made available, usually on a 36-hour stockholding basis. Everything ticks along nicely, with all of the right panels, trim items and mechanical components meshing together within the factory, the complete cars coming out of the other end, having been dyno-tuned to check that everything has been put together properly.

But when there is a strike, they do not stop the clocks and carry on where they left off—instead, they pick up again where the calendar says that they ought to be. In the case of Escort production, this meant that the last car before the strike was built at the Halewood factory in week seven—the workforce resumed work on week 14. The missing seven weeks' production was then slotted into any available gaps in the normal schedule! In the case of our own Mk IV Escort, it was being stitched together from a collection of bare, pressed-steel panels on the day that everybody went out on strike, but never made it to the spraybooths that day because everybody downed tools. The build-code letters within the chassis number confirm that the car was assembled in February 1986. Yet, according to our diaries from 1986, it was the middle of the last week in April before the car was actually completed, in Ford's week 16. We were by no means the only people thus affected; conversations with a number of dealerships elicited the information that their special-build orders placed before the strike had not been delivered in mid-May, despite being promised for the end of February at the latest.

In all other respects, the new model range was

The fascia of the new range was an improvement on that of the earlier model, bringing the auxiliary switches into reach of the driver's fingertips. The three switches on the left-hand edge of the binnacle controlled front and rear screen heaters and high-intensity rear lamps. Defrosting the windscreen also activated the heater elements of the mirror glasses when power mirrors were specified

applauded, mostly for Ford's radical attitude in offering anti-lock braking on what was already viewed as a small and, thus, relatively lowly car, and certainly not the type of machine which would be expected to come from the factory with such a major and sophisticated option. The redesign also seemed to go down well, bringing the car right up to date—and giving a slight aerodynamic advantage as well; the cd of the Escort saloon was given as 0.36 (compared to 0.39 for the earlier model), while for the Orion, it was 0.35 compared to 0.37. Ford was keen that the criticisms which followed the facelift of the Escort in the 1970s, when Brenda came along, were not to be repeated.

Ergonomics have always been one of Ford's strong points—even the jukebox-styled fascias of the 1960s cars were very user-friendly—and the newest Escort was complimented on its instrumentation and control layout; 'mini Granada' was how several publications described the car in the early part of 1986. The 'Hotscreen' facility also came in for much praise. Triplex, the automotive glazing division of the mighty Pilkington Glass Group, had developed this, and Ford was its first major customer, offering the 'Hotscreen' as an option on all models of Escort and Orion from GL grade upwards. Equipped with a series of tiny electric elements laminated into the glass, the 'Hotscreen' would clear a frosted windscreen in 60–90 seconds and stop it from freezing over again. As with the SCS, it was a feature which would not be expected on such a small car.

The economy levels of the cars were praised, as Ford had shown that its range was capable of extreme frugality without compromising performance levels unduly. The high-security locking was also often singled out in the reviews of the time as a worthwhile benefit—although at least one journalist expressed concern about the durability of the brass used for the keys. That same journalist was stranded several months later when filling up a test Orion 1.6i at a motorway service area and the only key snapped in the filler cap. At about the same time, Ford changed from brass to a hardened steel for the key shaft. I know, because I was that journalist.

What was less impressive was the ride quality of the revised car. Although there had been progressive fine-tuning of the system during the half-dozen years since its introduction, the major alterations in early 1983 being followed by a sequence of amendments to spring rates, there was still an overriding feeling of never being able to make a silk purse from a sow's ear. No matter how hard everybody in chassis engineering tried, there would never be an acceptable ride quality in the front-wheel-drive Escort range until the rear suspension design had been changed. Loading the boot with some ballast, or carrying a pair of passengers in the back seat of the Escort or Orion improved matters considerably. On smooth surfaces, the car rode well. The roadholding was good—especially by front-wheel-drive standards—but as with any front-driven car where the engine is overslung above the axle line, there was a good deal of understeer at higher speeds and some

The major technical breakthrough found on the 1986 model year Escorts and Orions was SCS. An acronym for Stop Control System, SCS was a low-cost form of anti-lock braking developed expressly for the car by Lucas Girling and Ford

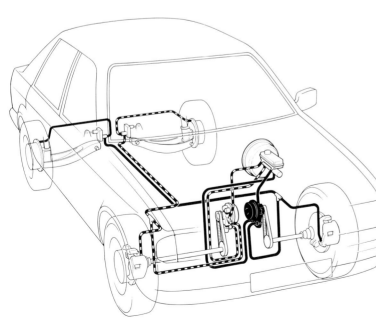

wheel tramp on hard acceleration out of tight corners.

The only other bone of contention, at the time of the car's launch, was the price structure; it was appreciably more expensive than the range which it had succeeded and, more importantly, was more expensive than rival products, model for model. However, what Ford had done was to build in a degree of inflation-proofing (a tactic which it has repeated on other new model launches), and within months, the products of other manufacturers had caught up with Escort and Orion prices.

Although the Escort was viewed by everybody as the 'Ford for the masses', the automotive giant had a different niche in mind for the Orion; although the car was the mechanical twin of the Escort, and while trim and equipment levels were broadly similar, Ford projected the car as being appreciably up-market. There was no Popular version, for example—trim packages started with the L, which could be had with the 1.3, 1.4 and 1.6 petrol engines or the 1.6 diesel. Prices were also a shade higher than equivalent Escort models, the 1.4L being a typical example and costing about £145 more than the hatchback equivalent.

'Class' was the word which Ford's advertising agency, Ogilvy & Mather, was using in the British-market advertising for the Orion, and much the same word was being used throughout Ford's brochures, along with such adjectives as 'elegant', 'stylish' and 'spacious'. Considering that the car had very much the same passenger space as the hatchback, the last term was perhaps a shade creative, but the other descriptions could honestly be applied to the Orion, for its styling was elegant; the proportions were better than most saloons derived from hatchbacks—and better than many purpose-designed saloon models.

At the top of the Orion range was a car which was to prove highly popular with the young, upwardly-mobile types who were a product of the mid 1980s, the 1.6i Ghia. This, as previously, shared its specification with the XR3i, but it had a couple of distinct advantages as business transport; it had a pair of extra doors which made it far more suitable for transporting clients, and it had a more useful overall gearing set than the XR3i. With its 3.84:1 final drive, high-speed cruising was far less frantic, the engine having to work less hard to sustain a given speed than the sportily-geared XR3i.

The Orion 1.6i also had more comfortable seats; the bucket-style front set of the XR3i required slim-hipped occupants. Ad-

Above The interior of the XR3i was set apart from lower-specification models by the use of a thicker-rimmed steering wheel. The fuel computer (right-hand side of binnacle) could be ordered as a £121 option. It monitored average consumption, range and fuel flow, as well as telling the driver when the tank contents were low. However, as this could occur with the tank still half full, it was often an annoying feature

Below left New for 1986 were these smart, five-spoke, twin-edged aluminium-alloy wheels, which took 185/60 × 14 in. tyres from a variety of different sources. As with all special Ford wheels, these were soon to be found on lesser models of Escort as owners sought to turn their 1.3 Populars into XR3i lookalikes

Below Following the trend set by the original XR3i, the second generation of the model had overtly sporting looks by virtue of its extensive colour keying, additional driving lamps and extra lower spoiler lip

One of the three special-edition Cabriolets produced between 1986 and 1990 was this all-white model with RS Turbo wheels, bootlid spoiler, white hood and leather interior. The occasion was nothing other than a desire to generate a few more deutschmarks or pounds sterling—it sold for £14,500!

ditionally, the Orion came with central locking, a sunroof, the ECU-2 electronic sound system (complete with amplifier), and the heated and power-adjusted mirrors as standard—all features which were considered *de rigueur* by the marketing people at Ford. By the time that a set of the pleasing 'pepper-pot' aluminium-alloy wheels (with 185/60 tyres), a heated front screen and Stop Control System had been added to the basic price, the car was still extremely good value at about £9700. Putting it another way, it could match the specification of a fully-loaded XR3i, provide its owner with the extra pair of doors, give as lively a performance as could be expected, yet still leave some change for a few months' petrol.

The Capri was in decline by the early 1980s, and although there had been a renewed surge of interest in the car when the 2.8i had arrived on the scene, the rest of the range had been sustained by putting together a package of specials, under a variety of names, for the European market. This really was continuing a tradition created by the Escort Mexico, but it was with the Capri that the marketing people really got their teeth into the specially-badged, 'added-value' models. To maintain interest in the Escort range, Marketing started to put together a major series of special-edition models throughout the latter part of the 1980s, starting in February 1987.

Announced just a year after the Mk IV had gone on sale, the Escort Bravo was available with either the 1.4 or 1.6 CVH engine and was based on the five-speed, L model five-door hatchback. Escort GL seats and door panels were installed, along with a cut-pile carpet. Tinted glass and a sunroof were standard, as was the higher-grade stereo radio-cassette unit. Continuing their foray into the parts bins, the marketing people decided that the car ought to have the body side mouldings of the Orion Ghia—complete with bright red bumper and side-moulding inserts. Available in six colours only (three of them extra-cost metallics), the car retailed at £6990 for the 1.4 litre model, and £7206 for the 1600 cc version.

A month later, the first of the Mk II Orion specials was announced, and this followed a similar format. However, it was available in only one shade of blue; both colour and the car were named Biscayne. Again, this was available with either the 1.4 or 1.6 CVH engine. It utilized cut-pile carpeting (with additional soundproofing—something which Escort Bravo owners would have liked), the Ghia body side mouldings with red inserts, the tinted glass, sunroof, and so forth. The price of this package was similarly competitive at £7399 for the smaller-engined version, and £7606 for the 1.6.

Obviously, these moves were successful, and they helped sustain interest in the range to the point where the Escort became the world's best-selling car for the sixth successive year. This was a world record, the latest in a string of records set by the model. In Britain, it outsold every other car for five successive years and had achieved 1,000,000 sales more quickly than any other car (taking the record away from the Ford Model A, which had taken 16 months to achieve what the Escort managed in 13). By the middle of 1987, production totalled 6,000,000 models. In 1986 alone, 963,000 Escorts had been produced world-wide.

Another significant milestone was reached in June 1987, when the 500,000th 1.6 litre diesel came off the production line at Dagenham, apparently aided by Mrs Mabel Arnold, the town's mayor—the vast majority of those engines went into Escort and Orion models.

The summer of 1987 saw another couple of special Escort and Orion models, which possibly bore the most unimaginative nomenclature of all time—Plus. 'Plus' means in addition to, and in addition to the regular specification of the GL models were added such extras as metallic paint, central locking and power windows—items which were worth £609 to the £7590 Escort and the

A power-operated hood was first offered to Cabriolet buyers (for a premium of £500) in late 1987. The time it took to raise or lower the hood was about 15 seconds, and the entire operation could be carried out without leaving the driver's seat. It would only work with the ignition off

£7830 Orion—for no extra charge. What they proved, above all else, was that if it so desired, Ford could have done quite a lot more to the Ghia models, because in comparison to these two cars, the Ghias showed little advantage.

A month later, Ford dropped the 1.1 litre engine from the range of Escort powerplants, presumably due to a lack of interest from the buying public, who had shown a preference for spending an extra £250 for the 1.3 litre Valencia engine. At the same time, Ford deleted the option of the Ghia Cabriolet; customer preferences had also proved this to be a less-desirable machine than the far sportier XR3i Cabriolet.

The special-edition formatting rolled on, and in September 1987, the most significant of all of the specials was announced, the LX. Developed originally for the Sierra range, the LX package would eventually be included in all the Ford model ranges. For the Escort and Orion, the basis was set with the L model, which was treated to a two-tone paint scheme (the lower side panels were painted

in a dark grey, chip-resistant finish which matched the grey plastic front and rear bumpers), waistline body mouldings with red inserts, and full wheel-covers. On the inside, the specification was upgraded by installing the tilt-and-slide sunroof, the up-market instrumentation, the rear heater element antenna and the better stereo equipment. As with other specials, only CVH-engined models were available.

Simultaneously, the rest of the Escort range was revised. The Popular gained the previously-optional wash-wipe unit and also was equipped with slightly wider-section 155/13 tyres. The L model continued (it was later to be dropped when the LX sales took off) and was given the improved stereo and the rear window-heater-mounted aerial.

The GL had the sunroof and central locking as standard, while the Ghia was upgraded with powered mirrors, an ECU–2 sound system and 175/70 tyres. The XR3i and Cabriolet came with central locking and driving lamps as standard, and the Cabriolet's previously-optional, electrically-operated aerial became a standard item.

The Orion's improvement list included the wholesale adoption of the five-speed transmission and wider-section tyres, as well as the Bi-Fi antenna. Central locking became a standard item on the GL, while the alloy wheels of the Ghia 1.6i also became standard, along with the fuel com-

The 1.8 litre diesel-powered Escort arrived in 1988. This was available in a wide variety of trim packages (including Ghia in Germany, France and Spain) and in the Orion as well. The engine offered more torque and was altogether better than its 1600 cc predecessor

puter. That computer, incidentally, had become increasingly reliable and no longer cried wolf; early customers who had specified it had been happy with its ability to monitor fuel consumption, but had been less than impressed by the way it would start to bleep that the range was down to about 50 miles (80 kilometers), when it was obvious that there was still a quarter of a tank full of fuel left.

The programme of 'added value' which Ford was pursuing at the time also benefited the commercial vehicle side, with a new 'added value' Escort van, the Laser, joining the fray against high-perceived-value imports to Europe from the Far East. With a 90 bhp, 1600 cc CVH engine and five-speed transmission, the van gave car-style performance—in fact, it could outsprint an equivalent saloon thanks to its better overall gearing. Duo-tone paintwork in either Diamond white with black lower section, or Rosso red with black, a cloth interior trim, and the same fascia as the saloons conspired to make the van a firm favourite with small businessmen, and with tradesmen who used it for work and for pleasure. The Laser van was getting back to Uwe Bahnsen's beloved XRV project.

One aspect of owning the Cabriolet model which had irritated a number of owners was that it was necessary to get out of the car to raise and lower the well-made hood. This was remedied in time for the 1987 British motor show (which was held in London and called Motorfair) when a power-operated hood mechanism was offered for the first time. This involved the driver in nothing more laborious than unclipping the two header-rail fasteners and pressing a console-mounted button. For £500, it was a worthwhile addition to the Cabriolet's specification. A small electric motor in the boot took up hardly any space at all and needed only 15 seconds of operation to raise or lower the roof of the car.

On the subject of the Cabriolet, the first of what would eventually be three special editions was announced in late October 1987. This was finished in a smart two-tone paint finish—the upper half of the car was in either Strato silver or Crystal blue, with the lower half in Mercury grey or Strato silver accordingly—and, as might be expected, came with the smart, radially-spoked aluminium-alloy wheels. On the boot of the Cabriolet was an aerofoil taken straight from the Rallye Sport accessories catalogue and finished in the same shade as the upper bodywork. The hood of the Duo-Tone (which, incidentally, had no special badging) was in blue, while blue Daytona fabric was used inside the car. At £11,234, the price of the Duo-Tone was higher than the listed cost of a standard example (which was £10,983, but the car was good value when the additional prices of the alloy rims, metallic paint and other little bits and pieces were added into the equation. Unlike most special editions, the Cabriolet Duo-Tone could still be ordered with the other available options, such as SCS, heated front screen and power windows.

1988 was a year of major significance for the Escort, because it celebrated its 20th birthday. It was also the year in which Halewood—described by Ford as the 'home of the Escort' (I wonder how that went down at Saarlouis and Valencia) celebrated its 25th birthday. By 1988, the overall, world-wide production figures for the Escort were

The estate car had been available in three- and five-door formats, but the latter was proving more popular. Thus, eventually, the three-door would be dropped. The 1600 cc version was a firm favourite among small businesses, as it combined a reasonable degree of pulling power with a practical load area

heading towards 10,000,000, and a sizeable proportion of those had been built at Halewood. To celebrate the Halewood birthday, a party was held for all of the workforce, complete with a flypast by a banner-towing aircraft. Rather surprisingly, the car-shaped cake which was presented to the plant depicted not an Escort, but an Anglia.

Totally unrelated to either birthday celebration, but simply created as a means of making a few extra pounds or deutschmarks, a special-edition, all-white Cabriolet was available in May 1988. Ford built 300 of the cars—150 each for Germany and for Britain—and they followed closely the theme set by the first, pre-facelift, white Cabriolet in that they used the special body kit of the RS Turbo, and even used the wheels from that car, although they were white-enamelled for the Cabriolet. Again, an RS rear spoiler was fitted and colour-keyed, and the car came with just about all of the available extras. It was upholstered in white leather, just to finish it off nicely. But at a price of £14,439, it needed to be special; this was the most expensive Escort yet.

Another year on and records kept falling to the Escort. In the middle of 1988, it was announced that up to the end of 1987, the car was still outselling every other model on the market by a sizeable margin; the nearest rival was the Golf, which was some 51,000 units behind the Escort during the 1987 sales year. At this point, production was taking place not just in the United States, Canada, Britain, Germany and Spain, but also in Brazil, Venezuela and Argentina. The last three countries were building European, rather than North American-specification cars, with the assistance of production planners from Ford of Europe; although some of the tooling was sourced in

Europe, other items were made locally from drawings supplied by Merkenich and Dunton. As with all of the Ford plants world-wide, there was a good degree of local content in the cars, especially in such areas as fasteners, plastic mouldings and other smaller items—supply lines for these items were overseen by Ford of Europe people.

Two new engines for the Escort and Orion ranges were announced in September 1988, along with a number of trim-package improvements. Well, they weren't exactly new engines, but rather evolutions of existing product lines.

The first of these was a further development of the Dagenham-built diesel unit, which had first been seen in 1983. Both bore and stroke were increased (the bore to 82.5 mm from 80 mm, and stroke to 82 mm from 80 mm), and there were a number of other major changes when the new engine was viewed alongside its six-year-old predecessor. Internally, the main bearing caps and sidewalls were stiffer to cope with the increased load, and the water jackets were thicker to improve cooling and reduce noise levels. These block changes had been designed with full use of the latest computer technology available to Ford at Dunton, facilities which included the very useful finite element analysis technique, which used computerized projections and extrapolations to

Two variants of light commercial vehicle were on offer by the middle of 1988. The original-style Escort van was carried over from the previous range (albeit with the new nose section and revised fascia), but this was joined by the Combi, a panel-sided estate car. Both were available with a range of engines, although the diesel unit has proved most popular; the 1.3 HCS petrol engine has also been widely specified

determine any possible weak spots. This technique saves a considerable amount of development time, as it is no longer necessary to build dozens of different dummy cylinder blocks.

The lubrication system was also modified, the main change being to install a spray bar in the lower section of the cylinder block which directed jets of oil on to the undersides of the pistons as a cooling measure. This had been used on the two-litre Cosworth engine to great effect and now was being applied to more mundane engines with equal success. The oil pump itself had been repositioned outside the engine block and was driven by a layshaft, which also served to improve the engine's balance. Other internal revisions included redesigned pistons with larger gudgeon pin holes, and new connecting rods which had larger gudgeon pins and a revised length to keep the angles within acceptable bounds despite the additional stroke. The crankshaft bearing surfaces were induction hardened for increased durability, and the piston rings were redesigned to minimize friction.

The camshaft was revised to increase lift on both inlet and exhaust valves, and the timing was set to extend the amount of time during which each valve remained open. At the front of the engine, the bearing was revised to allow the camshaft to run on rollers, and the belt drive mechanism was reworked so that the fuel injection pump had its own drive belt; henceforth, the camshaft belt drove only the oil and water pumps as well as the camshaft itself. The belts were given a new tooth design which reduced noise levels.

Oil sealing and water pump bearing surfaces were redesigned to improve their effectiveness, and a new end cover was designed to keep everything neat and tidy. In the interests of ecology, no asbestos was used in the engine's gaskets.

The top model of Orion was the 1600E, introduced as a limited-run model in 1989. This featured a full leather trimmed interior, wood cappings on the doors and fascia, two special exterior colours, aluminium wheels and special badging. The cars were built to Ford's specification by Tickford at Bedworth

In addition to the increased dimensions of the cylinder block, more power was released by reworking the induction system. A marginal increase in valve sizes (to 36.5 mm inlet and 32 mm exhaust, from 35 mm and 31 mm respectively) was matched by increased port dimensions and by a redesigned ram-intake manifold. This last item was made from a combination of aluminium and Dough Moulding Compound, a plastic 'alloy' of polyester resin, calcium carbonate and chopped glassfibre, which not only gave a useful shape, but also a small weight benefit. In net terms, the redesigned engine gave a substantial 17 per cent gain in power for an additional displacement of only 200 cc—power rose to 60 bhp and torque to 81 lb/ft, from 54 bhp and 70 lb/ft respectively. There were equal gains in fuel economy, as well; on the urban cycle, an Orion with the new engine gave an average mileage of 44.8 mpg, compared to the previous engine's 43.7 mpg.

At the same time as the engine was developed, Ford's policy to minimize noise, vibration and harshness was given a fresh airing, the engine mounts being reworked to improve insulation and the air intake system being resited to reduce the transmission of induction roar into the bodyshell. As well as being made available for the Escort and Orion, the new engine was also offered in the Escort van.

The other 'new' engine was a further refinement of the Valencia unit which, in turn, was a refined version of the old Kent engine that had powered the earliest Escorts. Of crossflow design, it had pushrod-operated valves, raised and lowered by a block-mounted camshaft, which was driven from the crankshaft by a simplex chain. Rechristened HCS (an acronym of High Compression Swirl), the Valencia-built engine incorporated many of the concepts already seen in the 1986 version of the CVH engine, such as low-friction piston ring packs and high-swirl combustion chambers which allowed the engine to run on a leaner air-fuel mixture than previously. Of particular significance was that the revised engine was designed to use unleaded petrol, having its valve seats hardened to cope with the absence of the toxic upper cylinder lubricant. Despite being detuned to run on low-octane fuel of 95RON (Super Plus high-octane unleaded fuel was unheard of at the time, and unleaded Premium grade was only just starting to appear on forecourts), the HCS engine displayed an ability to produce an extra 3 bhp (the previous 1.3 Valencia unit gave 60 bhp and also to give a nominal 1 lb/ft gain in torque. Most importantly, fuel economy rose; an Escort three-door gave 44.1 mpg on the urban cycle, compared to the old engine's 38.2 in the same configuration.

By this point in 1988, the L models were accounting for some 40 per cent of UK sales, so Ford decided that a degree of largesse was in order. This took the form of adding the tilt-and-slide sunroof (which previously was a £390 option) to the list of standard features, along with a mirror on the back of the passenger's sun visor. LX customers benefited from the provision of central locking as standard, and GL purchasers were given electrically-controlled and heated mirrors, and powered front windows. The XR3i's specification was improved by the standard issue of powered windows, too. The Ghia remained unchanged, however, despite the gap between it and the GL having closed considerably, but the Escort Popular benefited from the replacement of its old manually-tuned 'wireless' with a security-coded electronic radio. The radiator grilles of both Escorts and Orions were changed slightly at this point (which, as usual, was just in time for the British Motor Show), and the interior trim fabrics were changed slightly.

One further change was made to the range of Escorts and Orions at this stage, which Ford played down because to have made a song and dance about it would have been tantamount to an

The last major change to the MkIV range was the introduction of the EEC-IV engine management system for injected engines. This gave a small increase in net power, although its primary purpose was to improve the overall level of fuel economy

admission that there had previously been a problem; the steering rack was changed. One of the major complaints about the two models was the excessive weight of the steering at parking speeds, but Ford had always maintained that this was acceptable and unavoidable. Yet, in the autumn of 1988, the company showed that life could be better; the new rack was of variable ratio, which reduced parking-speed effort appreciably without affecting the directness of the rack at high road speeds. Although what many buyers would really have liked was power steering, the new variable-rate manual rack was a good substitute. Interestingly, at the time of the change to this rack, Ford already had a good power steering system designed

and working—but purchasers would have to wait until the end of 1990 before they could have it.

Another new bodystyle had appeared by this time, doubling the range of the available light commercial vehicles under the Escort banner; the new model was the Combi, and it was targeted even more precisely at the small businessman. Based on the three-door estate bodyshell, the Combi had panelled-in rear quarter-windows which offered a degree of privacy for the contents, without adversely affecting the load-carrying capacity of the estate. Instead of having rear seats, the Combi had a flat floor, and it was ideal for those who never needed to use the additional height offered by the van. Naturally, the new engines and the revised steering gear found their way into the two light commercials. Surprisingly, although the Escort van was a firm favourite in its class, comfortably outselling the similarly-sized vehicles from competing manufacturers, the Combi never really fired the imagination, and it is unlikely that the formula will be repeated.

Some years ago, in the latter part of the 1960s, Ford produced a special, up-market version of their Cortina, the 1600E. This car had combined such details as a wooden fascia with the running gear of the Cortina GT, augmented by some parts from the Mk II Cortina Lotus. This machine had been available only in a small variety of colours, and had gone on to achieve an envied cult status. Ford's marketing people, never ones to miss out on potential sales, decided that the time was ripe to revive the concept and that the Orion was the ideal machine upon which to base it. The Orion 1600E was born.

❋ Originally, the plan had been to produce 500 of these machines, but eventually double that number were built. The basic cars, which were the fuel injected 1.6i Ghia models, where shipped en bloc from Ford to Aston Martin Tickford's assembly plant in Bedworth, near Coventry. There, they were completed by having a full leather interior

The Rallye Sport name is not only applied to complete cars, but also to a lucrative range of aftermarket parts. This body kit for the MkIV Escort range is typical, providing an inexpensive means of changing the appearance of the car

trim installed, along with a set of wooden door cappings and a similar fillet for the dashboard roll, just above the stowage bin and oddments tray. A special steering wheel—which looked like that of the Granada—was installed, its leather rim being matched to a leather-trimmed gearknob. A Bedford cloth headlining was installed (very limousine-style), as were a handful of additional interior lights: one in the back, and one for each front and rear footwell.

In keeping with the style of the original 1600E, the car was originally available in only two metallic colours, Mercury grey and Raven, a deep blue-black shade. Later, white examples would also be available in the second batch. Special aluminium-alloy wheels were used on the car, too, but these were soon to become available through the RS accessories catalogue. Unfortunately, because of the way in which the £12,500 car was built, it was not possible to order one with anti-lock brakes, the 'Hotscreen', or any of the other extras normally offered for the Orion 1.6i Ghia. That quibble aside—a quibble which seemed not to affect sales at all, as all the cars found willing owners—the car was quite well-equipped, having all of the regular features of the 1.6i Ghia in addition to its special bucket-style front seats complete with map

pockets in their backs, and the graphic equalizer to offer extra colour to the Orion's six-speaker system.

According to a rumour (which has not been substantiated by anybody from Ford or Tickford, but which came from several reliable sources within the dealership network), there was a problem with the paint on quite a number of the second batch of cars. This was apparently caused by the close proximity to Tickford's Bedworth premises of a large chemical plant which had been raining corrosives on to the stockpiled cars that were waiting to be trimmed. It would appear that the cars were stripped and resprayed before being returned to their rightful owners.

As well as providing the means of creating special 'mini-limousines' for the affluent who wanted big-car comfort in a compact package, the Escort and Orion ranges also proved firm favourites with the disabled. In addition to a specially-adapted Escort van which had rear-mounted wheelchair ramps and a vista-style roof-line, Ford also produced hand-controlled versions of the Escort and Orion saloons, which came complete with a rise-and-fall, swivelling driver's seat. Ford established a special subsidized pricing structure, which helped absorb the cost of the special equipment and the normal price premium for the ATX automatic transmission. Quite a number of physically-handicapped drivers have taken advantage of the Ford Mobility Centres which are contactable through the normal dealer-ship network, and which offer a serious, civilized alternative to the dreadful old Invacar, which formerly was the only means of transport available to the handicapped. Ironically, Invacars were made by AC Cars (better known for their sensational Cobras), which became a majority-owned subsidiary of Ford in September 1988.

The next major advance in the Escort and Orion's running gear was the introduction of the CTX transmission. Evolved from a Dutch-designed transaxle, originally seen on the quirky little Daf cars of a couple of decades ago, the CTX used a series of belts and pulleys to maintain optimum power throughput from the engine to the road.

CTX was a fairly loose acronym for 'continuously variable transaxle', and it was the product of three major manufacturers, Van Doorne of Holland, Fiat of Italy and Ford of Europe. The development programme had begun a decade ago, when the Erika project was almost ready for unveiling, all three partners providing input; eventually both Fiat and Ford would use the system as an alternative to the usual, energy-sapping torque converter transmission. There are no gears within the CTX, nor is there a torque converter—conically-faced pairs of pulleys simply move closer to or further away from each other to vary the belt contact area and, thus, alter the overall ratios. A mite weird to drive because the normal correlating factors of engine speed and road speed no longer applied, the Bordeaux-built CTX transmission worked well, offering automatic speed selection without absorbing too much power. The CTX became available on 1.4 and 1.6 litre Orions and Escorts (with the exception of the injected models, which were available in only five-speed manual format) from the middle of 1989.

The final set of changes to the Escort and Orion came later in 1989, when the fuel and ignition systems of the CVH 1600 cc engines of the XR3i and Orion 1.6i were changed from a part-Bosch, part-Ford system to the Ford EEC–IV engine management computer. This was part of a policy of Ford's to adopt the computer to as many applications as humanly possible, and in the case of the CVH 1.6i, this yielded a net gain of 3 bhp and a nominal improvement in fuel economy (it allowed the engines to run on low-grade, unleaded petrol). At the same time, the cylinder head redesign, which had been a major feature of the newly-introduced XR2i Fiesta, was applied to both engines, along with that car's intake and exhaust manifolding.

The revised RS turbo was an appreciably softer package than its immediate predecessor, despite sharing the same basic format—spring rates were reduced, as was the fierceness of the viscous coupling. Although owners moving on to the new model were disappointed initially, the changes were sufficient to ensure a whole host of new fans for the car

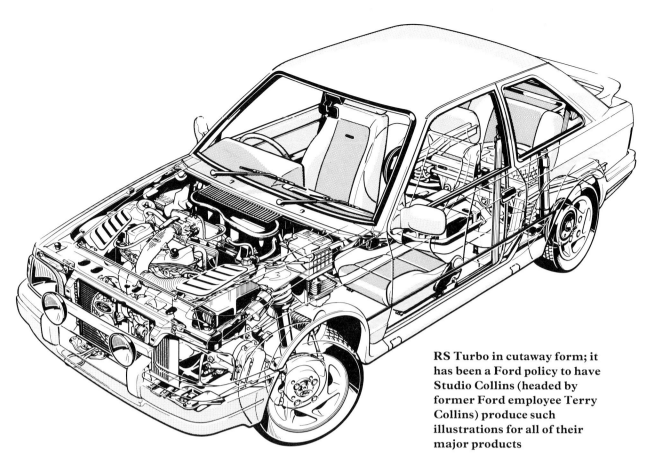

RS Turbo in cutaway form; it has been a Ford policy to have Studio Collins (headed by former Ford employee Terry Collins) produce such illustrations for all of their major products

At the same time as the EEC–IV was introduced, Ford announced that, in the near future, they would be offering catalytic converters for selected models in the Escort and Orion range. This proved to be a single model in each line-up, the 1.4 litre CVH. To offer the right level of control for the converter, the fuelling system was changed from the usual Weber carburettor to what Ford described as 'single point injection'. On closer inspection, this proved to be very similar to the hybrid carburettor/injection unit used with great success by BMW for some years on their 3-series cars. As might be expected, control of the fuel and ignition systems was handed over to the EEC–IV. The converter itself was a three-way unit which filtered and altered the usual noxious elements of carbon monoxide, unburnt hydrocarbons and nitrogen oxides into carbon dioxide, nitrogen and water vapour.

To go along with the engine revisions, a selection of other changes was put in hand. These included such detail touches as a variable intermittent sweep, an extended centre console, and one or two other bits and bobs.

The XR3i and Cabriolet came out best of all, appearing with a new set of wheels which closely followed those of the RS Cosworth Sapphire in style; although they looked great, they proved an absolute nightmare to clean, unless the owner

happened to possess a power washer. The XR3i gained a slightly redesigned rear spoiler, which was supposed to improve side-wind stability by virtue of its down-turned ends. In practice, however, the car proved to be less stable than its immediate predecessor. The XR3i Cabriolet gained tinted side glass to match the tinted windscreen. The GL and Ghia gained the wiper and centre console modifications, and they also benefited from (finally) having rear-door-operated courtesy lights mounted above the back seat. Finally, the L, LX and Sport all gained a light apiece in the load compartment, and grab handles over the rear side windows.

The Sport was mentioned in that last paragraph, for the first time. The Sport was one of Marketing's inspired moves and was, in cruel terms, a sheep in wolf's clothing. First announced in the autumn of 1989, the car had a three-door bodyshell equipped with the usual moulded plastic bumpers of the standard Escort range, and the painted lower sides of the LX. A black XR3i rear spoiler was added, more for effect than effectiveness, and under the bonnet was the standard, carburated, 90 bhp, 1600 cc CVH engine with five-speed transmission and tall final drive gearing. It came complete with sunroof, tinted glass, central locking and the mid-range stereo system. It also had the XR3i's seats trimmed in Daytona fabric.

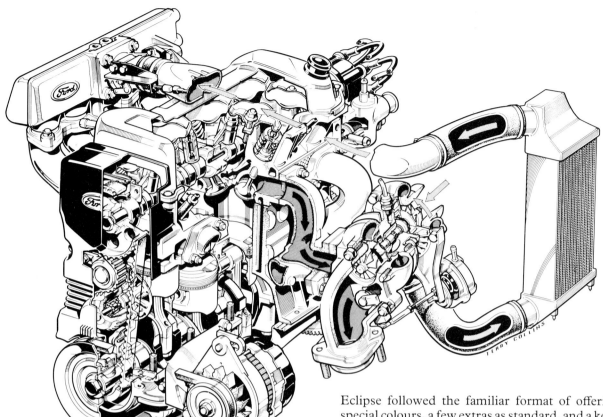

The RS Turbo powerplant. Producing 132 brake horsepower and a similar level of torque, the unit is force-fed a diet of high-octane, unleaded fuel through a Garrett AiResearch T.03 turbocharger with full intercooling. As the years rolled on, the original Motorola processor-based management system was eschewed in favour of a Ford EEC-IV computer. Power output was unchanged throughout the production life of the car

White enamelled wheeltrims and colour-keyed mirrors completed the illusion. To the prospective customer who was happy enough with the performance (which was reasonable, but hardly snappy), the £10,055 package proclaimed good value. To the more cynical observer, it smacked of Ford trying to use up large stocks of seats and spoilers before the Mk IV Escort went out of production.

The same sentiments applied to a pair of special, end-of-the-line cars which appeared at the beginning of 1990. The Escort Eclipse and the Orion

Eclipse followed the familiar format of offering special colours, a few extras as standard, and a keen package price. In the case of these cars, the colours were either red or blue metallic. Both came with spoilers (the Orion with one from the RS accessories catalogue, the Escort with the old-style XR3i item), and both had special wheel options; the Orion came with the Snowflake type first seen on the 1600E, and the Escort came with plastic trim covers. Both cars were available with either the 1.3 HCS or 1.4 CVH engine, both came with five-speed transmissions, and in both cases, the only optional extra was the Stop Control System. Prices ran from £8595 for the Escort, and from £9270 for the Orion.

There were what seemed like thousands of different trim and packaging options on offer from dealerships (with names that varied from the sublime to the ridiculous; Escort Manhattan was a typical example), many of which were based on the 1.3 Popular. There was, however, one other limited-edition car from Ford itself, which was based around the Cabriolet.

In the spring of 1990, Ford celebrated the production of 100,000 Cabriolets at Wilhelm Karmann by offering 600 lucky customers the chance to partake in the celebrations. Finished in Pacifica blue metallic paint—a fabulous shade that looked deep enough to swim in—the milestone Cabriolets

Above One of the main gripes from RS Turbo owners concerned the interior of the car. Although equipped with Recaro sports seats and a special fabric trim, the overall impression was that the car was insufficiently different from lesser models. The graphic equalizer, which features in this particular example, was an optional extra

were trimmed in blue hide upholstery, came complete with a full set of RS Turbo body styling panels, were colour-keyed throughout, and had the Turbo 15 × 6 in. wheels with 50-series tyres. The cars came with every extra available—power hood, 'Hotscreen', and so forth—except anti-lock braking. And the price? A cool £16,075.

There have been quite a number of dealer special Escorts over the years, but few were quite so dramatic as this one, built by Crown Cartec of Birmingham with widened arches, a special rear spoiler and unique graphics. The original intention was to produce a limited edition of 100 cars, which were sold as SunDay RS100 models exclusive to Bristol Street Motors in Birmingham. One car was given away through a competition in the colour supplement of the *News of The World* (hence SunDay), while another five or six were apparently sold before the project was wrapped up. The body kits are now produced by Fibresports of Basildon, a company which has been a Ford RS and Motorsport subcontractor for years

Which leaves but one Escort from the Mk IV range, the RS Turbo. Throughout the rest of the book, the RS cars have been treated to their own chapters, but in the case of the RS Turbo, it doesn't quite deserve such an accolade, so is not getting one.

The reason is that the car was only an RS car for the British market, and even then, it was a piece of badge engineering; to Ford—and especially to the production-line workers at Saarlouis—the car was an XR3i Turbo. Whereas the original, all-white Mk 1 RS Turbo was designed as a competition machine, and equipped with race-ready hardware from Day One, the second generation of the car was not intended for any kind of competitive activity. Consequently, it was toned down appreciably—sanitized is the word which springs to mind.

The basic running gear of the original car was carried over into the new one, with only a change in overall gearing; the final drive, at 4.27:1, had been deemed too racy for the different lifestyle of the new model, so this was swapped for a 3.82:1 set of gears. The viscous coupling, however, remained a feature of the car.

The suspension system was toned down, too, softer springs and dampers featuring on each corner of the car. The low-friction ball joints were integrated into the car's front suspension system, while the bottom linkages became exactly the same as those found beneath all Escorts, the anti-roll bar doing the job of fore-and-aft location of the struts. The Stop Control System became a standard feature of the car which, in all other respects, shared its braking system with the standard, less-powerful XR3i.

As might be expected, there were a few detail changes to the engine to smooth out its excesses a little. The first was that the turbocharger gained a watercooled centre bearing and an improved oil drainage system. The pistons were redesigned to reduce clearances—and, thus, reduce oil consumption—and the oil pump was reworked to improve flow and pressure. A new intake manifold was designed for the Bridgend-built powerplant, and the intercooler was also fine-tuned for smoother running. Despite the changes—which were mirrored by subtle changes to the management system programming—net power output was unchanged at 132 bhp.

Unlike the previous RS Turbo, which was available in any colour you liked, as long as it was white, the Mk II version could be had in Diamond white, black, red, or Mercury grey. To distinguish

A build-up of heat under the bonnet of the MkI RS Turbo led to Special Vehicle Engineering specifying these neat extractor vents. In addition to their practical application, they made the car's appearance more sporty!

it from the XR3i, the car had a colour-keyed rear spoiler, a pair of louvred cooling vents let into the bonnet, and special side panels which purported to make the car more aerodynamically efficient. A set of special 15 × 6 in. alloy rims was designed and used in conjunction with 195/50VR15 tyres from a variety of sources, including Goodyear, Pirelli and Dunlop. The wheels themselves were very close in appearance to the new XR3i items, but had single, rather than dual, spokes.

The inside of the car featured a pair of Recaro seats and a slightly different trim fabric, but apart from that, it was too similar for comfort to the XR3i for many people.

On the road, the car was a lively performer, giving sub-nine-second sprints to 60 mph and a top speed of almost 130 mph, and zappy performance through the gears. When compared to the XR3i, it was impressively fast. Yet those who moved up to the car from its predecessor were less impressed; gone was that special tingle that had typified the white car, and in its place was the feeling of being in a souped-up XR3i.

Rod Mansfield of Special Vehicle Engineering still feels that the car was better than its predecessor and, talking to the author a matter of weeks before this chapter was written in the middle of 1990, was philosophical; his department has long since given up trying to be all things to all men, and instead simply does the best it can within the restrictions placed upon it by the accountants who tend to run Ford in Europe. 'We took out the worst excesses of the earlier car,' he told me, referring to the RS Turbo, 'and got a panning for it. The later car was definitely safer, and the sales figures have proven it was more popular. The newer car appealed to a different type of buyer than the old Turbo.' There is little to dispute in those comments. The sudden sharp behaviour of the old car, which had thrilled some and frightened more, had been replaced by a far more progressive feel. Suspension compliance was greater in the new car, and what tended to happen to the driver pressing on hard was that the body roll would generate a desire to back off a little before the car actually reached the limit of its considerable grip.

What bears this out is the industry which has grown up in tuning cars such as the RS Turbo, primarily by altering the turbocharger system. Although appreciably more Mk II than Mk I RS Turbos have been produced (remember the early

The research and development centre at Dunton has a recently-added facility which allows simulated heavy road use to be programmed into any car. This has been particularly helpful in developing the low noise, vibration and harshness levels which are a feature of the latest generation of Escorts and Orions. Although the car shown here is a MkIV Escort, by the time that the facility was installed in late 1989, the MkV would have been undergoing the treatment, and not its predecessor

car was a limited-run machine, whereas the later car was in series production as a mainstream model), the number of earlier-type Turbos which have been modified for faster roadwork is still disproportionately lower than the number of later cars.

Originally, the RS Turbo was available in two forms, the base model and the Custom Pack; this was a tradition carried over from the days of the RS2000. However, in July 1987, Ford altered the structure so that the base model was deleted, offering only the RS Turbo with central locking, powered front windows and sunroof. In September 1988, another small item was added to the specification of the car when the 'Hotscreen' became a standard fitment. A year later, it gained the intermittent-wipe adjuster, the extended centre console and the modified XR3i rear spoiler. But by then, the price had gone up from its original launch price of £10,950 to more than £13,000, only some of which could be accounted for by inflation.

But the RS Turbo's days were numbered, anyway, even before the Mk II version hit the showroom floors a few months after the rest of the range of revised Escorts had gone on sale. Ford had already decided that if it was to keep up with the competition, it needed to produce something a good deal more radical than the 132 bhp machine—and, boy, was its projected replacement radical. But that was for Ford of Europe. In America, they had abandoned the entire notion of the Escort being a serious world car.

14 Separation

The Americans go their own way

Ford's interest in Toyo Kogyo, the company which manufactures Mazda cars in Japan, was already being used to great effect in the Far East, where the equivalent model to the Escort for the South Pacific Basin, from 1980 onwards, had been a Mazda with Ford oval badges on its nose and tail. Although Erika had been a successful package in terms of overall sales for Ford North America, the next generation of Escort for the United States and Canada would need to be radically improved compared to the old model if the success story was to continue. Casting their eyes around the empire, it soon became apparent to Ford's Dearborn management that the answer to the problem of replacing the entire range of Escort and Lynx models could lie in Hiroshima, at Toyo Kogyo's headquarters.

The new generation of compact Fords was displayed to the public for the first time on 22 April 1990, in an orchestrated blitz of national television commercials; it was a Sunday, and Sunday night is prime viewing time for the entire population of the United States. What the viewers saw were two commercials, both of which used the common theme of a team of engineers huddled around a cluster of computer design equipment, interspersed with footage of the new model range. Produced by J. Walter Thompson in Detroit, the advertisements concluded with the ongoing (for the previous year or two) punch line: 'Have you driven a Ford lately?' This was coupled to a new theme: 'A new line of thought, a new line of cars.' Targeted by Ford, with crosshairs firmly set on the major Japanese marques of Toyota, Honda and Mazda(!), the new model was projected by Ford as being of major importance.

According to Thomas J. Wagner, the new project (which had been coded CT–20) was even more important to the fortunes of Ford North America than had been the Taurus—or even that legend of recent times, the Mustang. The total investment in the programme had run to $2,000,000,000, and Ford was even allocating some $65–70,000,000 to the television advertising budget. Wagner had been Vice President of Ford Division for two years by the time that the advertising campaign started to roll, having already served his time in various divisions of the Ford group. And his reason why CT–20 was so important to the company's future? Quite simply, 'because it will usher in a new era at Ford in terms of quality, manufacturing and design,' said Mr Wagner in a special preview pack issued on 4 January. 'The 1991 Escort is much more than a new car. It represents a new way of doing business.'

Which sounds like the sort of sales hype one might expect from a man who has spent part of his career selling Ford products to dealers in the Mid-West—which is precisely what he had done. That statement didn't really answer the question of the car's importance, so perhaps this is an opportune moment to look at the product itself, and return to the car's *raison d'être* later in this chapter.

The Escort is available in three body styles—two- and four-door hatchbacks and a wagon (estate car to us on the left-hand side of the Atlantic)—and its stablemate, the Mercury Tracer, is available as only a four-door conventional sedan (saloon), which echoes the European range of Escort and Orion models. The bodywork has been styled by a team from Dearborn who had decamped to Hir-

Early design sketches for the CT-20 programme were produced by a team from Dearborn, which moved *en bloc* to Hiroshima as the project evolved from the sketchpad to reality. As always happens, the realities of manufacturing techniques meant that some of the early concepts needed to be modified—if only it was possible to make cars which are as sleek as these early design studies!

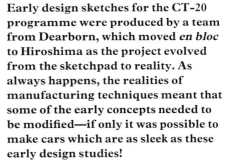

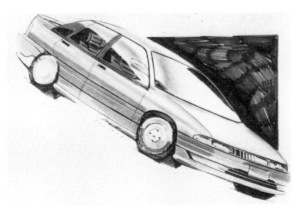

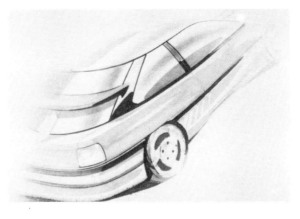

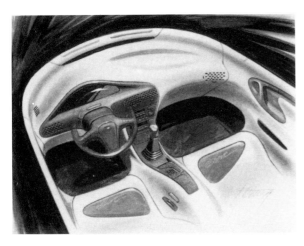

oshima to work closely with Mazda's engineering people; the idea was to use as much of the Mazda 323 floorpan as possible, to design a new suit of clothes around that car's skeleton. If the car has ended up bearing a close resemblance to the new European models featured in the next chapter, it is not surprising. Given the finite number of designs which can be produced around a set overall length, width, height, accommodation package and drag coefficient, it was inevitable that the new Escort and Tracer models would share much conceptual styling trends with the CE–14 programme being developed simultaneously in Europe.

The glass area of the American car has been made as large as is practical without exacting undue penalties in the form of weight; square inch for square inch, glass weighs more than sheet-metal. Although encumbered with the unenviable task of integrating large, impact-resistant federal bumpers, the design team has managed to produce a range of sleek cars whose lower bodyline flows neatly into the upper styling. The target coefficient of drag was set at an average of 0.35, and the team has also managed to fulfil that objective; the cars vary from 0.34 cd for the sports model to 0.36 for the wagon. This has been achieved by such detail touches as a smoothed-off air intake grille (which follows the corporate styling found on virtually all North American Fords), flush-fitting as much of

Despite concessions to manufacturing methods, the models launched in 1990 are still good looking—especially so considering that they have those dreadful Federal bumper assemblies integrated into their appearance. This is the two-door LX, the mid-range contender and, thus, the projected biggest single-badge seller

the glazing as possible, and by eliminating the usual wheelarch lips. Light clusters are slim and smooth, and even such details as the licence plate detents have been designed to offer as little wind resistance as possible. All three styles (hatch, sedan and wagon) are equally successful and pleasing, and have won immediate approval from Mr and Mrs Middle America and their teenage offspring.

Interestingly, although the new models are the product of the American design team, controlled by Fritz Mayhew, a number of components are common to the bodyshells of both Escort and Mazda 323—the windscreen and the forward section of the roofline are typical. A key member of the Ford team in Japan was Toshiaki Saito, a Japanese-born designer who was educated initially in his native land, but qualified as an automotive stylist and designer in Pasadena, California. He was able to act as interpreter, not just of linguistics, but also of ideas, between the Ford and the Mazda people because of his intimate knowledge of both cultures. He was also able to correlate that most important of factors, cost accounting, for Ford, whose *modus operandi* is totally different to Mazda's way of doing business. Working closely with Ford's Arthur Hyde, a key player in the small car development programme, who had been de-spatched to Hiroshima in 1985 for a three-year period, Mr Saito was able to ensure that all costs were kept under strict control in the way that Dearborn likes them to be.

Underpinning the panelwork is the 323 floor-pan, but Ford has not merely taken it to Michigan and duplicated it.

The suspension system, for instance, follows Mazda's original format of having a strut at each

corner, but Ford's chassis engineers have developed their own blends of spring and damper rates; not once, but three times. The first of these is the softest and is intended for the main product run, which is to be sold to the masses. Although Ford has gone as far as possible with handling and roadholding on that package, its emphasis is most definitely on maximum ride comfort; a colleague, who has been able to test-drive the new range, reported that the Escort Pony offered a ride quality on a par with an appreciably bigger car, at the expense of gradually-increasing understeer. Next up from that series of struts is the system found on the Tracer LTS, the 'GT' version of the Mercury, which is probably best-likened to the Orion 1.6i Ghia of the European range. This has a sharper edge to its handling, according to my colleague, but still displays a pleasantly comfortable ride quality. Finally, there is the Escort GT's market pitch at younger, sportier drivers. As might be expected, the words 'Noise', 'Vibration' and 'Harshness' were written large across the minds of the chassis engineering team, just as they have been for all Ford products since the 1960s.

A major contributory factor to the quality of ride, to the good NVH factors which the new cars are able to display, is the neat and effective lower linkage arrangement which Mazda had designed for the rear suspension. Whereas the Erika project had been evolved with all research into suspension being based on two rear seat passengers, that of the CT–20 had been based on having three adults in the back of the car. To provide insurance against the rear wheels adopting lurid angles (and thus creating instability) when the car is fully-laden and travelling through curves and corners at speed, the Mazda engineers devised a trapezoidal arrangement which comprises two pairs of transverse swinging arms, a pair on each end of the main rear crossmember which runs between the hub centres. These are augmented by a pair of forward-running compression struts and by an anti-roll bar, the diameter of which varies, depending upon application; the GT has one measuring 22 mm, while the rest of the range come with a 20 mm item. To avoid stiction, the damper mounts are offset from the hub centres, and to ensure a constant ride level, regardless of the number of occupants in the rear seat of the car, compound (rising-rate) springs are employed. These, for the uninitiated, become harder as more pressure is applied to them; in practice, the car will start to roll gently as it begins to corner, but will then level out.

At the front of the car, the lower link takes the

The Mercury Tracer LTS, the North American equivalent of Europe's Orion, shares its floorpan with the Escort. This particular model is the GT member of the line-up and is powered by the 1800 cc, twin-overhead-camshaft engine, which was developed by Mazda for their world-wide operations

form of a substantial pressed-steel, delta-shaped affair which has one pivot point on the bottom of the strut, while the other two are spaced widely apart on the front rails. This minimizes the chance of torque-steer effect by precluding any fore-and-aft movement of the struts under hard acceleration.

The arrangement also helps reduce the chances of the car's nose diving towards the tarmac under hard braking. Unlike the rear, the forward suspension system has a predictable weight load, so rising-rate springs are unnecessary, conventional, evenly-spaced coil springs being used around the damper units. Again, there is an anti-roll bar and, again, this varies in size depending on the application. Most of the range have a 19 mm diameter item, but the GT has a 22 mm bar. As with the rear suspension, the strut mounts are offset in the interests of smooth operation of the hydraulic dampers.

Rather than employ the Japanese steering rack, the 1991 Escort family makes use of an all-American system, which is available with or without power assistance. One of the main criticisms of the Erika Escorts was the car's abysmal turning circle, and Ford was keen to overcome that complaint. Therefore, the new rack is capable of turning the car around in 31.5 ft—this cuts a quarter off the old radius. The manual steering

With four valves per cylinder and the variable inertia charging system (a dual-action, gated intake manifold which ensures optimum gasflow speeds), the 1.8 dohc engine produces 127 bhp and 114 lb/ft of torque, despite being restricted by its emission system. The windage tray, seen through the cutaway sump pan, is a feature previously only found on race cars

rack requires 4.3 turns of the wheel from one lock to the other, in the interests of minimizing the input required at parking speeds, but the assisted rack needs only 3.1 turns to achieve its lock range. For the first time on a Ford of the Escort's size, the powered rack has a variable rate of assistance engineered into it, to do away with any tendency to over-lightness at speed. European Ford owners, those with Sierras and Scorpios, will already be familiar with the concept, as their cars have been equipped in this manner for several years.

To ensure that the car stopped well—essential in any country, but especially one where litigation over product liability is a national sport, the Escort and Tracer models come with a front-disc, rear-drum braking arrangement. There are 9.25 in. discs and 9 in. drums on the standard range, and 10.1 in. front discs, 9.88 in. rear discs on the GT model. Servo assistance and split circuitry are provided, but rather surprisingly, there has been no attempt to utilize the mechanical anti-lock system pioneered on the British Escorts of 1986.

The choice of engines was something of a problem for Ford, because the CVH engine, even

in its later guise, was hardly the sort of powerplant suitable for the entire range of cars which were aimed at matching the packages being put together by Toyota, Honda and the other competitors in the same market sector. Although efficient enough in terms of power output, its coarseness at high speeds—anything beyond 5000 rpm—was close to infamous. Probably, Ford could have got away with using it in the less-prestigious models, but for the flagships, the GT and the LTS? Clearly, something more sophisticated was called for.

Once again, the sun rose in the East, when Mazda came to the rescue with its newest powerplant, which had been designed for the 323. A sophisticated twin-camshaft unit, based around a short-skirt, cast-iron cylinder block, the new engine displaces 1.8 litres and —very important to Ford—displays excellent NVH suppression characteristics. A single toothed drivebelt rotates the pair of camshafts which, in turn, open and close four valves in each of the four cylinders. Hydraulic cam followers are used to reduce noise levels and servicing chores, while at the other end, the valves locate into a pentroof-shaped combustion chamber above each pocketed piston. The spark plug is located centrally, but unlike many dohc engines, it is channelled into the chamber from the side, rather than from directly overhead. The valves themselves are relatively large for a multiple arrangement, at 33 mm for the intake and 28 mm for the exhaust. Normally, such large inlet valves would lead to a drop in gas velocity at low engine speeds (thus harming low-speed torque delivery), but with typical Japanese ingenuity, Mazda has designed the inlet manifold to counter this risk; the intake charge is fed through a dual-channel arrangement of pipes, which halves the swept area at low speeds by closing off one tract with a vacuum-activated butterfly. This effectively raises the gas speed and maintains good torque figures. Beyond 550 rpm, the butterfly opens and allows enough air to maintain power delivery. Peak power is 127 bhp at 6500 rpm, peak torque 114 lb/ft at 4500 rpm.

The engine's crankshaft is a five-bearing, eight-counterweight design which is damped torsionally and restrained by a complex steel plate which also adds torsional stiffness to the cylinder block. At the other end of the engine, fuelling is taken care of by a Bosch L-Jetronic system with twinned delivery (pistons one and three get a shot of fuel into their manifolds at their port faces, then numbers two and four get their share of the unleaded petrol), whilst an electronic control unit governs the camshaft-driven distributor.

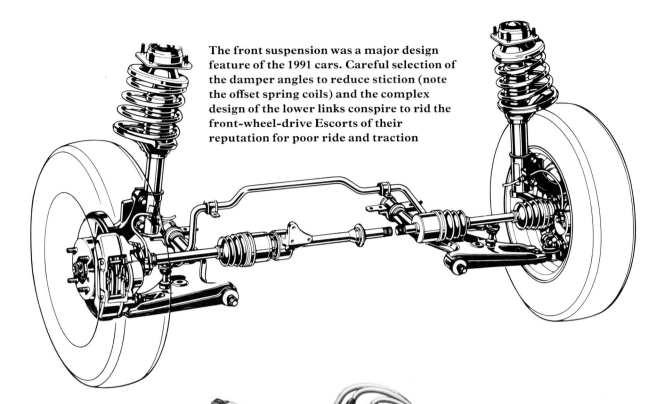

The front suspension was a major design feature of the 1991 cars. Careful selection of the damper angles to reduce stiction (note the offset spring coils) and the complex design of the lower links conspire to rid the front-wheel-drive Escorts of their reputation for poor ride and traction

Right The dohc engine has been reserved for use in the sporting variants of CT-20, so a redeveloped version of the familiar CVH engine has been adopted for the rest of the range. This uses long intake manifold runners to enhance low-speed torque and is equipped with sequential electronic fuel injection, controlled by the EEC-IV management computer

This engine is found beneath the gently-raked bonnets of the LTS Tracer and the GT Escort, and it is powerful enough to provide acceleration to 60 mph in 8.3 seconds, and a top speed of a shade over 120 mph. Which is not bad at all, when you consider that the cars are equipped with catalytic converters which hamper ultimate power delivery because of the back-pressures that are created.

Escort GT for 1991 is based on the two-door bodyshell and has a rear spoiler which is heavily Mazda-influenced. Despite looking like plastic trim covers, those are actually aluminium-alloy wheels. Clean and uncluttered lines are something of a novelty for the North American market, and the car has been praised for its simplicity of styling

The rest of the range is propelled by the 1.9 CVH engine which, for 1991, has a totally revised fuelling system; rather than the multi-point constant electronic injection of the older engine, the new unit has sequentially-timed injection. Specific power outputs are down very slightly (110 bhp at 5400 rpm), but the torque is improved—thus aiding drivability—with a peak figure of 115 lb/ft at 4200 rpm.

The revised engine is immediately identifiable by its long-runner intake manifold (which increases the velocity of the incoming charge), and by its cast-aluminium camshaft cover—the latter item has been designed to insulate as much of the noise as possible from the valvetrain. Interestingly, the intake manifold is fabricated from aluminium tubing rather than being cast; this saves weight and is also claimed to improve airflow. The end of the engine is distinguished by a coil pack, which replaces the usual distributor—the ignition is crankshaft-triggered and controlled by the same EEC–IV microprocessor which manages the fuel system. The cylinder block has been redesigned slightly to increase torsional stiffness and to decrease noise levels, and the bottom of the powerplant is now a cast-aluminium piece which bolts to the transaxle as well as to the engine block. This increases torsional stiffness. Finally, the engine

mountings have been redesigned with NVH priorities in mind.

Having mentioned the transaxle, two are offered for the new Escort and Tracer models. The first is a development of the existing transaxle (which Mazda had designed in the first place) and which features a tall, overdriven fourth and fifth gear set in conjunction with a 3.41:1 final drive. This is an economy-motivated package, as exemplary mileage figures were essential to Ford since the introduction of the CAFE measuring system, which requires every manufacturer in the United States to give a Corporate Average Fuel Economy figure for their entire passenger car range. By having good mileage figures from the smaller cars, the CAFE figure can be raised as it counters the thirsty, older and larger cars. Just for the record, Ford's CAFE figure is 27.5 miles per gallon, the Escort 1.9 SEFI CVH giving 34 mpg.

The other transaxle, for the 1.8 dohc engined cars, is a beefed-up derivative of the Mazda five-speed unit with a closer-ratio set of gears and a 3.62:1 final drive. This transaxle offers synchromesh on reverse gear as well as the forward clusters. The clutch assembly, which is hydraulically activated, has been uprated in size from that of the previous generation and is self-adjusting.

The automatic transmission is still a firm favourite in the States, and obviously Ford would need to offer one if the car's sales were to achieve the required (rather than desired) levels. Once again, it is a Mazda-designed unit, which has four forward speeds and a choice of final drive gearing to suit specific applications. Unlike Europe, the GT variants are available with the self-shifting transmission.

The CT–20 programe was designed from the

outset to compete head-to-head with the Japanese imports, so a strong launch line was a prerequisite. At the bottom of the range—the one which offers a high perceived value by dint of it being cheap—is the Pony; obviously Hyundai do not sell their small hatchback in the States! The Escort Pony is available in only two-door hatchback format, and with the 1.9 SEFI engine and the five-speed transaxle as standard—the four-speed automatic transaxle is an option for this car. Although mechanically similar to the rest of the range, the car is downgraded by the absence of such features within its cabin as a radio (the car is wired for a stereo and has a speaker grille and a screen-pillar-mounted aerial) and by its interior trim quality: moulded, rather than woven, carpeting and functional, rather than luxurious, seat covering fabrics. The Pony also has the down-market instrumentation (no tachometer, no trip meter) and the bare minimum of interior lighting. Prices start in the region of $7500, although they rise quite rapidly if the option list is looked at seriously.

The Pony is expected to achieve a good proportion of fleet sales to rental companies, government departments and larger businesses which provide either personally-assigned cars or pool cars, but its appeal to private buyers is expected to be limited. The main thrust of direct consumer (i.e. private) sales is to be achieved by the LX model. This is available in two- and four-door Escort hatchback form, and also in the wagon; the equivalent model in the Mercury series is sold simply as the Tracer.

Externally, the LX is distinguishable by its full-cover wheel trims (the Pony has only centre caps) and by its silver-grey lower body side mouldings, as well as its special badging. Inside the car, the distinctions are more marked. The down-market instrumentation features ahead of the driver, but in the centre of the car is a console with a bin and a pair of cup holders.

The interior trim level of the car is appreciably more luxurious—although by European standards it looks a shade cheap and nasty. The door liner panels are trimmed in fabric to match the seats (those of the Pony are vinyl), and the rear seat of the car has a split, folding backrest. A stereo system comes as standard in this car, but it does not have a cassette deck—no sense in being too generous, obviously! As might be detected, much of the higher perceived quality of the LX is achieved by sleight of hand, rather than by spending large amounts of money. Again, it is necessary to dig into the option list if the car is to be equipped with a power steering rack, automatic trans-

mission, a tilting steering column, remote-controlled tailgate and fuel filler flap, cruise control, air conditioning, and so forth.

The top-of-the-line Escort is the GT, and in comparison to the rest of the range, this is positively luxurious. It comes with sports seats, full instrumentation, a radio-cassette unit, power steering, and so on and so forth. Much the same packaging is applied to the Mercury Tracer LTS, and both cars come as standard with aluminium-alloy wheels which, at 14 × 6 in., are an inch bigger in each dimension than the pressed-steel items of the lesser Escorts and Tracer. Interestingly, the Tracer has a different fascia design to that of the Escort, having a wider binnacle with the clock and mirror adjustment control for the powered unit (in both cases where fitted) located on each side of the instrument panel—in the Escort, the clock is a part of the stereo system's display functions, and the mirror switch is on the panel and partially concealed by the lighting stalk. Other vital differences between the two models include the steering wheel (two-spoke on the Escort, four-spoke on the LTS) and the arrangement of the air ventilation grilles.

As well as providing a good, comprehensive and keenly-priced range of models from which the buying public can make their choice, it was also essential for Ford to produce both model ranges to a quality which at least matched, and hopefully exceeded, the build-standard of the Japanese imports, which were the rising threat at the time the car was being planned in 1985. Accordingly, a major part of the two-billion dollar budget was directed into the plants where the cars would be built—not just into the manufacturing process, but also in worker training.

The Escorts are primarily built in Wayne, Michigan, at the plant where the majority of the Erika-class cars had been built during the previous decade. From May 1990, this became the only facility within the United States for production of the model, because from that date the former second plant in Edison, New Jersey, changed over to the manufacture of Ranger pickup trucks. Escorts are also produced for the North American market in Hermosillo (the name translates literally as 'Little Beauty'), Northern Mexico, a medium-sized town which is just inland from the Gulf of California. All Mercury Tracer production is taken care of at Hermosillo.

Wayne is a suburb of Detroit, and the Ford plant dominates its landscape, just as it dominates the land on each side of the Rouge River where that stretch of water tumbles into the Great Lakes, around which the American motor industry has made its home. For many years, Wayne had been an assembly plant, but very early in the CT–20 programme's gestation period, Ford decided that much would be gained from making a major investment alongside the existing plant which could supply the new panels. This would make Wayne the only plant in Ford's North American operations which would have sheetmetal stock rolling in at one end, and finished cars coming out of the other—logistically, it would be sensible, and it would also allow far tighter control of quality. And 'quality' was the byword of the entire CT–20 project.

Once again, Mazda provided much of the groundwork for this major new facility—Ford effectively copied (albeit on a different scale) the way in which the Toyo Kogyo plant in Flat Rock worked. The closest point of the new stamping plant in Wayne sits some 687 ft from the original assembly plant, a distance across which the newly-stamped and welded-together metal would need to travel. To ensure that the panels remain unexposed to the atmosphere, they travel through a large bridge, being carried by automated transportation units.

The stamping plant itself is truly massive, with no less than 625,000 sq. ft of floor space. As befits its technological background, much of the equipment installed is of Japanese origin, such companies as Komatsu, IHI and Amino Iron Co all supplying presses, blanking equipment and pilot presses. American companies, though, were used for materials-handling equipment and computer control gear. The great majority of the welding work—in excess of 90 per cent—is by robot, and this is a major contributor to the consistently good panel fits displayed by the finished vehicles. Again, the technology was shipped in from the Land Of

The Rising Sun for that aspect of the production process. But that was nothing compared to the other thing which has been shipped in from Japan; before crossing the bridge to be completed, the bodyshells are assembled in the pressing plant on a team-build basis. For years, Ford boasted of its expertise, virtuosity even, in line production techniques. Yet here is Ford in Wayne, a relative stone's throw from the final resting place of the man who actually created the production line, putting together bodyshells with teams!

Once again, this was a move inspired by the Japanese. Teamwork has been a feature of the Japanese automobile industry for many years, but the major Western manufacturers had been cynical of it, preferring the tried-and-tested method of sending the car along a line where bits would be added by workers who never left their stations. But wait. Weren't the Japanese manufacturers putting together cars and vans which oozed consistently high build quality? Weren't they running rings around the American auto industry? Perhaps there was something to this team-build idea after all.

Naturally, there was much more to introducing the technique than merely convincing the management that it would result in higher-quality vehicles, and convincing the accountants that the sums would still add up to a suitable profit margin; the major obstacle was to convince the production workers that the scheme was not only feasible, but also that life would be generally better—

The Mercury Tracer wagon. The sleek styling has given the machine a commendable coefficient of drag of only 0.36—presumably, this is without the roof rack. A smooth grille and a low waistline with lots of glass indicate almost European styling influences

understandably, Ford's personnel people were concerned at the prospect of trying to persuade a man who, for the last 17 years of shiftwork, had done little more than stitch together two pieces of metal (duplicates of the same pieces, year in year out) that he could suddenly become part of a team, that he would mesh neatly into a democratic unit of workers who, between them, would have control over the way that their products would go together.

Whilst the new plant was being completed, the machinery installed and made ready for the new Escort, Ford took small teams of production workers (in all, there are some 600 people employed in the pressing plant) to quiet corners of the buildings, sat them around in small groups, and started them off making flashlights. Yes, flashlights. The technique is described by the Japanese as *kaizen*—a word which literally translates to mean 'constant improvement', but which also encompasses working in groups to analyse and improve team spirit when making a product jointly.

But that was close to the production point in terms of time; before they had got that far, Ford's personnel team had to convince the unions that the scheme would work, and that their members would gain, not lose from the radical change in working practice. The main blue-collar body, the Union of Automotive Workers, had been dubious about accepting the changes at first—in the words of their local President, Jeff Washington, 'We were always sceptical when Ford told us they wanted to try something new. We'd say "Um, we'd better watch our backs."' Ford, however, was deadly serious in its intent, and as a major peace offering to the UAW, it abolished the usual management privileges of special dining areas and reserved parking spaces. This appeased the union, but nobody has been able to tell me how it went down with the plant management.

As a part of the scheme, Ford even went as far as to send groups of workers to Japan to study team-build techniques in action, as well as inviting comments from whoever had anything to say on the subject—apparently, there were frank discussions in the early stages, but by the time that the flashlight programme was under way (with a series of competitions between the various groups to see which could build a set of 18 flashlights of varying designs and colours, and box them up ready for dispatch, in the shortest time—the record was under three minutes), the worth of the exercise was already starting to prove itself, because employee grievances had dropped off dramatically; from an average of 350 unresolved disputes, the figure dropped to less than ten in a matter of a couple of weeks.

Having started from scratch, Ford was also able to introduce a totally new set of working practices into the stamping plant—such as each team being able to elect its own leader, to decide the best place for the parts bins, tools and equipment, and so forth. Unlike the Flat Rock Mazda plant, which employed staff who had never worked in a car manufacturing plant before, the staff of the Wayne pressing plant were obviously veterans of the automobile industry and that, thought Ford, might cause problems when the new practices were being mooted. However, the flexibility—and mental agility—of all concerned have greatly surprised Ford, and the company is planning to extend the team concept further through the empire as opportunities arise.

Most importantly, though, it has worked. The build quality of the new Escort is excellent, the bodyshells going together precisely as the drawings said that they ought, while the customer gets a car in which the doors, bonnet and bootlid open and close precisely.

When the bodyshells have made their way across the bridge, and gone through the new dust-free, fully-robotized paint booths, they are put back on to a line-build, but at the time of writing, there

One of the main selling points of the typical American station wagon is a two-way split tailgate: the bottom half folds down, whilst the glass is either dropped into the metalwork by a power winder mechanism, or raised on gas struts. On the Tracer wagon, the one-piece tailgate breaks with that convention by opening upwards, in the manner of European estate cars

The fascia of the Tracer LTS, in automatic form. Ford's world-standardized four instruments are well placed and readable, through the upper section of the four-spoke steering wheel. Cruise controls are mounted on the wheel, while primary switchgear is column-mounted. A footrest (just visible) is provided for the driver's left foot in automatic variants

were plans to offer the main assembly workforce the opportunity to change over to the team-build way of working. It looks as though the offer will be taken up, inspired by the success of the teams on the far side of the bridge.

Even though there is a production line in the assembly plant, that too has been altered from the old way of doing things; ergonomics have entered into the scheme of things, and the bodyshells rise and fall on their cradles to allow the operative to carry out his or her task at the most comfortable level. Operatives have also been given appreciably

more authority over their tasks and can move from one task to another without too much red tape.

To a lesser degree, the same principles are applied at Hermosillo, a plant which has the considerable advantage of being relatively new; production of Mercurys started there as soon as the plant was completed in 1986. Having a workforce which, like the Mazda employees in Flat Rock, was unused to car factory work was a help, as Ford was able to introduce novel working practices without having to undertake a re-education programme. Robotics feature prominently at the Mexican plant (although not quite to the same level as seen inside Wayne's cavernous buildings) and, again, the accent is on maintaining the best possible quality control.

In common with the European plants, Ford operates 'just in time' stock levels at both plants, with a steady through-flow of components straight to the assembly stations. Ford's official reason for this policy is that components are exposed to the

The Escort GT's fascia is less comprehensive than that of its Tracer stablemate: no cruise control, no digital clock, and an altogether less tidy installation. A dead pedal is provided for the driver's clutch foot in manual versions of the car. The steering wheel bears a striking resemblance to that of Europe's Escort range

minimum amount of handling and in-plant traffic and, thus, are less likely to become damaged or dirty. The more cynical view is that Ford's stock investment levels are minimized—why have cash sitting in a warehouse in the form of a stack of components, when it can be in the bank earning money?

As with all recent new-product launches from Ford, the entire programme has been timed precisely, virtually to the day. From the basis of the plan being laid in 1985, a timetable was set out, specific tasks being matched to deadlines. The engineering aspects of the chassis, for example, would have to be signed off—given final approval—for tooling up and manufacture by the middle of 1988, and the final body styling programme approved at a similar time. The timetable even extends to the dates at which the various departments within Ford, such as Public Affairs, Marketing, Advertising, Labor Relations, Merchandising, and so forth, would become involved in their specific areas of activity. For example, in December 1989 (three months before production of the Escort was to begin at Wayne), special marketing programmes would be instigated to arouse the interest of minority groups, as well as the targeted priority groups of dealers. Sometimes, things were cut on the fine side, such as the brochure which would be available at each of the selected motor show launch platforms; in one case, the brochures arrived from the printing plant only five days before the car was unveiled!

And heaven help anybody who did not deliver on time.

It takes a lot of searching to discover the real reason why the CT–20 programme is of such importance to Ford North America. Cutting a swathe through the hype and the wordy reams of literature, I have finally been able to pinpoint precisely what is so important. First and foremost, the range has to demonstrate to an increasingly hostile American public that Ford is able to build cars which will compete with the Japanese imports in terms of quality, styling, fuel efficiency and customer satisfaction. It must provide products that appeal to a broad range of customers—those who are existing owners of Escort and Lynx models, those who normally buy imported cars (such as the equivalent Honda and Toyota models), and those who habitually buy the similarly-sized products of General Motors and Chrysler Corporation. Furthermore, the new car must also appeal to first-time buyers. Ford has the capacity to build more than 500,000 of these machines each year at the two plants, and 500,000 cars need 500,000 customers. The car range must also illustrate that Ford's 'Centers of Responsibility' design and production process, which utilizes the global approach of pulling in expertise from any appropriate corner of the empire, works; this involves showing the public a product range which is of high build quality and of high perceived value. The latter point is crucial to the acceptance by the public of future world cars. Most important of all, though, is that the car must achieve a high mpg figure to ensure a good CAFE rating—this will allow Ford to continue to sell bigger, thirstier cars without fear of recrimination from the government. And big cars mean big profits.

The four-door version of the Escort is a pleasing 'eight-lite' design (Fordspeak for four panes of glass on each side of the car), with wide doors for both front and rear passengers. A smooth grille design bearing the familiar blue oval is a feature of all Escort models—this is the LX variant

In the short term, if the CT–20 programme flops, Ford stands to lose an almost unimaginably large amount of money. If the company gets it right, it is in clover, but if it gets it wrong, the financial ramifications are dire. That is why the programme is so important.

Rather surprisingly, after a decade of selling rebadged Mazdas in the Escort market sector in the Pacific Basin, Ford is about to make a complete volte-face and start to produce CT–20 in Australia. Having already spent two billion dollars on the models, it is highly unlikely that Ford will be changing much on the car, but as production is still some way off, it may be too early to say. What is likely is that the main power unit offered for the new model will be the twin-camshaft Mazda engine; whichever way it is looked at, the engine for the Australian Escort, circa 1991, will have to be brought in from outside Australia, so it might as well be the better unit from Japan. The only reason that Ford does not make more use of the Mazda unit in North America is because it would constitute too great a proportion of the car being imported and, thus, affect that oh-so-valuable CAFE rating. That requires some 80 per cent of a car to be local in origin before it can be included in the government's equation.

In building cars in Australia, the benefits to Ford will be high; once past the break-even point, the profits will be greater than they are on bought-in Mazdas with separate badging. And anyway, in certain areas of the Pacific Basin, the Mazda badge has greater credibility than the familiar blue oval! The other vital thing to bear in mind is the Australian car taxation system, which is weighted heavily against imported cars in a bid to maintain a sensible balance of international trade; as with all major economies, the attitude is to maximize exports and to minimize imports. The Australian motor industry is not renowned for its exports, so a penalizing structure to discourage more imports is the next best thing. To illustrate the point, every foreign car landing on Australian soil is subjected to a 40 per cent duty. Then sales tax is applied to the car when it passes into the hands of the end-user which, on standard-sized cars, is a further 20 per cent—it rises to 50 per cent if the car is a luxury model with a price tag of A$43,000! By building cars at their Campbellfield, Victoria, NSW, facility, Ford is able to undercut the Japanese opposition by a substantial sum. By way of example, a Honda coming in from Japan with a base price of A$10,000 will actually cost the purchaser A$16,800, whereas an Australian-built Escort costing the same basic figure of A$10,000 will net out to A$12,000. And if that incentive isn't good enough for Ford to revitalize their production facilities for smaller cars in Australia, what is?

There was even a suggestion by the now-retired Chairman of Ford Motor Company, Donald E. Petersen (who surprised everybody by stepping down from his lofty seat two years before he was supposed to, early in 1990), that the CT–20 programme would be extended into Europe. This is patently not so, as Ford of Europe has its own CE–14 cars ready to roll out of Halewood, Saarlouis and Valencia, but what is about to happen is that the Escort will be going on sale in Asia, right alongside the car from which it was developed, the new Mazda 323. May the best car win.

But back to America. Just how well has the new model been received? The Tracer has yet to hit the streets, and at the time of writing test examples had not made their way to the magazines. But the Escort certainly has—the press was first given the chance to sample the cars in the spring of 1990. Initial reactions were generally good, although testers were not exactly overawed by the newest Ford. One major newspaper, for example, described it as 'an improvement, but not perfect', stating that the styling was bland, the interior ugly and 'distressingly cheap' looking, the older CVH

The Escort wagon shares its bodyshell with that of the Hermosillo-built Mercury model—a classic example of badge engineering. Such features as the rear wash-wipe, central locking and the roofrack are optional extras; the American public like to buy a bargain car and then load it with options to their original budget level, rather than buying a ready-to-roll package determined by the manufacturer

engine still sounding coarse despite its revisions, and the brakes feeling spongy. Interestingly, back on the subject of styling, that particular reviewer felt that the GT's spoiler looked as though it had been tacked on rather than designed integrally, and his overall impression was that the most stylish of the three bodyshells available was the four-door LX model. The same journalist also offered some praise for the car, though, in particular liking the clutch and transmission's actions, the twin-camshaft engine's behaviour in every respect, the interior accommodation, and the (optional) top-grade stereo system.

Another transatlantic colleague was more generous, praising particularly the GT's nimble agility—the extended wheelbase of the car (which is 98.4 in. compared to the Erika's 94.2 in.) and the dramatically improved suspension arrangement have apparently endowed the car with a poise akin to the best European and Japanese cars. The dual-camshaft engine also merited praise, as did the power steering system, which comes as standard on the GT.

Ford's entire marketing programme is based around the question: 'why buy an import when you can buy a Ford?' Looking at the specification of the range, and the amount of background effort which has gone into it, Ford ought to succeed. The company feels that the car will be able to hold its own against the competition in terms of quality, dynamics and accommodation. All that remains to be seen is whether the great car-buying public of the North American and Australian continents agree.

Meanwhile, in Europe, the Anglo-German interpretation of what was needed to replace the Erika range was about to be shown for the first time.

15 Carrying on

Meanwhile in Europe, a small revolution

DISINFORMATION is a way of life within the European automotive industry; that and speculation. Sometimes, magazines are given occasional hints at what might be happening by some of Ford's people, just as they are by the employees of other major manufacturers. Sometimes, these become realities, whilst in other cases, it eventually becomes apparent that the information was simply a red herring, something to throw an inquisitive journalist off the trail. Quite often, these snippets will be embroidered upon (and many motoring journalists have done it), while at other times, they will be taken with a pinch of salt. There is one rule to apply in this game, and that is to believe nothing until it is confirmed in the form of a press briefing, officially staged by the manufacturer.

The car market in Europe is fiercely competitive, and every manufacturer is desperately keen to know what the rest of the competition is up to, hence the shroud of secrecy that surrounds every new model. Even at the road-test stage, long after the final designs have been signed off for production and cars are out being tried on the highway, they will be as heavily disguised as possible—the usual trick is to tape cardboard panels over as much of the bodywork as possible to mask the lines. That way, if the cars should be spotted by anybody with an interest that is keener than the

manufacturer would like, there is still a deal of scope for confusion. It is these cars which form the basis for the artists' impressions which so often illustrate a scoop story, proclaiming the car to be the new Smith Superspeed, the Bloggs Bounder— or the Ford Escort.

There has probably been more press speculation concerning the 1991 Escort and Orion models for

In charge of the CE-14 development programme in Europe was Nick Fry, an affable character who epitomizes the rising stars within the Ford empire. His role was to co-ordinate the activities of the various teams involved in the range during its gestation period

The launch line-up of the CE-14 models. The estate car did not actually go on sale at the same time as the main models, but followed a couple of months after the 18 September 1990 'on-sale' date. The date was chosen because it coincided with the opening of the British Motor Show—the first time that Ford has launched an entirely new model range at the show for years

the European market than has ever surrounded any other car from a major manufacturer—and, yes, the magazine which I edit is just as guilty as the rest of combining snippets from indiscreet employees with informed guesswork to draw a sketch in words of what the car will be. The amount of speculation is not surprising, given the success stories which the Mk III and Mk IV cars have been; only rarely in the decade of their production were they knocked off the best-selling

list in Britain, and in Germany also the cars have sold extraordinarily well. It amuses me at this moment to sit at my desk, surrounded by cuttings and magazines (both British and German) from the past couple of years, to see how none of us managed to get it completely right.

Because of the large amount of dis-information/speculation, call it what you will, and partly because of his different way of doing things, the Director of Ford of Britain's Public Affairs Department, Kenneth Cannell, took the unprecedented step of inviting a small number of journalists to the inner sanctum of the Dunton Research and Development Centre almost two months ahead of the scheduled press launch date so that we might actually see what the new range would be like.

The Escort accounts for a major proportion of Ford's European sales; in the four years from 1985

A light van derivative has featured throughout the Escort's lifetime, and the fifth generation was no exception; the latest version has a raised rear roof section (after the style of the GM Astra van), which improves load-carrying capacity. As with earlier vans, a number of different models were offered, the variations being brought about by mixing different cocktails of engine size and cab trim packages

to 1988, there were no less than 664,871 Escorts registered in the United Kingdom alone—which accounted for 30.76 per cent of all Ford registrations. Assuming an average price of £7500 per car, a quick bit of fingerwork with the Casio calculator produces a figure of £4,986,532,500—so we are dealing with a major money-spinner which, obviously, Ford will not let fall from favour with the public by making a mess of its successor.

In its early days, the Sierra had come up against quite a degree of resistance from customers who, hitherto, had been quite happy to buy Cortinas; in comparison, the Sierra was too radical for many to accept, and it took a couple of years for the car to become as popular as Ford had hoped it would be. Therefore, there was no way that the company could make a similar mistake with the successor to Erika—whatever they put on show in the autumn of 1990, at the British Motor Show, would have to be identifiable as an Escort. Yet, at the same time, it had to be styled in such a way that it would endure for a decade, with only a relatively minor facelift on or about its fifth birthday.

But beneath its skin, it was obvious to Ford that much new thought would be needed, for the Erika, although undoubtedly popular, had attracted much the same criticisms in Europe as it had in the United States. Despite the revisions made by Chassis Engineering, the ride quality had never been as good as it ought, and the steering, although much-improved in terms of effort required, had still been considered unsatisfactory in view of its

lamentably large turning circle. Most of all, though, the CVH engine's noise levels were wholly unacceptable. Each problem area has been addressed in turn, along with several others that were less widely shouted. These included the torque-steer problems of the more powerful models, and the way in which the performance levels of the sportier models had been progressively eclipsed by offerings from the competition.

Although everybody in the design facilities denies any collusion whatsoever, the new Escort and Orion models bear an uncanny family likeness to the CT–20 cars on sale in North America. The European cars are slightly more curvaceous and, of course, do not have the substantial bumper mouldings, but the similarity is there for all to see—especially in the wagon and Orion derivatives. In keeping with Ford's policy of recent years, the new bodyshells have been heavily 'clinicked' during the design period, with unmarked examples of the new model proposals—quite often full-scale mock-ups—being shown alongside what Ford see as the major competitors to a select, invited audience. These clinics took place across Europe, and were repeated after the feedback from the audience had been analysed and, where appropriate, integrated into the designs. One major magazine representative was heard to mutter something to the effect that Ford had paid too much attention to the clinics and not enough to the design team when we were first shown the cars at Dunton.

In common with the American cars, the new European models have had their dimensions shuffled about to accommodate a longer wheelbase and to create a greater amount of internal space, along with more glass area. The other principal areas of commonality with the American cars are that they have no protruding wheelarch lips and the familiar little Escort 'bustleback' is still there.

As a purely personal observation, I feel that the designs of the European car range are even more successful then those of the American models, although I am also duty-bound to add that the car looks appreciably better in the metal than it does in photographs; this is extremely rare for Ford, whose cars are normally extremely photogenic. Obviously, the family likeness is there, with the slim, wide headlamps and the wedge-shaped nose, along with the expected long, single-pane rear side windows of the two-door hatchback, and six-light styling featuring on the side elevation of the four-door hatch. The main difference between the European and American cars is that the latter have smooth side panels from window line to knee level, whereas the former have been swaged along their length at the car's widest point.

When Erika arrived in 1980, the Cabriolet did not exist, but it has since gone on to achieve a great deal of success in terms of both kudos and sales. Therefore, it is not surprising to discover that there was a replacement for that particular model right from Day One of the CE–14 programme. This joins two- and four-door hatchbacks, an estate car and a saloon. Add to those five bodyshells, the six trim series, the three engine families, and the three transmissions, and immediately it becomes apparent that the European offerings are appreciably broader-ranged than the American cars. As is the norm, the products will be released progressively, the main range being scheduled for release in October 1990—immediately following the British Motor Show—with the sports models rolling out progressively over the following year. There is nothing surprising in that, nor are there any surprises in the line-up of the main range. What has raised eyebrows is the choice of powerplants for the 1991-season cars.

Ford has been experiencing the same criticisms on both sides of the Atlantic concerning the CVH engine; its relative lack of refinement and its eclipsed power levels have become increasing causes for dissatisfaction among owners and operators. To remedy matters, Ford instigated a design programme for a completely new engine range (codenamed Zeta), which offers multi-valve technology (the heads will take two, three or four valves per cylinder) with twin overhead camshafts and alloy castings for block and head. The new engines were originally slated to be built in both Wales and Detroit, the two centres between them supplying Europe and North America. Ford even went as far as issuing a press release in October 1988, saying that there would be a brand-new £725 million production plant alongside the existing CVH plant in Bridgend, which would create 3000 new jobs, and which would be able to produce in excess of 750,000 engines each year.

With this knowledge, the CE–14 programme was developed with the design team working around the dimensions of the Zeta—the engine has been designed to encompass a range of capacities from 1.4 litres up to two litres by varying the bore and stroke dimensions, all of which will be achieved using a common block size. That powerplant would be used in the majority of applications, but smaller-engined Mk V Escorts and Mk III Orions would continue to use the Valencia-built HCS pushrod engines for several years, until the second phase of Ford's engine programme was completed, and the proposed Sigma range of small-capacity engines (1000 cc to 1400 cc) was ready for service. These engines will be all-aluminium units with three or four valves in each chamber, and dual camshafts operating them.

The CE–14 programme was first laid down in the early part of 1986 (just as the facelift Erika models were being dusted down for final presentation) and, as usual, development was carried on in tandem; Chassis Engineering laid down the basic dimensions, Body Design worked around them, and the Interior Design team commenced their work. A four-year, ten-month schedule was laid out, with specific dates linked in—adherence to the timetable was sacrosanct, and as Ford of Europe's Program (sic) Manager of the Medium Car Group Body Engineering Group, Hans Fleischer, informed me, 'if anybody was running a little adrift we (the Product Development Group) would spot it and put on a little pressure or persuasion. Nobody actually failed to meet a deadline.'

But all did not flow quite as smoothly as some would have liked. The major hiccup came part way into the programme when the team which had been developing the floorpan was directed to change its plans. In keeping with the formula laid down at the inception of the Erika programme, the CE–14 cars were all to be front-wheel-drive (utilizing the same transaxle arrangements as

Luggage space in the new models is greater than at first appears, due to the useful shape of the boot. This large camera bag takes up only a small area of the available space. The spare tyre has been accommodated under the floor, to save space—which is all very well, until a puncture occurs and the entire contents of the boot need to be emptied out!

Erika), and the team was working around this. It had laid down the basic dimensions, arranged the revised suspension layouts and designed in the stiffening and stress-point compensation, when it was asked to alter the car to accept four-wheel-drive.

There are several reasons why, eventually, we will see Escorts (and probably at least one Orion) which put their power out through the rear as well as the front roadwheels. The first is because quad-drive allows increased engine power levels—trying to put anything more than, say, a 150 bhp through the same wheels that steer the car is inviting trouble. The second is that having a four-wheel-drive CE–14 car gives Ford a good marketing platform; the technical appeal of such a drive system has already been used to bolster the image of the Sierra and Granada models, and such

Instrumentation is Ford's standard selection, although the provision of a 150 mph speedometer smacks of crass optimism. The switchgear was criticized for the scattered locations along the main body. The stereo system in the Ghia includes an 80 watt amplifier as standard

companies as Audi have found that four-wheel-drive models have done wonders for their images. The most important factor, though, is to be found with Ford of Europe's Motorsport supremo, Stuart Turner.

In short, Ford's entire motorsport reputation, from the late 1960s to the early 1980s was made by the Escort; here were cars for the masses that trounced the opposition. Even today, the image of the RS1600 and RS1800 Escorts in competition conjures an image of overwhelming success—and the person in the street could go out and buy a car which looked like those rally- and race-winning machines. The Mk III Escort never quite managed to repeat the same trick, and in the mid 1980s the emphasis at Ford Motorsport had shifted to the bewinged RS Cosworth Sierra, and then its successor, the Sapphire Cosworth. These have been successful, but in terms of selling Sierras and Sapphires, the effect has been less dramatic than with the Escorts. It would be totally illogical not to take an opportunity to revitalize the Escort as a serious competition machine—and Stuart Turner is anything but illogical.

Thus, the rear section of the floorpan has been revised to allow the replacement of the standard

rear suspension assembly with a driven axle. In fact, the redesigned floorpan, which features on the finished cars, will (with strategic modifications) even allow an inline engine installation instead of the standard transverse arrangement.

Then another problem arose when, for a variety of reasons, it was decided that the Zeta engine range would not be ready in time for the launch of the new Escort and Orion; instead, the older CVH engine would have its production life extended until the new powerplant was fully developed. Then the CVH-powered models would be gradually re-engined. An immediate side-effect of this was that the desperately needed increase in power for the XR3i and Orion 1.6i models would not be extractable from the existing 1.6 CVH unit—even if Ford brought in the 88 mm stroke crankshaft for the block (which is an American part already used in the Escort in the USA and the 1.8 Sierra in Europe), the engine would still be some way short of the required 140 + bhp which would restore the supremacy of the XR3i. The answer to that one came in the form of a revised version of the two-litre I–4 engine, which is built at Dagenham for use in Sierra and Scorpio models. The upshot was that the engine bay of the CE–14 project would have to be versatile enough to accept no less than five engine family types—a tall order by anybody's standards.

Engineering has pulled it off, however. At the bottom of the new range of powerplants is the 1.3 HCS engine, then comes the 1.4 CVH unit in either of two forms: with or without a catalytic converter. As previously, both of these engines are available with only carburation at present, in their normal emission standard. The catalytic 1.4 engine uses the Ford single-point injection system, as previously.

Up from the 1.4 is the 1.6 CVH, again available with a choice of injection or carburation. Then there is the diesel engine. Diesels are of major importance in mainland Europe, and they are becoming increasingly popular in Britain; the signs are that within a year or two, the diesel-powered saloon will account for as many sales in Britain as it already does in such countries as Germany and France. Fine engine though it was, the naturally-aspirated Dagenham 1.8 diesel's power output, at 60 bhp and 81 lb/ft of torque, needed to be increased if the Escort Diesel was to remain competitive against the rival products from Peugeot, Volkswagen and the like. In the middle of 1987, Ford was already laying a new production line within its engine plant at Dagenham for a new

Unlike previous models of Escort and Orion, there is no discernible difference between the grille designs—both cars use the same arrangement of slots above and below the bumper to allow cooling air into the engine bay

generation of this engine, which had started life as a 1600 cc unit before being enlarged. By bolting a turbocharger on to the induction side of the engine, and making the other necessary changes, such as fuelling, Ford was able to offer a 25 per cent increase in bhp, and a 38 per cent boost in torque. The engine was designed for multiple applications—the P100 pickup truck is one—and was a natural choice for the new Escort and Orion models.

Unfortunately, although slated for use in the CE–14 range, the new forced-induction diesel has followed the lead set by the Zeta petrol unit and missed its launch date; early examples of the new Escort and Orion models can be had only with the naturally-aspirated diesel. The turbocharged version is not due to join the fray until the latter part of 1991.

Although there has been a degree of shuffling about, the overall marketing stance is not far from that of the old range; the lower-specification models get the HCS engine, the middle-specification cars gain the 1.4 or 1.4ci (catalyst injection) engines, and the fuel-injected 1.6 engine is reserved for the upper-specification cars. At last, the injection engine is beneath the 1.6 Ghia's curving bonnet, and the same mechanical package is also offered for the Orion Ghia. There is also a completely new model, inspired by one of the Fiesta range, the Escort 1.6S; this uses the tuned, carburated, 1600 cc CVH engine which first appeared in the old XR3. At least, it was that engine when we were first shown the car at Dunton. Magically, by the time the car became a production model, the carburated engine had been

The term 'limousine doors' cropped up time and again during Ford's press presentation of the new range. Whilst nobody has been able to determine precisely what was meant by this term, it was clear that the design of the seals was fiendishly clever—they incorporate a rain gutter. Ford is obviously so proud of this that a special illustration was commissioned from Herr Schrader's styling people in Merkenich!

dropped in favour of the 108 bhp, XR3i, 1600 cc CVH powerplant.

Mentioning the Fiesta leads me neatly to the main improvement to be found beneath the new skin of the Escort—its suspension system. As mentioned earlier, the Erika project was famed not so much for what its suspension had to offer, but for what it lacked. The Fiesta had also attracted a broadly similar range of criticisms, and they had been remedied by a total revision of thinking. Therefore, it seemed an obvious move to investigate the possibilities of utilizing as much as possible of the Fiesta Mk III technology in the CE–14 programme.

As with the Fiesta before it, the first move with the CE–14 was to extend the wheelbase; the old Escort and Orion's 94.5 in. dimension from wheel centre to wheel centre was no longer satisfactory in a car of that class. The new cars feature a wheelbase increased by almost 5 in. (125 mm, to be precise) which makes for a new dimension of 99.4 in., or 2525 mm in Continental measure-ments. Despite this increase in space between the wheels, the overall dimensions of the Escort hatch-back bodyshell have been increased by only 6 mm (the Orion and the estate bodyshells are some 100 mm longer than the hatchback models), which means that the poise of the car is much-improved due to its greater load spread.

Again, with the Fiesta, the bottom links of the front suspension system have been revised to do away with the poor location offered by the old arrangement of a single track control arm on each side and the anti-roll bar. Instead, the CE–14 features an L-shaped bottom linkage, which really is just another interpretation of the tried-and-trusted A-linkage, long favoured by other manu-facturers. The L-frame is joined to the strut base at one point (the shorter end of the 'L') and to the car's frame at the other two points with a pair of vertical bushes, which are made from double-bonded rubber and which have their axes aligned vertically—the norm is for such bushes to be horizontal. The main advantage of the L-linkage is that it offers better fore-and-aft location than that of the traditional Ford strut bottom mounts; no longer would the bottom linkage be forced back-wards as the anti-roll bar scribed its arc under compression, or forwards as it moved down below its centre-line. There is another advantage to the L-bracket linkage, which is that the anti-roll bar is free to carry out its intended role as a secondary spring. This, in turn, allows the use of rubber bushes with a greater insulation value, which means less noise, vibration and harshness making their way from the chassis to the cabin.

Also taken straight from the Fiesta—which had been overhauled completely and put on sale in April 1989—was the rear suspension design. Ford of Europe was keen to rid itself of that dreadful design which Dearborn had thrust upon it a decade previously, and had already designed and applied a far more effective arrangement, which was semi-independent rather than fully independ-ent, and which was far better-suited to front-wheel-drive cars. A combination of torsion beam and coil-over-damper strut springing, the system offers consistent wheel alignment which, in turn, benefits not only roadholding, but also tyre wear rates.

At the heart of the system is an inverted V-section steel beam, located at each end by trailing arms fabricated from light-alloyed, high-strength steel—all components have been designed using Ford's finite element stress analysis computer programmes to ensure that minimum weight and maximum strength were balanced to the optimum ratio. As with the American Escort, variable-rate springs have been used in the car (actual rates vary to suit specific model applications), and all research has been carried out with three, rather than two, rear seat passengers in mind. Outboard of the torsion beam are the strut units, which are close to vertical to minimize sticking and friction. These join the bodyshell in turrets which are situated on the outboard ends of the rear seatback to minimize their intrusion into the cabin. As with the front suspension arrangement, the chassis engineers have been guided throughout their task by the tenet of noise, vibration and harshness—the old Escort's reputation for a harsh and jolting ride would take a lot of living down, and the company had to be able to demonstrate that the new models of Escort and Orion would represent a quantum leap forwards from the Erika models.

Steering effort also needed attending to and, as with the American cars, this has led to two forms of treatment. The first was to revise the positioning of the steering rack's pivot points to give them a more vertical position, thus reducing the amount of friction which they need to overcome—naturally, the manual rack is the variable-rate one which was quietly introduced on to Erika a couple of years previously. As well as reducing friction, the resit-

An X-ray-type shot of the Cabriolet shows the amount of stiffening which was designed into the car by Special Vehicle Engineering, the team headed by Rod Mansfield. In time, the car will gain a new twin-overhead-camshaft engine, and thus become a proper sporting roadster

ing of the track control arm ends has also helped reduce both steering effort at parking speeds and the overall turning circle. Did you notice that reference to manual rack? The reason for the more detailed description is that, for the first time in a mid-sized European model, Ford has made available a power-assisted steering rack for the CE–14 cars—or, at least, certain models within the line-up. This is a development of the system already in use on the Sierra range and is of proportional-assistance design; as road speeds decrease, the level of hydraulic assistance increases. The main advantage of a powered rack—in addition to the obvious reduction in effort on the part of the driver—is that a much higher steering ratio can be used. Whereas a manual Escort rack needs four-and-a-quarter turns from one lock to the other, the power rack requires only three turns to achieve the same manoeuvre. Ford anticipate this to be one of the major option take-ups of the new range, especially in two distinct market sectors; more mature owners who will be most appreciative of the system's reduced wheel effort, and the sports model drivers who will most benefit from its fast-ratio action.

When the Escort Mk IV arrived on the scene in 1986, its major breakthrough, and unique selling point, was the Stop Control System. A purely mechanical system, the Lucas-Girling/Ford co-developed system was an immediate success. Naturally, this concept would have to be carried over to the CE–14 cars if credibility was to be maintained. But Ford could not merely carry over the existing system, for that had already been overtaken in technological terms by the system in use on the Fiesta—which, incidentally, made Ford

the only major manufacturer of cars for the masses to offer anti-lock braking on every car in their product range. A criticism of the Escort IV system had been that the pulse rate—that is the length of time during which the pressure was released to prevent wheel locking—was too slow, and this was amended on the Fiesta by altering the valving to increase the pulse rate. However, even that system was not quite good enough for the Ford team assigned to sort out the braking system of the new model range. Therefore, the CE–14 cars have eschewed the purely mechanical system in favour of one with microprocessor control; this is not a true Teves-style ABS in the Sierra Cosworth mould, but instead is a hybrid of the two systems, many of the mechanical components originally designed for the Escort being retained, but with ultimate control being assigned to a small on-board computer system. Again, 'borrowing' from the Fiesta programme, the entire range features front disc brakes made to a revised alloy formula which is able to offer a far greater resistance to the problem of brake rotor distortion. This had plagued not just the XR2 Fiestas, but also the harder-working sports models within the Escort and Orion series of cars.

The picture that is starting to emerge of the new Escort and Orion models is that they are an integral part of a much larger picture, that they have been developed as the contenders in what, in Europe, is considered to be Class C, alongside the Scorpio (Class A), Sierra (Class B) and Fiesta (Class D). Each member of that line-up will use what it can of the technology developed for the rest, rather than going its own way; any major breakthroughs, whether they are the development

Deft use of a wide-angle lens, and the absence of the B-pillar, accentuates the amount of space available in the CE-14 Escort. The Orion model shares the same cabin—only the rear quarterlight sets this apart from the car's booted stablemate

of anti-lock braking systems, or something as apparently trivial as the design of new secondary switchgear, will be applied as far across the range as possible, in the interests of spreading development budgets.

Such rationalization of resources makes itself apparent within the cabins of the new CE–14 cars. For the Fiesta, Ford worked closely with Imperial Chemical Industries' Polyurethanes Division and with Grammer Seating Systems to develop a completely new method of producing seats, which saved both materials and time. In brief, a moulded shell is produced which carries the sub-assembly (tilt mechanism, rise-and-fall subframe mounts and reclining gears), then the seat cushions are dropped into place, already upholstered. This method has reaped several benefits over conventional seat manufacturing methods. Firstly, the overall shape of a complete series of trim packages can be rationalized by using a single design of moulding press for the outer shell; the shells are made by vacuum-forming which, although expensive to tool up for, is extremely inexpensive to use once a line is up and running. Shell colours can be changed almost at a whim, and can be designed in such a way that the perceived value of the trim can be enhanced by simply clipping into place such items as pockets in the seat backs or, should they return to popularity, picnic tables which fold down.

Another major benefit to the new system of seat manufacture—which has probably been patented to high heaven by now—is the way in which the seat cushions are produced. Whereas the traditional method of manufacture started with the fabrication of a tubular frame followed by the addition of blocks of foam in strategic positions before pulling over and fixing pre-sewn seat covers, the new method is totally different. The trim fabric—which can be velour cloth, woven fabric, vinyl or even leather, depending upon the intended status of the finished vehicle—is first treated to a barrier film, which is applied to the reverse side of the material to seal it. Then the material is inserted face-down into a mould and held lightly under vacuum whilst the semi-liquid foam padding is added. Any strategic blocks of shaping foam are then applied to the underside of the seat before a second former is added to the assembly and vacuum pressure applied until the seat is cured to its finished shape. Once moulded, the new seat cushion assembly is simply clipped into place and the seat is finished. By varying the shape of the blocks of pre-cured foam which are

Although not available until the latter part of 1991, the turbocharged diesel unit was announced at the car's launch in mid 1990. As all of Ford's major European competitors already have Td units, Ford could not afford to be without one

dropped into the mould, the seat shape can be varied—so now a bucket-style sports seat can be made on the same equipment as a wide 'comfort' seat, whereas previously separate lines would have been required. Again, this is a major cost-saving factor, as designing different seats for different models within a range is now a much simpler procedure. Furthermore, Dunlopillo, one of Ford's main seating sub-contractors is already proving adept at coming up with different foam densities and shapes to order.

Given the level of investment in the seating system, it is hardly surprising that all the main-stream models of Escort and Orion come thus equipped. The top-of-the-line sports models, however, will continue to use brought-in seats from Europe's leading aftermarket supplier, Keiper Recaro of Kirchheim in West Germany; that company also supplies the rise-and-fall mech-anisms for the seating range.

Following the ergonomics of the previous range of Escorts was a tough act; a driver needed a distinctly abnormal shape if he or she could not achieve a good driving position, with all controls in easy reach, on that range of cars. But the CE–14

cars had to look distinctly fresh and different. The fascia design in the new range, unlike the Amer-ican cars, is basically the same, although there are two series of instrumentation—the lower-specification cars do not enjoy the luxury of a tachometer (although the same applies to high-specification diesel-engined models, as a suitable instrument would prove far too costly), whereas the more expensive and higher-powered Escorts and Orions will advise their drivers of the engine's speed. It all comes down to perceived values, to giving the more senior members of a company the opportunity to score a few points over their juniors who will also be driving Escorts or Orions.

A main criticism of cars in the past decade and a half has been that the major application of plastics in dashboard design has led to a dramatic increase in the number of squeaks and rattles experienced by drivers. Anybody who owns a Mk IV Escort, or its equivalent booted Orion, will be familiar with the most common one, which gives a passable impression of a canary in season and is caused by the thin piece of black plastic, which forms the detent in the instrument panel, rubbing against the clear plastic that covers the instruments. Although remedying this is a simple matter of placing a hand on each side of the offending black plastic moulding and pulling it slightly forwards, such errant sounds are inconsistent with cars that cost anything from £7500 to more than double that — anyway, so many of the BMW models which use a similar amount of plastic in their fascia mouldings do not squeak and rattle anything like as much. To prevent this happening, Ford has moulded the fascia in a single piece; that way, there is nothing to create a squeak or a rattle. The mouldings themselves are designed to accommodate all of the little bits and pieces which drivers like to have with them on a journey, and this is one of the more praised features of the Mk IV cabin. Ford has even gone as far as to make provision for two DIN-sized in-car entertainment units; the standard radio or radio-cassette unit can be joined by a graphic equalizer, an amplifier unit or a compact disc player without the loss of storage facilities.

Ergonomically, the interior is good—very good. The ability to choose an ideal seating position is enhanced by the provision of an adjustable steer-

The styling of the estate version is very close to that for the American market (Chapter 14), with a neat wrap-over roofline at the rear. Unlike many such cars, it looks as though the estate was styled at the same time as the rest of the range, rather than being an afterthought. The estate is longer that the other cars in the range to maximize its load area

ing column, which can be tilted (but there is no telescopic feature; no sense in going overboard with corporate largesse), and by providing the drivers of the more up-market models with seat-height adjustment as well as variable seatback angles. The primary controls all fall to hand, as they ought, and are lightly balanced in that way for which Ford is almost as famous as its blue oval trademark. The only aspect of the driver's area which has drawn criticism is the placement of the secondary switches for such equipment as the heated front and rear screens, the high-intensity rear lamps and additional driving lamps. These look as though they have been tacked into the inner side of the main moulding as afterthoughts, and they are at odds with the integrity of the rest of the fascia design.

To manufacture the cars, Ford are using the three main European centres of Halewood, Saarlouis and Valencia—all three have been the subject of major overhauls in readiness for the new model ranges. The aim throughout the CE–14 development programme has been to take on the Japanese opposition, just as it has been in America. The threat from the East is a world-wide phenomenon, and those manufacturers who choose to ignore it and carry on in their own sweet way will be on a rapid decline.

The Toyota Corolla is the car which best typifies the build quality being sought, and it goes almost without saying that this car has been scrutinized by every division of Ford world-wide. Much of the Corolla's success starts in the earliest stages of production, the quality of raw materials and of bought-in components being extremely high. The presses upon which the sheetmetal panels are created are state-of-the-art, allowing rapid die changes; the dies wear out quickly and need to be replaced at regular intervals without interrupting production flow for longer than absolutely necessary. The panels need to be fixed together with absolute precision, with all the shut lines and panel joins being aligned exactly. The process continues right down the line, each operation involved in turning a skipful of parts and a collection of

The Orion 1.6 Ghia, seen here in injected and catalyzed form, was perceived as following in the 'performance incognito' role assumed by its predecessor. In due course, it is expected that the Orion range will gain a 16-valve 2.0i model, and also a four-wheel-drive variant. These will be pushed as serious GT models and are expected to retain limited-production status

stamped panels into a finished car being accomplished in accordance with the master plan.

Ford has a team which is responsible for installing first the pilot lines (which are used for pre-production runs to ensure that everybody involved in final engineering has got the calculations right and that all parts fit as they ought) and then the finished production lines. This team visited each of the factories during the late spring of 1990. It started in Saarlouis, then went on to Valencia and finally to Halewood. Essentially Germans—although there are some British and Spanish members—the team started by familiarizing itself with all of the equipment before going to Saarlouis, and was working under the overall control of Hans Fleischer of Body Engineering. Apparently, it takes the team a mere three weeks from start to finish on each plant—and on the day it leaves the entire new-model range is ready to roll off the line. Impressive stuff—especially when employee training and retraining is taken into account. Much of the difficulty, according to the affable Herr Fleischer, is not so much in getting the equipment in and running (much of the initial work on new hardware and computer systems is carried out jointly by Ford and its many equipment suppliers, and nothing is accepted by Ford until it is working perfectly), but rather in persuading the production-line workers of the importance of perfecting such details as lock and catch settings and hinge adjustments.

Although the three plants are essentially similar, there are differences between Saarlouis, Halewood and Valencia. Automation at both Halewood and Saarlouis is similar, both plants having more than 70 per cent of body assembly tasks carried out by robotic machines; the Saarlouis plant's 82 per cent automation is the highest. All three plants use robotics in final assembly, too, but the amount for Valencia is lower because local labour costs are lower—and it is cheaper to hire more hands than to pay for automatons!

A major part of the reasoning behind Ford operating at three plants in Europe is the single market which will take effect from 1992, when traditional barriers throughout Western Europe will cease to exist and all member countries of the European Community will be able to trade freely with each other. As a part of this, the level of national protectionism which, at present, exists in a number of member states of the EC, will have to cease; no longer will Spain, Italy and France be able virtually to exclude Japanese manufacturers, and even the 'voluntary code' which exists in Britain, whereby Japanese importers agree to keep their products to within 12 per cent of the total vehicle registration figures, will probably disappear. By having strategically-placed plants around Europe, Ford will be able to capitalize on the low transportation costs made available by having factories either in, or on the doorsteps of, member states of the European Community. Additionally, it means that should there be a local supply difficulty, that hole in production can be filled quickly and easily by either of the other two Escort and Orion manufacturing plants.

It was this philosophy that led to the delays in the Zeta engine range. At present, Escort and Orion engines are manufactured in two European plants: Bridgend and Valencia—the Welsh plant produces the CVH engines, while the Spanish location is the source for the HCS power units which carry the plant's name. A hiccup in production at either could wreak absolute havoc, especially given Ford's 'just-in-time' stock-control system. Occasional bursts of industrial action are not

As a foil to underwhelming press reaction to the new range, Ford showed this Ghia-designed alternative version of the estate car. Known as the Seeka, it positively bristled with features, such as a roll-out canopy, barbecue, ski and pushbike racks, and so forth. Mechanically, the machine was diesel-powered and featured heavy-duty suspension, special alloy wheels, off-road tyres and skid guards on the underside

unknown at any major manufacturing plant, and Ford's two engine factories are no exceptions, so the decision to concentrate not just CVH production, but also the forthcoming Zeta unit's production, in the same area of South Wales would be very risky. Therefore, the decision was taken to redirect a sizeable chunk of the proposed Bridgend investment to Köln, thus halving the risk of a hiatus in production because if one plant went out of production, there would still be an alternative source of supply. Not a popular decision in Wales, but Dearborn was a lot happier with the idea of building a new plant in Köln.

Whilst on the subject of supply and the essential nature of maintaining it, I am reminded of a tale—which I was assured was absolutely true—that concerned the Bridgend and Treforest plants. Being situated on the western side of Wales, these two component factories (Bridgend for engines, and Treforest for ignition parts) are in some danger of being cut off from the rest of the country when winter's teeth bite deeply. When the roads are impassable, the components can be sent to Halewood by ship, but in the hardest of winters, even this route can be made impossible for a day or two. So Ford is prepared to resort to the expense of chartering freight helicopters. Accordingly, one winter in the early 1980s, this means of carrying parts to Merseyside was brought into play, and even though the weather conditions were very severe, the no-nonsense pilots carried out their sterling work on a round-the-clock basis until less expensive routes were reopened. One pilot even clung on to his sense of humour whilst working; when asked how he would navigate the short route from Bridgend to Treforest in near-blind conditions, the pilot replied, 'Oh, every time I come to a junction on the road I'm following and I'm not sure which way to turn, I drop down to blow the snow off the roadsign, and read the directions.'

The entire Ford supply network is a complicated one, which relies on accurately-timed logistics from not only its own factories and plants, but also from those of its outside suppliers. Every one of these is expected to deliver first-class goods on time, every time. In all, there are 35 major Ford sites throughout Europe, and a large number of these are involved in the CE–14 programme.

One outside contractor that gets, perhaps, a shade more tangible business (at least more when viewed from the customer's end) is Wilhelm Karmann, for again, this company has been employed to produce the sleek and stylish Cabriolet version of the new car. As with earlier Cabriolets,

A key figure in the technical development of the Escort and Orion models was Clive Ennos, who was Director of Product Engineering at Ford of Europe until he moved to Jaguar in the autumn of 1990. Clive's last major product at Ford was the Zeta engine family, due to go into cars a year after his move to Coventry

the cars are sent to Osnabrück in partially-built form, but not as complete shells. The Cabriolet was designed into the range from the very beginning, and this shows in the finished product's integrity; whereas the rear quarter glass of the earlier Escort wound down only partially, that of the new model drops down flush with the bodywork, giving the open car a smoother line, interrupted only by the roll-over bar. The Cabriolet's panels are common to those of the three-door hatchback only as far back as the B-pillars; from that point rearwards, they are unique to the car, although the same light clusters feature on all models with the longer floorpan.

Much work has gone into minimizing buffeting and turbulence within the passenger compartment when the roof is down, and a lot of effort has also gone into one of those little detail touches which were requested by a surprising number of existing Cabriolet owners—a roof rack. Yes, I know it sounds bizarre to want a roof rack on an open-topped car, and I said as much to one of the design team, only to be gently put right in a clipped and

Germanic tone: 'Ja, I see your point, but it seems that a lot of our owners use their cars all-year round—and that includes taking them up into the mountains, during the winter months, for skiing holidays. And they wanted a way of carrying their skis.' The solution is a fiendishly neat and tidy pop-up mechanism attached to the roll-over bar which does not interfere with the hood operation, but which does allow a ski-rack to be fitted to the car.

Other criticisms of the earlier models of Cabriolet were also attended to before the CE–14 roadster went into production, principally the hood sealing mechanism and the tendency of the earlier style of hood to buffet at high speed when the windows were down. It is not certain just how much of an effect on European sales the provision

In times past, Ford needed to send 'troops' to Finland or Northern Sweden to carry out driveability tests in arctic conditions, then down to Africa for a similar exercise in the tropics. Today, the same exercises can be carried out in a chamber at Dunton which simulates those conditions without having to take the car off a rolling-road dynamometer

of a ski-rack mounting will have, but it is nice to know that Ford has attended to what might have been viewed as a trivial request. Or perhaps one of the team at the Merkenich Design Studio has a company Cabrio and goes off to Kitsbuhl every January . . . ?

When the Erika models were unveiled, the absence of a serious sports version of the car, an RS model for the British market and its equivalent (but differently badged, because RS means little or nothing elsewhere in Europe) for Germany and the other main EC consumers of fast cars, was much lamented. There is no way that Ford was prepared to let that happen again, if only because of the showroom-draw potential of such a car. I have already made mention of the 1.6S model and the place which that is to occupy in the line-up; this is a more serious version of the Sport model which was introduced during the Mk IV's dotage, and it promises to be a lively performer with a high fun quotient. Obviously, there is no way that such a machine would be acceptable as a flagship sporting saloon. No, what is needed is something a little more radical, something with a good deal of fizz, something which will take on everything up to and including such devices as the Golf GTi in its

latest supercharged format, the GTE 16v Astra, and suchlike. Ford's answer to these casually-tossed gauntlets is the XR3i 16v in Europe, the same car being known in Britain by the far more emotive name of RS2000/16v.

Scheduled for sale to the public in October 1991, the model is based on the three-door hatch-

Robotics are a way of life. This machine, jointly developed by Ford and ASEA, plucks out the crankshafts for the RS2000-16v engine and drops them neatly on to the assembly line so that they are facing in the right direction. This saves a few seconds per crankshaft, and that saves money

back bodyshell, as might be expected. The original plan was for the car to be powered by the top-of-the-line Zeta engine, but when it became apparent that the engine would not be ready for the 1991 model year, another engine was rapidly seconded—the Dagenham-built I-4 dual-overhead-camshaft unit, which has been in service in both the Sierra and Scorpio model families since its introduction in August 1989. In its most potent form, the I-4 produces 125 bhp, with a similar torque figure. Whilst this would represent a gain of almost 16 per cent on the powerplant of the old XR3i, it would still fall below the level of horse-power needed to propel a serious replacement RS

model. Yet wasn't the I–4 originally designed to be a more powerful unit, designed to be able to accept not just its standard eight-valve cylinder head, but also twin-spark, 16-valve heads?

That is where the answer to the quest lay; make use of the 16-valve cylinder head (which had been in existence as a casting-blank form since the latter part of 1987), and the net power output would rise to somewhere in the region of 150 bhp. Nobody in Engineering exactly shrieked 'Eureka!', but it had the answer just the same.

Whereas the Zeta block—which eventually will supersede the I–4 in this particular car, according to an informed source—is a short-block, the I–4 is tall. Too tall. The first thing that Engineering did after installing a set of the correct-sized valves was to redesign the cam covers, reducing the overall dimensions as far as possible; the net result is a neat aluminium casting which wraps snugly over the pair of chain-driven camshafts. Even with this modification, a small amount of engine—the two ends—still protruded above the bonnet line. Not by a great deal, but enough to make a pair of nasty dents in the sheetmetalwork should anybody attempt to close the bonnet. As this is a sports model, Design felt it acceptable to revise the nose section to incorporate a neat pair of teardrop-shaped 'blisters' in the bonnet panel. These just clear the offending bits of engine and aid the aggressive nature of the model by alluding to flared nostrils. Aided by a five-speed manual transmission (as with previous European sporting Escorts, the automatic option is not available), the performance of the beast promises to beat the marginally more powerful Astra GTE/16v, with a 0–60 mph time in the region of 7.5 seconds, and a maximum speed in excess of 135 mph. This also ought to go hand-in-hand with a worthwhile fuel economy figure, for while there is no Corporate Average Fuel Economy figure to chase on this side of the Atlantic (yet), all of Europe's major manufacturers are ecology conscious, and they know well that to produce a car with fuel figures which are as unimpressive as the performance figures are impressive would attract undesirable attention from an ever-increasing 'green' movement. Different manufacturers take different actions to appease the 'greens'—BMW and Mercedes-Benz have both introduced maximum-speed governors to their top-of-the-range cars for this reason; programmes within the management systems preclude their big-engined cars from exceeding a mere 155 mph, even though those cars will easily surpass that velocity. Ford has yet to yield to such temptation,

Stuart Turner, head of motorsport for Ford of Europe, made a great effort to get full-scale approval for the sensational RS Cosworth Escort, which is due to go on sale in 1992. The car is an amalgamation of the mechanical parts of the Sapphire Cosworth 4 × 4, an Escort centre section with modified floorpan and suspension pickup points, and specially-pressed aluminium wings. That whaletail spoiler is a 'delete option'

preferring instead to use the time-honoured technique of extracting the best-possible mpg figures from their more powerful cars.

Mind you, there will quite possibly be an outcry when the intended flagship to the range arrives, a little over a year after the RS2000/16v . . .

In comparison, the RS2000/16v will be a pussycat; the Escort Cosworth will be the real tiger. The car is an evolution special, which will be sold in strictly limited numbers; once the required number have been manufactured and the necessary motorsport papers gained, production will cease. Unless, that is, the machine proves to be lucrative enough to be continued, in which case it will remain in the catalogues for some time to come.

The Escort XR3i/RS2000/16v (this is getting to be the written equivalent of a mouthful, so henceforth, I'll refer to the car as the 16v) makes use of the familiar packaging so successfully used in the past by Ford to distinguish its sporting saloons. To the basic three-door shell is added a special bumper/spoiler moulding with the required additional number of brake cooling ducts and a pair of extra driving lamps, while at the rear of the car is a matching bumper unit and a special rear deck aerofoil. In the case of the 16v, the last item is of

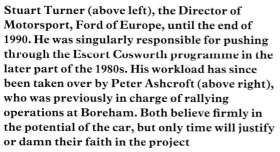

Stuart Turner (above left), the Director of Motorsport, Ford of Europe, until the end of 1990. He was singularly responsible for pushing through the Escort Cosworth programme in the later part of the 1980s. His workload has since been taken over by Peter Ashcroft (above right), who was previously in charge of rallying operations at Boreham. Both believe firmly in the potential of the car, but only time will justify or damn their faith in the project

most pleasing design, wrapping neatly into the rear wings and being raised some 3 in. above the 'bustleback'. It is wider than previous XR3i elevated aerofoils. Just how effective it is has yet to be disclosed, but it certainly looks the part! By the time that the alloy rims (again, 15 in. diameter items on the early examples which I have been able to view) and their low-profile tyres have been added, and the image completed by the use of strategic colour-coding and contrasting strip inserts in the rubbing strakes and bumpers, the nature of the beast has been declared to all, without Ford having to go overboard on the build budget. The only aspect of the car which jars—again, this is a personal observation—is in the badging. On the pre-production examples, the various messages (Escort, XR3i, 2000i, 16v) are all laid out, or rather scattered, across the back panel of the car, each in a different typeface; the overall effect is of somebody rampaging through the studio's Letraset catalogue.

Inside the car, the sports seats are trimmed in a

dedicated fabric which does not appear anywhere else in the Escort or Orion ranges. As previously, the 16v gets a special, smaller and thicker-rimmed version of the newly-designed, three-spoke steering wheel (as do the Orion 1.6i Ghia and the Sport) and also gets the more senior level of sound equipment. For the Cosworth, the trim of the prototype was in leather; as the car is not scheduled for launch until the latter part of 1991—or even the spring of 1992—only time will tell if that is the way the finished production cars will appear in the showrooms.

Reverting, for a moment, to the range as a whole, the level of equipment on offer (on some models items are standard, on others they are paid-for options, while on the lesser models unavailable) is on a par with what the public has come to expect. In addition to the three transmissions—four- and five-speed units plus the CTX variable-ratio automatic—there are such features as a tilt-and-slide sunroof (although none yet has power assistance—you have to buy a Scorpio for that), the Triplex 'Hotscreen', rear wash-wipe on virtually all hatchback and estate models and also the Orion Ghia injection, heated and electrically-adjustable door mirrors, air conditioning (for certain markets, such as the Mediterranean countries), tinted glass, power window lifters (including the rear windows on certain models of four-door car), and central locking. Aah, the locking mechanisms. Ford was publicly applauded for its adoption of the Chubb disc-tumbler system in 1986, but the applause paled rather when it was discovered that the use of a suitable lever would overcome the lock's resistance. Failing that, a felon could gain access by inserting a wire hook down the outside of the window channel and tugging on the rod which connected the system's various components.

To overcome such criticisms—which proves that Ford listens, even if it feigns deaf ears—the security moves on the Escort involve extending the door locks so that they can be deadlocked, and replacing the connecting rods with cables concealed behind screening plates. Ford feels that this ought to silence those critics of the earlier moves towards a more secure Escort—moves which had been almost forced upon the company by the way in which just about any pre-1986 example of the car could be opened by anybody armed with only a nailfile. As added security, Ford has also introduced a range of optional alarm systems to suit the CE–14 models.

I mentioned earlier that the floorpan of CE–14 was designed to accept four-wheel-drive, and the first example of the machine to be thus equipped is scheduled to arrive in the autumn of 1991. This

The RS2000 name has been revived for use in Britain. This time around, it will be stuck on the stern of a compact, front-wheel-drive car with a 2.0 litre, 16-valve engine (which will also be found in the Granada and Sierra models from mid 1991), developing 150 bhp, despite being equipped with a catalytic converter. A 4 × 4 version is scheduled to follow within a year of the RS2000's spring 1991 début

will be a 4 × 4 version of the 16v, and although an evolution from a front-wheel-drive car (which, incidentally, uses a new transaxle, the MTX–75), the power split will not be biased towards the front pair of wheels, but will be weighted in favour of the rear set; final figures have yet to be decided, but they are expected to be in the region of 40 per cent front, 60 per cent rear. A number—said to be in excess of 40—of all-wheel-drive Mk IV Escorts have existed for several years, as pre-production prototypes which made use of an additional transfer box on the main five-speed transaxle. Drive then passed back to an independent rear axle (similar in design to that of the Sierra, but suitably narrower), the transfer box apportioning the torque. Various systems have been tried, some with viscous coupling front and rear (the 16v-engined car will have a viscous coupling as standard to help smooth out power delivery), some with couplings only in the transfer box, and some with a coupling apiece for the transfer box and the rear axle. Whilst those cars were chopped into little (and not so little) pieces and scattered to the four corners of the breaker's yard, the data gathered from testing them formed the basis of the forthcoming model. In mechanical terms, the car will effectively be a 16v with additional drive to the back wheels, the rear suspension retaining the standard car's outboard struts, but with additional trapezoidal lower links replacing the normal assembly.

If the prototype is to be believed, the Cosworth will differ radically from the 16v 4 × 4, as the turbocharged, twin-camshaft machine which we

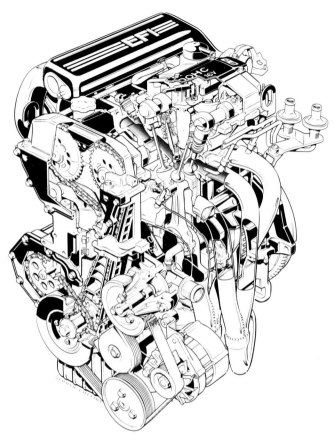

Featuring a classic, compound-angled valvetrain, driven by overhead camshafts (one apiece for the intake and exhaust valves), and with the spark plug situated centrally in the hemispherical lean-burn chamber, the RS2000 engine (which is sold as the XR3i-16v in mainland Europe) is a direct development of the Dagenham-built I-4 engine. The camshafts are chain driven in the interests of longevity—a belt snapping would certainly prove hellishly expensive to Ford!

were shown at Dunton on that sunny June morning in 1990 had an inline engine and what amounted to the same running gear as the Sapphire Cosworth 4 × 4 underpinning its radiant red bodywork. The last is as radical as the car's 160 mph performance suggests; the Cosworth is a serious street-racer of a machine with beautifully-styled, spaced-out arches providing for the car's wider track and 16 in. aluminium-alloy wheels. Although following the overall styling line of the standard car, the revised wings give the car an additional 3 in. of width in total, and there are open slots to duct cooling air to and from the four substantial brake discs. If the team at Special

Vehicle Engineering gets its way, these wings will be stamped to order from aluminium sheet in the interests of saving weight.

If the wings look radical, then raise your eyes a few degrees and look at the back end of the car. The same neat aerofoil as the 16v model is still in place, but just above it is another massive device that runs at roof height and trails backwards to finish flush with the tailgate's rearmost point. This aerofoil measures a good 12 in. across its main section; its ends flow neatly into the rear tailgate window pillars, and there is a central support to prevent it drooping under its own weight, which will increase radically with aerodynamic downforce at speed.

And speed is what this machine is all about. It has been conceived purely to win rallies and races, which is why the Cosworth powerplant has been installed beneath its louvred bonnet—as the aftermarket has already proved, the twin-camshaft development of the old Pinto cylinder block can be made to produce as much as 600 bhp—and in racing form, it has been consistently reliable at close to that figure, even in endurance races lasting for four hours. Should Ford decide, at some point, to develop a similar package around either the I–4 (which, incidentally, can be taken out to as much as 2400 cc by juggling with bore and stroke dimensions) or the Zeta, then the chances are that the equipment found in and on the Cosworth BDT–YBF engine can be transferred or adapted to suit without too much difficulty, which means that similar power levels are within range. The only part of the entire programme which leaves Ford with all of its eggs in one basket is its retention of Cosworth Engineering, now a division of Vickers, for engine development on the turbocharged 16-valve units.

According to an informed source, Ford has taken the car to several test facilities (both rally stages and race and test tracks) and pitched it against examples of the types of cars which it will be up against in serious competition. Even in standard trim, with a 225 bhp example of the Cosworth engine, it has trounced the lot of them—which bodes very well indeed.

It is, of course, easy to be cynical and to draw parallels with the RS1700T from the Erika programme, a car which was similarly radical when compared to the rest of the range, and which was unceremoniously axed when Stuart Turner took his present role as Director of Motorsport, Ford of Europe. The seasoned Ford-watcher might well view the equivalent CE–14 model as heading towards a similar fate once it has finished its initial duties as a grabber of headlines in the international motoring press. Only time will tell, but my personal feelings are that the car will proceed into its intentionally limited-production run for two very good reasons. One is that Ford's replacement for the Sierra is due a year or so after the 1991 Escort and Orion models appear in the showrooms, while the life of the present Sapphire Cosworth will reach an end—and Ford needs to maintain its very high profile in motorsport because it sells more mundane models with the same nameplate. The other reason is that Derek Barron, Chairman and Chief Executive of Ford of Britain, has already made it public knowledge that the company will have Cosworth versions of each model range by the mid 1990s. To perform a volte face and not put the Escort Cosworth into production would be sheer folly, having already gone on record with that statement.

Perhaps the most succinct comment on this aspect of corporate philosophy came from Stuart Turner who, watching the Motorsport version of the car (complete with heavily-stylized stripes by Ford's French studio) being off-loaded from a covered transporter at the CE–14 gala ball launch, at Blenheim Palace in June 1990, turned to me and said, with deep conviction, 'There. They daren't drop the project now, not now that all the press have seen it.'

The other great unknown in the future for CE–14 concerns the Orion. In the launch line-up, the range of the booted car is much as previously, with a 1.6i CVH-powered example heading the list; mechanically, this is much the same as before, apart from the obvious changes shared with the rest of the CE–14 cars. A year before the new cars became available, the RACMSA, British motorsport's governing body, reworked its eligibility classes for the British Touring Car Championships to create only two classes, the lower one of which was for models with a maximum engine size of two litres, and natural aspiration as distinct from turbocharged or supercharged induction. And there, in the middle of the list, was the Orion 2.0. So does this mean that there will be a twin-cam, two-litre version of the model in due course? And if so, will there be a sports version of it?

The Orion was conceived and marketed as an executive car, while the serious sporting models from the Erika were invariably based on the three-door Escort hatchback. The marketing stance for the new car is much the same as previously—in spite of the fact that dealers reported that a sizeable

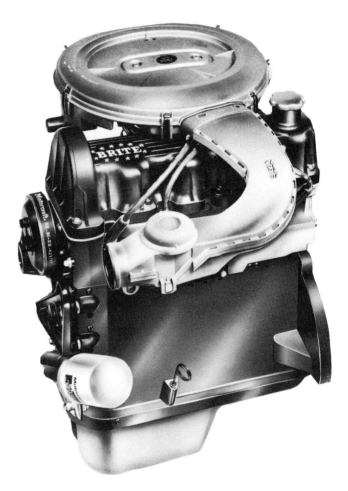

The shape of things to come? This engine, which will appear in a prototype Escort in 1992, is made from plastic with a minimum of metal parts. It offers savings in both weight and building costs, so it can be expected in series production before too long

number of Erika/Orion 1.6i purchasers made their choice because the car offered XR3i performance, but with improved access, security and accommodation offered by the extra pair of doors and a separate boot. So why no 16v engine for the latest Orion?

As expected, the official response to the question, when put to various members of Ford's Marketing and Public Affairs departments, was a series of statistics which placed performance fairly low on the list of requirements brought to the company's attention by the many market research programmes. More likely, though, is that the change of plan caused by rescheduling the Zeta engine brought about the decision to wait until that particular powerplant was ready—for the first year or two of Orion's sale period, the absence of a two-litre version is hardly likely to affect sales by any great amount. Then, when the 16v Escort gets its new engine, so will Orion—and also the Cabriolet. According to a senior member of the engineering staff, the reason why the Orion had not already been given the 16v I–4 engine is quite simply that the special cylinder heads can only be made in relatively small quantities of 20,000 units per year, and all of those will be needed for the Escort RS2000/XR3i. As an aside, this also deflates the hopes of Sierra drivers, who were expecting the GLS version of that car to gain the additional set of valves in the near future.

In conclusion, once again, Ford has followed the path of evolution rather than revolution; although CE–14 has been designed from scratch, and is a totally new car in many respects, it still makes use of the engine and transaxle arrangements from the

The three-door Escort. Whilst, in the author's view, it is not as successful a piece of styling as the five-door, nonetheless, it is clean and tidy— and it will sell consistently well, especially to fleet buyers who appreciate the fact that it is less expensive to build (and, thus, to buy) than the five-door model

earlier cars in most of its models—and the new engines for which it was designed will not be installed beneath the aerodynamically-efficient bonnets of Escort and Orion models for another year or two. The body styling, although totally new, still follows the same format, and the car is unmistakably an Escort—although the Orion does tend to look more like a Mitsubishi or Peugeot from the rear quarters. Having seen some of the conceptual sketches produced for the car when the CE–14 programme first started 58 months before the launch date, it is obvious that the designs have been toned down substantially, and the main culprits behind that are The Great European Public, whose opinions and sentiments, expressed at the clinics, were taken as gospel.

Yet despite the fact that the car is considered to have broken precious little new ground in terms of styling and design, it will sell; it is such a good overall package that, undoubtedly, it will go on to outsell its predecessor, which was itself a record breaker. And if Ford achieves its aim of beating the build quality displayed by the major Japanese manufacturers—including Mazda, its own part-subsidiary—the European buyers will be happy with their purchases.

Once again, only time will tell.

16 Epilogue

So what went wrong?

HAVING got this far, having looked into all of the Escort models and their derivatives on a global scale, the question still remains—in part, at least, unanswered—just why did the Escort never actually become the world car?

The crux of the answer lies in its size—not so much its market suitability in that respect, but rather its profitability. Small cars cost very little less to develop than large cars, and not that much less to produce; the number of components in a Fiesta, in an Escort or in a Sierra all total up to about the same figure (although, obviously, different trim standards determine different total figures), and the sums turn out to be surprisingly similar. This makes a project such as the world car concept make sense—until somebody starts messing about with the components.

When Erika was first conceived in the mid 1970s, the idea was to produce, via Ford's acclaimed use of transatlantic links, a car which would fulfil the same role in each of the company's major marketing areas. What nobody reckoned on was local demand. Whilst Erika, in her purest form, went on sale throughout Europe, the version which North America gained was different in quite a number of areas; the overall dimensions were similar and the appearance and formatting were also very much alike—but of interchangeable parts, there were few.

Indicative of just how little commonality there was between the two models is The Grey Book. Quite literally, this is a grey-covered book, in loose-leaf form, which was started at the beginning of the project and which listed each of the many components which come together to make up a car—it is worth noting that an engine counts as many hundreds in its own right, not just one unit. Slowly, one by one, the list of common components was whittled away as the Americans decided that pieces such as track control arms, in their European form, were far too flimsy, that the 1.3 engine was unacceptable for North America, that the gear ratio clusters needed to differ on each side of the Atlantic, and so forth. All that remained of The Grey Book by the time that the two opposing camps in Europe and in North America had finished was a single sheet of A4 paper, listing what amounted to a few trim clips and a half-dozen self-tapping screws.

Meanwhile, the Pacific Basin area of operations had already decided that the future lay not in using either of the two alternative Erikas, but instead in selling a variation on the local delicacy, the Mazda 323.

Strangely, as has been detailed in Chapter 14, in part, that situation has been reversed, because the latest American models will also be built in Australia for sale in the Far East—but the European models will go their own sweet way.

So does this mean the end of the world car concept as we know it? In a word, no. In fact, there is a true world car waiting in the wings, even as I write this conclusion to my tale. As might be expected, it is bigger than the Escort and, thus, more profitable. The new Sierra model in Europe is due to go on sale about a year and a half after the Escort and Orion models. Like the American Escort, it will call heavily upon the Japanese for its concept beneath the skin, and this time, it will sell in virtually identical form in all of Ford's major market zones around the globe. You didn't think, for a moment, that Ford would waste all of that investment in intercontinental communications equipment, did you?

But the Sierra is another story entirely, for another time and another book. For now, we have a new range of Escorts on both sides of the Atlantic Ocean—and both seem set to continue the trend set by their predecessors. Both, in turn, will receive their facelifts and their replacements, but from where I am sitting, one thing seems certain: nobody involved in the conceptual work in the early 1960s, when Ford of Britain was looking for a replacement for the Anglia, could have had any idea just how much of a major driving force the Escort would become during the next two decades!

Index